The Twelve Stories
of Christmas

The Twelve Stories of Christmas

by

Joe Wheeler

RIVER
OAK
PUBLISHING

Tulsa, Oklahoma

The Twelve Stories of Christmas
ISBN 1-58919-991-X
Copyright © 2001 by Joe Wheeler

Published by RiverOak Publishing
P.O. Box 700143
Tulsa, Oklahoma 74170-0143

DEDICATION

Mother — on earth, the ultimate source, the bedrock
Of our existence. She is the soil one germinates in,
The inner sun and rain one flowers to.

Her voice is the first ever heard. She is the moon that
Summons and dismisses the tides of life, the pitch pipe
That sets the melodic base, the rhythm that sets the beat.

These words began my book *Heart to Heart Stories for Moms* and
reflect how I feel about my mother, the true author of this book
of Christmas stories, the flame that lit my Christmas torch.

Thus it gives me great joy to dedicate this collection to
Barbara Leininger Wheeler
of
Canyonville, Oregon.

❈   ❈   ❈

ACKNOWLEDGMENTS

"The Snow of Christmas." Copyright © 1989. Reprinted by permission of the author.

"The Bells of Christmas Eve." Copyright © 1990. Reprinted by permission of the author.

"'Meditation' in a Minor Key." Copyright © 1991. Reprinted by permission of the author.

"The Third Rose." Copyright © 1993. Reprinted by permission of the author.

"Luther." By Joe Wheeler and Michelle Wheeler Culmore. Copyright © 1994. Reprinted by permission of the authors.

"Hans and the Trading Game." Copyright © 1995. Reprinted by permission of the author.

"Pandora's Books." Copyright © 1997. Reprinted by permission of the author.

"His Last Christmas." Copyright © 1997. Reprinted by permission of the author.

"Legacy." Copyright © 1999. Reprinted by permission of the author.

"City of Dreams." Copyright © 1999. Reprinted by permission of the author.

"White Wings." Copyright © 2000. Reprinted by permission of the author.

"Evensong." Copyright © 2001. Reprinted by permission of the author.

TABLE OF CONTENTS

Introduction 10

1. The Snow of Christmas...................................13

2. The Bells of Christmas Eve..................................23

3. "Meditation" in a Minor Key 33

4. The Third Rose 65

5. Luther..91

6. Hans and the Trading Game................................99

7. Pandora's Books..123

8. His Last Christmas 153

9. Legacy 165

10. City of Dreams...179

11. White Wings 201

12. Evensong 225

About the Author...265

INTRODUCTION

L ife plays funny tricks on us. Not in my wildest dreams did I ever expect to be writing an introduction to a book featuring twelve Christmas stories that *I* had written. In fact, if the truth must be told, I never expected to write a Christmas story at all—much less sire two series of annual Christmas books.

Nevertheless, as I wrote each year's Christmas story, I couldn't help noticing that I was achieving a critical mass of sorts. Even so, it was a bit of a shock when my agent, Greg Johnson, phoned me about putting together a collection of my own Christmas stories for RiverOak Publishing. "How many have you written?" Greg asked. After checking, I phoned him back, saying, "I just completed my eleventh for *Christmas in My Heart 10.* "Guess you'll have to write next year's early then, for the title of your collection is going to be *The Twelve Stories of Christmas.* " So over the last few months, I wrote that twelfth story, "Evensong," which will also appear in *Christmas in My Heart 11,* in 2002.

I certainly don't have the *chutzpa* to contend that these twelve stories are *the* twelve stories of Christmas; only that they represent twelve doors into my past (for these stories reflect my own journey, my own changing philosophy of what Christmas is all about). My attitudes have shifted as I have gotten older, for I now perceive life from a broader span of years. But there are tradeoffs: While it is great to be able to see life from the perspective of a sixty-year-old, it is not great to be losing the ability to conceptualize clearly and accurately life as a forty-year-old, a twenty-five-year-old, or a ten-year-old might see it.

In teaching creative writing to students down through the years, I have always urged them to write from known experience, for the other kind isn't worth the paper it's written on. As I scrutinize each of my dozen Christmas stories, it's clear to me that I've followed my own advice. Each story represents either a stage in my own life or a reenactment of what was occurring in the lives of some of those dear to me.

All of them have been written in an attitude of prayer; thus if they are convincing and deeply moving, the thanks should go to God, for His has been the guiding hand.

People measure the stories in my anthologies by the tissue quotient: "How many Kleenex will it take me to get through this story?" they ask. A five-Kleenexer is the ultimate tearjerker. I frankly admit to being a confirmed softy where stories are concerned. I cry easily. Yet I've noticed that I'm anything but alone in that respect, even in terms of other men. Sentimentality is not determined by what sex a person may be.

Furthermore, I feel that unless a given story takes me somewhere, makes me a better, a kinder, a more empathetic person than I was before I read it, then I shouldn't have read it. Life is too short to read stories or books that nudge you towards darkness rather than the light.

It is my hope that you will find each of these stories to be a blessing, not only personally but in terms of your family and friends. I will be interested in your reactions, and will appreciate very much any stories you send to us, stories you feel touch the heart. Not just stories about Christmas but stories from all genres. When the story's origins are known, please relay them as well. You may write me at:

Joe L. Wheeler, Ph.D.
P.O. Box 1246
Conifer, CO 80433

The Snow of
CHRISTMAS

A h, it seems so easy there at the altar: starry-eyed bride, a groom who can't take his eyes away from her loveliness, supporting family and friends. "As long as you both shall live" has a nice ring to it, but the real significance, the daunting odds against making those seven words come true, escapes the man and woman standing there.

It is only later, when the honeymoon high has worn off, when the real world intrudes more and more, when the personal idiosyncrasies and tics of the other begin to grate — it is only later that the marital foundations begin to shake.

And so it was with John and Cathy . . . and Julie, that long ago Christmas. So easy to walk away.

❄   ❄   ❄

Three doors he had slammed on her: the bedroom, the front, and the car. What started it all, he really couldn't say; it was just one of those misunderstandings that grow up into quarrels. In a matter of minutes he had unraveled a relationship that had taken years to build. His tongue, out of control, appeared to have a life of its own — divorced as it was from his accusing mind and withdrawing heart.

"Catherine . . . it's all been a big mistake . . . you and me. I've tried and tried — Heaven knows I've tried — but it just won't work. You're . . . you're wrong for me . . . and I'm wrong for you."

"John!"

"Don't interrupt me. I mean it. We're through. What we thought was love—wasn't. It just wasn't. . . . No sense in prolonging a dead thing. . . . Don't worry, I'll see to it that you don't suffer financially. I'll keep making the house payments . . . and uh . . . and uh, you can keep what's in the checking and savings accounts. . . . And us, uh, don't worry, I'll send child support for Julie!"

"John!"

Almost he came to his senses as he looked into Catherine's anguished eyes and saw the shock and the tears. But his pride was at stake; so ignoring the wounded appeal of those azure eyes, he had stormed out—his leaving punctuated by the three slammed doors.

Three weeks later, here he was, pacing a lonely motel room three thousand miles from home. "Home?" He had no home. He had only his job—a very good one—and his Mercedes. That's all.

Unable to face the prosecuting attorney of his mind, he turned on the television—but that didn't help much. There were Christmas-related commercials or programming on every channel—one of these ads featured a golden-haired little girl who reminded him far too much of Julie.

He remembered Julie's wide-eyed anticipation of every Christmas. The presents under the tree that she'd surreptitiously pick up, evaluate by weight and size and sound, and the finesse with which she unwrapped and rewrapped them . . . ; he found it hard to be stern with her, for did not Catherine too unwrap them on the sly? Catherine had always been constitutionally unable to wait until Christmas should reveal what hid within gaily-wrapped packages bearing her name—so poor Julie came about this affliction naturally.

Again, he switched channels. Wouldn't you know it—yet another Christmas special. Had to be Perry Como . . . *still* at it. Why, the Christmas special advertised as Como's farewell performance was a number of years back—in fact, he and Catherine heard it the Christmas season of Julie's birth. . . . Como no longer had the range, but his middle tones still carried him through.

Oh no! Not "I'll Be Home for Christmas . . . You can count on me. . . ." On the wings of Como's voice he soared backwards in time, all the way back to his own childhood.

Was it his seventh Christmas, or his eighth? "The Eighth!" . . . for that was the year his parents had surprised him with an adorable shaded-silver Persian kitten—which he promptly named "Samantha." Samantha had lived a long time—fifteen years, in fact. It was hard to envision life without that bundle of purring fur which cuddled up next to his feet every night—until he left for college. And even then, whenever he returned home, every night like clockwork, within sixty seconds from when he turned out the light and slipped into bed, he would sense a slight vibration resulting from the four-point landing, hear a loud purr, and feel a whiskered head searching for a head-scratching.

❄ ❄ ❄

Memories flooded in upon him in torrents now. How he had loved Christmas at home. His had always been the responsibility of decorating the Christmas tree—a tree he got to pick out himself. A *real* tree—never a fake! The fragrance of a real tree, the sticky feel of a real tree, even the shedding of a real tree, were all intertwined in the memories of the years.

Strange . . . passing strange . . . how he measured the years by specific Christmases.

The Christmas of the "Broken Phonograph Records" with its now legendary "Lean-to" . . . by . . . uh . . . Mari Sandoz—yeah, Sandoz wrote it. How everyone had laughed and cried over that Nebraska frontier tale. "Lean-to" had gone into the family lexicon of memories. And, as usual, all four of his grandparents had been there, and numerous aunts, uncles, cousins, and family friends.

Then there was the Christmas when Dad, for the first time, read *all* of Dickens' *A Christmas Carol*—he had thought it would never end. But strangely, ever since that first reading, the story of Scrooge and the Cratchits seemed shorter every time it was read. And theater and movie renditions? They but reinforced the impact of the core story.

And how could he ever forget the first time he had heard Henry Van Dyke's *The Other Wise Man*? Like Dickens' tale, it normally took several evenings to read. That poignant conclusion where the dying Artaban, under the extended shadow of Golgotha, at last finds his king . . . never failed to bring tears to his eyes.

"That's *enough*, John! . . . You've got to put all that behind you. Christmas? What is it but Madison Avenue's annual process of grafting sales to sentiment? That's why the first Christmas sale now takes place the day after Independence Day."—But it wasn't enough: he just could not convince himself that Christmas meant no more than that. Instead, his mind flung open a door and replayed the scene in his folks' kitchen three weeks before.

It had been anything but easy—rather, it had been perhaps the hardest thing he had ever done: telling them about their separation and impending divorce. And he had begged off for this Christmas, telling them that a very important business meeting on the East Coast would make going home impossible.

❖   ❖   ❖

Mother had broken down when she heard about the end of his marriage, for Catherine had slipped into their hearts, becoming the daughter they had always yearned for, that first Christmas when he brought her home from college. Catherine had taken it all in: the warmth and radiance of the *real* tree; the crudely carved nativity scene (John had made it when he was twelve); the exterior Christmas lights; the Christmas decorations everywhere; the Christmas music played on the stereo and sung around the piano; the Christmas stories read during the week; the puns, jokes, kidding, and ever-present laughter; the crazy annual trading game—which was more fun than the usual exchange of presents; the bounteous table groaning with delicious food day after day; parlor games such as Monopoly, Caroms, Dominoes, Anagrams; the crackling fire every evening; the remembering of the Christ Child; and the warmth and love that permeated every corner of the modest home.

When he had proposed—on Christmas Eve —and apologized for the plainness of the home and compared it to the Marin County estate where she grew up, her eyes had blazed, and she had hushed his lips with her fingers.

"Don't you *ever* apologize for your home, John! she exclaimed. There is *love* here, and Christ, and Father, *and* Mother—not just my lonely embittered father rattling around in all those endless rooms, *alone.* No, this," . . . and she paused as her gaze took it all in again . . . "this is the kind of home I've longed for all my life." Then her eyes, reflecting the firelight glow, softened and emanated such tender, trusting love— unqualified and unreserved—that time stopped for him as he gathered into his arms what had once seemed virtually unattainable.

"This has got to stop!" he admonished himself. "There can be no turning back!" Out of the room he strode, down the hall, down the stairs, and out into the city. It being December 23, the streets were crowded with people, all with one goal: get those last-minute gifts. He passed two Salvation Army bell-ringers, and left a ten-dollar bill with each one.

Happiness and seasonal good humor were all around him. Strangers wished him a very merry Christmas. Christmas carols were piped into almost every store.

His attention was caught by a crowd in front of Macy's biggest window; he pushed himself far enough in to be able to see what they were all looking at. What he saw, in a fairyland setting, were hundreds of cashmere teddy bears in varying costumes. Julie had fallen in love with them the first time she saw them (long before they had become the rage of the season). And he had planned to surprise her on Christmas morning by bringing it to her at the breakfast table rather than putting it under the tree. Oh, well, perhaps Catherine would remember to buy it; that is—which he rather doubted—if she was in the mood to have Christmas at all.

He moved on, but seemed to feel an invisible gravitational force pulling him back to Macy's. Two hours later, unable to resist any longer, he went back, bought one of the last three in stock—even the window had been cleaned out—and returned to the motel. He shook his head, not understanding in the least why he had bought it, for he was a continent away from Julie—and tomorrow was Christmas Eve.

❄   ❄   ❄

After depositing the teddy bear in his room, he returned to the street. This time, he walked away from the downtown district. He came to a large, white, New England-style church. The front doors were open, and floating out on the night air were the celestial strains of "Ave Maria." He stopped, transfixed; then he walked up the steps and into the church. There, down candle-lit aisles, at the front of the church, was a live nativity scene. Off to the side, a lovely brunette, eyes luminous with the illusion of the moment, was singing the same song he had first heard Catherine sing, and with the same intensity, forgetfulness of self, and sincerity.

When she reached those last few measures, and her pure voice seemed to commingle with the angels', chills went up and down his spine; and when the last note died away into infinity, there was the ultimate accolade of total silence . . . followed by a storm of applause.

John closed his eyes, soothed yet tormented by what he had just experienced, by whom the singer reminded him of, and the significance of that mother's love and sacrifice two thousand years ago.

Out of the sanctuary he strode and down the street, mile after mile, until he had left even the residential district behind. On and on he walked; he did not stop until the city lights no longer kept him from seeing the stars. As he looked up into the cold December sky, for the first time in three traumatic weeks, he faced his inner self.

And he did not like what he saw.

Etched for all time in the grooves of his memory were the terrible words he had spoken to the woman he had pledged his life to. How could he have been so cruel—even if he no longer loved her? That brought him face to face with the rest of his life. The question, the answer, and what he would do about it, would, one way or another, dramatically affect every member of his immediate family from now until the day they died.

What was his answer to be?

❧   ❧   ❧

It was snowing! For the first time in ten years, declared the radio announcer, there would be snow on Christmas. The windshield-wipers kept time with Bing Crosby, who comes back to life every December just to sing "I'm Dreaming of a White Christmas." The lump in his throat was almost more than he could handle. Would this be a Christmas "just like the ones I used to know"? Could she—*would* she—consider taking him back?

Although bone-weary from staying up all night and from the frantic search for airline reservations, he was far too tense to be sleepy. The flight had been a noisy one, and a colicky baby right behind him had ensured a wide-awake trip. He'd rented a car, and now . . . his heart pounded louder as each mile clicked past on the odometer.

Now that he had thrown away the most precious things in life—his wife and child—he no longer even had a home. Belatedly, he realized that without that, life's skies for him would lose their blue. How odd that his mind meshed the graying of his personal skies with the cold-graying of Cathy's eyes when he mentioned divorce:

the blue of both was now as silvery as the ice- and snow-bedecked trees that flashed by.

The road became icier, and he narrowly averted accidents several times. Occasionally a vehicle would spin out of control in front of him, but somehow he got around them safely.

At last! The city limits. He could hardly keep his runaway heart from jumping its tracks.

Had the road to his house ever seemed so long? Then he turned that last corner. . . . Darkness: no lights, no car! He fought panic as he skidded into the driveway, got out, and fought the bitterly cold wind and snow to the back door. Inside, all appeared normal— nothing to indicate that Cathy and Julie had left on a long trip.

Maybe they were at his parents' house! He rushed back to the car, backed out onto the street, and sped out of town, hoping against hope that he was guessing right. He didn't dare to trust his fate to a telephone call.

❅   ❅   ❅

About an hour later he saw the cheery lights of his folks' place. Through the front window he could see the multicolored lights on the Christmas tree. And *there*, in the driveway, was his wife's car.

He passed the house, then circled back on an alley road, cutting his lights as he reapproached the house. His heart now shuddering like a jackhammer, he brushed off his clothes and shoes and ever so quietly opened the back door and stepped into the gloom of the dark hall.

He heard a child's voice . . . singing. He edged around the corner into the foyer. Kerosene lanterns, as always, gave to the room a dreamy serenity. His folks sat on the couch intensely watching their grandchild as she softly sang, kneeling by his nativity stable,

> "Silent night, holy night
> All is calm, all is bright . . .,"

a look of ethereal beauty about her, lost as she was in her Bethlehem world.

Oh God, he prayed, *shield her from trouble, from pain —from growing up too soon.*

Then, like a sword-thrust through his chest, came the realization that he—her own father—had thrust her out of that protected world children need so desperately if they are to retain their illusions, that child-like trust without which none of us will ever reach Heaven's gate.

The sweet but slightly wobbly voice continued, then died away with the almost whispered
"Jesus, Lord at Thy birth
Jesus, Lord at Thy birth."

❄ ❄ ❄

His heart wrenched as he drank in every inch of that frail flowering of the love he and Cathy had planted. Oh how little it would take to blight that fragile blossom!

He wondered what his daughter had been told. . . . Would she still love him? Would she ever again trust him completely?

Upon completion of the beloved Austrian hymn, Julie sank down to the level of the nativity figures and, propping her head on her elbows, gazed fixedly into another time.

John now turned to an older version of Julie; this one leaned against the window frame. She was wearing a rose-colored gown that, in the flickering light from the oak logs in the fireplace, revealed rare beauty of face and form. But her face—such total desolation John had never seen before. In all the long years that followed, that image of suffering was so indelibly burned into his memory . . . this hell of his own making . . . that he would be unable to bury it in his subconscious.

How woebegone, how utterly weary, she appeared. A lone tear glistened as it trickled down that cheek he loved to kiss.

Oh, how he loved her!

He could hold back no longer. Silently, he approached her. Was it too late?

Suddenly, she sensed his presence and turned away from the vista of falling snow to look at him. She delayed the moment of reckoning by initially refusing to meet his eyes . . . then, very slowly, she raised her wounded eyes to his . . . and searched for an answer.

Oh, the relief which flooded over him when he saw her eyes widen as they were engulfed by the tidal wave of love that thundered across the five-foot abyss between them. In fact, it was so overwhelming that neither could ever remember how the distance was bridged—only that, through his tears, he kept saying, as he crushed her to him,

"Oh, Cathy! Oh, Cathy!
Forgive me, Cathy.
Oh, Cathy, I love you so!"

And then there were three at the window—not counting the snow-coated teddy bear—the rest of the world forgotten in the regained heaven of their own.

And the snow of Christmas Eve continued to fall.

❄   ❄   ❄

HOW THIS FIRST STORY CAME TO BE

In truth, this story started it all. And I had precious little to do with it. God had everything to do with it. With more than a little help from one of my English majors at Columbia Union College in Takoma Park, Maryland. Tired of dormitory regulations and cafeteria food, she asked if she could come home with me that December 15-17, 1989 weekend. Connie having agreed to her coming, there she was on that memorable Friday evening, sitting across from me in an easy chair, the fire crackling in the fireplace, and the snow softly falling outside.

Exhausted from the week's teaching, counseling, and administration, all I wanted to do was rest and dream there by the fire. Suddenly our visitor jolted me out of my reverie, with these words:

"Dr. Wheeler, have you ever thought of writing a Christmas story?"

I answered, rather lazily, "Yes . . . , I've thought of it."

Not at all satisfied with my answer, she asked, "Well, why don't you?"

Still unaware of my doom, I responded with the ambiguous, "I will . . . someday."

Then she bored in for the kill: "Why don't you—tonight? I want to proof your story as you write it."

Thoroughly awake to my peril now, I struggled mightily to get off her hook. But she was inexorable. For an entire semester she had been in my creative writing class, and I had been utterly inflexible in my writing assignments: come a given Monday, Wednesday, or Friday, she'd jolly well better have a certain piece of writing ready at class time. Now she had the unmitigated gall to reverse roles with me.

So I hoped the good Lord would be on my side and grant me, in His great mercy, writer's block, so I wouldn't have to write it. Unfortunately, the Lord ganged up on me, too, and almost instantly gave me a story plot. So what could I do but surrender? In recent weeks and months, separation and divorce having shattered the lives of some of those we loved most, I was impressed that

I should write a story about a man who walked out on his wife and daughter. It snowed all that Friday; it snowed Saturday and Sunday. We couldn't have gone anywhere had we tried. Outside, the wind shrieked down the icy Severn River towards the Annapolis Naval Academy only two miles away.

As I got further into the story, the fire in the fireplace and the snowstorm outside combined to bring back torrents of Christmas memories. For the first time in my life, as I took on the persona of my protagonist, John, I began to realize that I not only was, but always had been, a Christmas child. Memory after memory poured into the story, so that, in a very special way, my story became John's story.

Meanwhile, my guest continued to take sadistic delight in slashing my story, and scribbling suggestions about how to improve it in the margins. It was mighty humbling for me to be "done to" as I had "done to" others (more specifically, the creative writing class).

Because of the unceasing snow outside, snow was woven into the very fabric of the story, hence its title. After I had completed it, my guest suggested I give copies of the stories to students, family, and friends. I did, and it was very well received, thus setting mighty forces in motion.

                    ❧   ❧   ❧

As the years passed, this simple little story has gone on to become one of the most beloved stories I have ever helped to write, eliciting mail that has continued for over ten years now. More significantly, it proved to be the catalyst for our year-round involvement in the Christmas season today. It first appeared in Review & Herald Publishing Association's trade paper Christmas in My Heart 1 *(as the lead story) in 1992, and again in Doubleday/Random House's second hardback* Christmas in My Heart Treasury *in 1997. It was also included in the Tyndale House/Focus on the Family* Heart to Heart Stories of Love *in 2000.*

The Second Story of Christmas

The Bells of
CHRISTMAS EVE

Two women sat at the feet of Christ: Mary and Martha. There is something in most of us that identifies with the beautiful Mary—so effusive, appreciative, responsive, and filled with the joy of life!

But there was the second sister, not nearly as flamboyant, whose love manifested itself not in mere rhetoric but in service. It is the Marthas among us who carry on their shoulders the burdens of the world. It is the Marthas who nurture and sustain the eagles who fly so perilously close to the sun.

But Marthas have their dreams too.

❀   ❀   ❀

"When will the bells ring?"

"Midnight, Miss Louisa . . . midnight."

"Thank you, Jacques. I'll . . . I'll be waiting. Don't forget the carriage."

"I won't, Miss Louisa."

She turned and walked to the hotel window, leaned against the sill, and waited. Waited, as was her custom, for the dying of the day. She sighed, with a faint feeling of loss, for the sudden disappearance of the silver path to the sun that had so recently spanned the deep blue Mediterranean sea and sky.

Losing all track of time, her soul's lens recorded on archival film every detail as the master scene painter of the universe splashed all the colors and hues on His palette across the gilding sky. At the peak of intensity, she felt like a child again, watching that last heart-stopping explosion of fireworks which transforms mundane evening darkness into a Twilight of the Gods.

Then, as suddenly as it had come, it was over—and the curtain of night was drawn down to the darkening sea.

It was only then that the icy blade of loneliness slashed across her heart . . . and time ceased to be.

❊ ❊ ❊

How much time passed before awareness returned, she never knew, for the breakers of awareness came in soft and slow, seemingly in unison with those breaking on the French Riviera shore outside the window.

Fully awakened at last, she slipped into her heavy coat, stepped outside, and walked across lawn and sand to her favorite rocky shelf. After snuggling down into a natural hollow out of the path of the winter wind, she spread her coat over her legs and wrapped a small blanket around her shoulders.

The tide was ebbing now, and with its departure she again realized how terribly lonely were the shores of her inner world. . . . If only *he* were here to hold her, to commune with her, to fill that void in her life that only he could fill, achieve that sense of completeness that only he could induce.

Scenes from last summer flashed on the screens of her mind: his arrival in a huge carriage at the Pension Victoria; her almost instant recognition of his weakened health; his stories detailing his involvement in the ill-fated Polish revolt against Russian tyranny, his capture and incarceration in a damp airless dungeon, and his eventual release.

Fresh from her service as a nurse in Washington during the recent American Civil War, she noted the same battle symptoms that marked tens of thousands of her own countrymen: the tell-tale signs of a weakened constitution and the lingering evidence of recent illness and almost unendurable stress and pain. Instinctively, she steered the newcomer over to a table near the largest porcelain stove. That simple act of kindness supplied the spark which short-circuited the stuffy formalities of the day: one moment, they were complete strangers; a moment later, they were friends.

She was a thirty-three-year-old June to his twenty-one-year-old April. But hers was a young-at-heart thirty-three and his a maturity far beyond his years, forged by the crucible of war and imprisonment. But it was his seared, but cheerful still, spirit that won her heart. In spite of his recent residence in hell, this bruised and battered lark was a living embodiment of the poetical portrayal of two men looking out through selfsame bars, one seeing walls, the other stars. Ladislas Wisniewski saw the stars.

Used to the cold formality and austerity of new England, she was totally unprepared for warm-hearted Ladislas, who smashed through conventions and formalities as though they were so much kindling: a Mozart minuet stormed by a Liszt rhapsody.

In truth, Louisa had been the object of many a lovesick swain through the years, but none had been able to break through her self-imposed barriers of reserve and indifference; prior to Ladislas, not one had been able to raise her temperature so much as one degree.

❊   ❊   ❊

The days and evenings that followed were full of adventures, large and small: he taught her French, and she taught him English; he regaled her with the culture, history, and lore of the alpine country of Switzerland and France, and she introduced him to the New World of America; they rowed almost daily on beautiful Lake Geneva (framed by the snowcapped Alps); they explored the grounds of the chateau and area sights of interest such as the nearby Castle of Chillon which Byron had immortalized; they took frequent tramps along the mountainsides, pausing often to drink in the stunning deep blue sheet of water spread out below them, the verdant hills around them, and the saw-tooth mountains above them, cutting notches in the sky.

And woven into the fabric of that never-to-be-forgotten summer of Sixty-five was talk—talk when talk added color, silence when talk was superfluous. Their talk recognized no barriers, no constraints. The subject was life, life with all its complexities, inequities, and unanswered questions. In the evenings, Ladislas would perform in the parlor (he was an accomplished professional musician), and Louisa would join the others and listen—deep, deep within her, seas long dead would be stirred into tempests by Ladislas's fomenting fingers.

He was good for her—far better than she knew—for Louisa was (and always had been) a caregiver, a Martha, one who sublimated her own dreams and desires so others could fulfill theirs. All her life, others had always come first. She had grown up early, realizing while yet a child that it was her beloved mother who bore the full weight of the family's financial problems, for her father—bless him!—seemingly dwelt in another world. Like Dickens' immortal Micawber, he blithely assumed that something would always "turn up" to enable the family to muddle through. Certainly God would provide. Somehow, some way, God always did, but her mother Abba grew old before her time, in the process.

❊   ❊   ❊

Louisa had early recognized that she, by nature and temperament, was born to be an extension of her mother—she had sometimes resisted and resented this burden, but not for long, for hers was a sunny disposition, and duty was not an ugly Puritan word but something you shouldered with a song in your heart.

Rummaging around in her mind, Louisa took off of a dusty, cobwebby shelf a Christmas reel of her childhood: images of that bitterly cold New England winter flooded the walls of memory. They had been down to their last few sticks of wood, and the winter wind howled around the snow-flocked house, icy fingers reaching in through every crack and crevice and chink. Besides the three sisters, a newborn was now at risk when the firewood was gone. "God will provide" was her father's rejoinder to his wife's worried importuning. "God will provide as He always has."

Just then, there was a knock on the door. A neighbor had braved the banshee winds to bring over a load of wood, unable to escape the conviction that the Alcott family needed firewood. "Needed firewood?" Abba's face resembled a rainbow on a golden morning.

Later that memorable evening, Father had disappeared for some time; when he returned, stomping his half frozen feet on the fireside hearth to restore circulation, he jubilantly announced that a neighbor, with a sick baby in the near-freezing house, had asked for help—how providential that the Lord had sent them wood. Abba's face grew coldly pale: "You . . . you didn't . . . certainly, you *didn't!*" But she knew even before he answered that he had. How *could* he? *They* had a baby too! This was just more than flesh and blood could bear.

But before her pent-up wrath could erupt there was another knock on the door—and another load of wood waited outside. "I told you that we would not suffer," was her father's trusting response. Abba and her girls just looked at each other—absolutely mute.

❊   ❊   ❊

Louisa stirred, aware of a change in the tide: it was beginning to return. A dream-like full moon had risen and the breakers rolling in were now luminous with a ghostly beauty. The wind had died down at last.

Truant-like, before she knew they had slipped away, her thoughts returned to that golden summer in Vevey. How lonely she had been. At first, the mere idea of seeing Europe had entranced her; all she had to do was care for a family friend's invalid daughter: be a companion. But the girl was so insensitive to the beauty and history Louisa reveled in that her joie du vivre had begun to fade.

And then came Ladislas.

He filled a long-aching void in her life, for growing up, she had been so tall, coltish, and tomboyish that romance, for her, could be found only in story books and in dreams. Her sisters it was . . . who were the soft, the feminine, the lovely ones.

Then, when she had grown up, this ugly duckling self-image refused to go away, in spite of the refutation in her mirror and in the eyes of men. As a result, she remained shy and unsure of herself— and certainly, so far, success in her chosen career was mighty slow in coming.

Ladislas unlocked an inner Louisa even she had never seen before. Free, for the first time in her life, to be young without heavy responsibilities and worries, her day-by-day interactions with Ladislas brought new gentleness and vivacity to her face, and his open adoration, stars to her eyes. The older travelers staying at the pension watched the couple, subconsciously envying their youth and happiness. In the evening, Louisa's face, in the flickering candlelight, was graced by that inner radiance that comes but once in a woman's life: from the full knowledge that she is loved and adored by the man she perceives to be her world.

She borrowed not from the future but accepted each day, each hour, each minute, as a gift from God. The realities of life were swept aside to dissipate in the mists of the mountains as they lived each moment with the intensity of those who live on the slopes of a volcano or on an earthquake fault. Time enough for harsh realities later, when the cherubim of circumstance barred them from Eden with their flaming swords.

But like all Shangri-las, this one too had to end. As the cool autumn winds swept down from Mont Blanc, Louisa's invalid charge decided it was time to move to a warmer climate: southern France would be ideal.

As Louisa tearfully packed her trunks, it was no longer possible to pretend that this idyllic island in time would be their home. The age differential, Ladislas's lack of livelihood prospects and weakened health, their cultural differences, Louisa's commitments to her family as well as her own career uncertainties—and, of course, the slight tincture of the maternal in her love for him—all added up to a gradually growing conviction that it would never be. Even as they rowed together, it was her sister May she envisioned opposite Ladislas down through the years; her age equating with his, her love of music and art responding to his, her infectious love of life feeding upon his boyish blandishments, impulsiveness, and warm and tender heart.

But none of this took away from the bittersweet parting. Masking his intense feeling, he kissed her hand in the European manner. As she watched his waving scarf recede into a blur down the train tracks, her eyes filled with tears.

For what right had she to dream of marriage? She, who had vowed to shore up her mother's failing strength, assisting her in every way possible; and then, when that beloved caregiver could no longer function very well, quietly and cheerfully taking her place.

Then, too, Louisa vaguely realized that she was out of step with most of the women of her age, in that marriage, children, and domesticity were really not her all in all, for she had career dreams of her own, and had little inclination to turn over her life to a man, becoming old before her time by repeated pregnancies and brutally heavy housework.

But even that could not check the tears running down her cheeks . . . for love is not governed by the mind.

❈   ❈   ❈

She pulled out her watch and, by the light of the climbing moon, discovered it was almost eleven. Just before midnight, she planned to take a carriage to the ancient cathedral and see the nativity scene everyone had been talking about. And she hungered to hear the choir and pipe organ celebrate the birth of Jesus eighteen and a half centuries ago.

In her pocket was a letter from home (worn and tattered from many readings) that her fingers touched in the darkness. She had no need to reread it for she knew it by heart: Father's lecture tours were not doing very well; Anna had just given birth to her second son (how good John was to her!); Mother continued to weaken, her gradual buckling to the resistless juggernaut of the years becoming ever more apparent to the writer of the letter, May; and as for May— how much she needed a chance to flower, to become a real artist: she must be given the opportunity to experience Europe too.

And never far from mind was Beth—little Beth with her endearing ways whose untimely death seven years before had left an aching void that time would never fill or completely heal. What a *dear* family she had! And how they loved each other! Wouldn't it be wonderful if she could use her writing talents to somehow recapture those magical childhood years, so permeated with sunlight and shadow, laughter and tears.

But every story, *especially* a story of four girls, has to have a hero too. Perhaps—the image of a dark-haired Polish musician, forever teasing, laughing, and cajoling . . . she could no more resist him than she could the incoming tide now lapping at her feet. Brother, sweetheart, and friend. But "Ladislas" would never do. Um-m . . . how about "Lawrence" . . . but she'd call him "Laurie."

She sank into a reverie outside the stream of time. She had no way of foreseeing the future: of knowing that four months later, "Laurie" would be waiting for her at a train station, and that for two wonderful weeks he, she, and Paris in the spring would coalesce in memories that would never die. Nor could she have known that three years later, her book—the first half of the story—would be published, and a year later the second-half sequel would be snapped up by a constantly growing audience, an audience that would but grow with the years. The book would become the most beloved story ever written about an American girl. For, in spite of all her efforts to show off her sisters, offsetting their portraits with unvarnished depictions of her own frailties, mistakes, and weaknesses, she would fail in her purpose—for it would be Jo with whom generations of readers would fall in love.

And who among us could ever read that unforgettable passage, set in the eternally flowering gardens of Vevey, wherein Amy, still mourning the recent death of her sister Beth, looks up . . . and sees him standing there:

"Dropping everything, she ran to him, exclaiming, in a tone of unmistakable love and longing, 'Oh, Laurie, Laurie, I knew you'd come to me!'"

Yes, who among us can ever read that without sensing that the words were really Jo's, that the broken heart was really Jo's, and that the longing for a love that would forever remain imprisoned in the bud of might-have-been, never blossoming into the rose of marriage, was Jo's. Who among us can read that heartbroken call without tears?

✽   ✽   ✽

"Miss Louisa? . . . uh, Miss Alcott?"

"Uh. . . I'm sorry, Jacques, I guess I . . . I must have dozed off. What is it?"

"You asked me to have the carriage ready at fifteen minutes before midnight."

"Oh, yes! Thank you—just give me a minute."

Soon Louisa was settled within the carriage. The horses snorted in the cold night air, and the wheels complained as they chattered and clattered over the cobblestone streets. She looked out her window and took in the festive crowd and air of expectancy that hovered over the city. She realized that she regretted nothing—even if she had the opportunity to live her life over again, she would change not one line. Joy and pain, hand in hand—without both she would have but a one-dimensional ditty or dirge; with both, a multidimensional symphony of life.

She could ask for no more.

Then she heard them, faint at first, then gathering power as they were joined by other bells across the city. The crescendo continued until the ringing and the clanging swallowed up every other sound on earth.

It was Christmas. . . . Christ was born in a manger.

✽   ✽   ✽

HOW THIS SECOND STORY CAME TO BE

*It was fall 1990, almost a year after I had written "The Snow of Christmas."
One of the assigned books for my American literature class was Louisa May
Alcott's* Little Women. *As I was preparing my lecture on Alcott, it came home
to me that I had never delved deeply into her life. So I went searching for a
biography and found Cornelia Miegs' moving* Invincible Louisa. *Having
loved Alcott ever since I'd read through her as a child, I was fascinated by this
biography which opened a door to the world where Alcott's books were born.*

But the story that interested me most had to do with the antecedent of
Little Women's *protagonist, Laurie. I had not known that after the terrible
Civil War was finally over, Alcott had traveled to Europe as a companion for
a friend's invalid daughter. How Alcott reveled in this world she had heretofore
only read about: the scenery, the folklore, the people. In Vevey, on
Switzerland's Lake Geneva, the two women settled down for a time.*

*One day, at Pension Victoria, a thin, rather young Pole by the name of
Ladislas Wisniewski arrived. The young man was weak from illness,
malnutrition, and suffering, for as a Polish patriot, he had been imprisoned
by the Russians. Poland did not exist on the map of Europe in those days,
having been gobbled up by Prussia, Austro-Hungary, and Russia, but still the
Poles yearned to be free. This particular revolt had failed too, and Ladislas
had paid the price. Now, finally released from prison, he was in Switzerland
trying to regain his shattered health. He and Louisa quickly became
friends—then, soul mates. Ladislas taught Louisa French, and she instructed
him in English. They explored the grounds of the chateau, rowed on the lake,
hiked along the mountainsides, and talked unceasingly. In the evenings,
Ladislas would play the piano in the pension parlor.*

*Apparently, never before had any male near her own age come to mean so
much to Louisa. Now, Ladislas's admiration and love bolstered her self-esteem.
Growing up, Louisa had always felt unattractive because of her height and
gangliness, but, now in the warmth of Ladislas's approval, Louisa blossomed.*

*After two months in Vevey, Louisa was informed that it was time to move on.
The separation from Ladislas almost tore her in two. Yet she knew, for a number
of reasons (not least being the age differential: he was twelve years her junior),
that marriage with him would never be. Yet, he had so captured her heart and
soul that she would later on give him immortality with her creation, Laurie.*

*My students were so captivated by the story that as winter rolled around
and people said, "Well, you wrote a Christmas story last year; what's keeping*

you from writing another?" the conviction grew on me that I ought to tell the story of Louisa and Ladislas, but as a bittersweet Christmas romance. "The Bells of Christmas Eve" was the result. Having stayed in the Lake Geneva area for nine days twelve years before, I could picture perfectly the scene in my mind. Also, at the time I wrote the story (December 7-9, 1990), our daughter Michelle was studying abroad for a year at Collognes, France, only a few miles from Lake Geneva, so the setting was never far from my mind.

I had quite a bit of trouble figuring out how to make the story work — especially how to keep Louisa's true identity obscured until the very end of the story. But finally it came together. Afterwards, I had my creative writing class attack it and point out to me any flaws they perceived. At the end, I printed up a limited edition and gave them out to students and friends. It proved to be almost as popular as the first had been.

❋ ❋ ❋

This story first appeared in Review & Herald Publishing Association's trade paperback Christmas in My Heart 2 in 1993, and then in Doubleday's first Christmas in My Heart 1 hardback treasury, in 1996.

The Third Story of Christmas

'Meditation' in a
MINOR KEY

Can a person's life be dominated by a single piece of music? Two people's lives?

❊ ❊ ❊

"Eight minutes until curtain time, Mr. Devereaux."

"How's it looking?"

"Full house. No. *More* than full house—they're already turning away those who'll accept Standing Room Only tickets."

"Frankly, I'm a bit surprised, Mr. Schobel. My last concert here was not much of a success."

"I remember, sir. . . . The house was barely a third full."

"Hmm. I wonder . . . uh . . . what do you suppose has made the difference?"

"Well, for one thing, sir, it's your first-ever Christmas concert. For another, people are regaining interest—that Deutsche Gramophone recording has all Europe talking. But pardon me, sir. I'd better let you get ready. Good luck, sir."

And he was gone.

❊ ❊ ❊

No question about it, he mused as he bowed to acknowledge the applause, the venerable Opera House was indeed full. As always, his eyes panned the sea of faces as he vainly searched for the one who never came—had not in ten long years. He had so hoped tonight would be different. That package—it hadn't done the job after all.

Ten years ago . . . tonight . . . it was. Right here in Old Vienna. It was to have been the happiest Christmas Eve in his life: was not Ginevra to become his bride the next day?

What a fairy-tale courtship that had been. It had all started at the Salzburg Music Festival, where he was the center of attention—not only of the city but of the world. Had he not stunned concert-goers by his incredible coup? The first pianist to ever win grand piano's Triple Crown: the Van Cliburn, the Queen Elizabeth, and the Tchaikovsky competitions?

Fame had built steadily for him as one after another of the great prizes had fallen to him. Now, as reporters, interviewers, and cameramen followed his every move, he grew drunk on the wine of adulation.

It happened as he leaned over the parapet of Salzburg Castle, watching the morning sun gild the rooftops of the city below. He had risen early in order to hike up the hill to the castle and watch the sunrise. A cool alpine breeze ruffled the trees just above; but it also displaced a few strands of raven black hair only a few feet to his left. Their glances met—and they both glanced away, only to blush as they glanced back. She was the most beautiful girl he had ever seen. But beautiful in more than mere appearance: beautiful in poise and grace as well. Later, he would gradually discover her beauty of soul.

With uncharacteristic shyness, he introduced himself to her. And then she withdrew in confusion as she tied the name to the cover stories. Disarming her with a smile, he quickly changed the subject: What was *she* doing in Salzburg?

As it turned out, she was in Europe for a summer-long study tour—and how his heart leaped when she admitted that her study group was staying in Salzburg the entire week. He made the most of it: before her bus had moved on he had pried from her not very reluctant fingers a copy of the tour itinerary.

And like Jean Valjean's inexorable nemesis, Javert, he pursued her all over Europe, driving his concert manager into towering rages. Had he forgotten that there was the long and arduous fall schedule to prepare for? Had he forgotten the time it took to memorize a new repertoire? No, he hadn't forgotten: the truth of the matter was that his priorities had suddenly changed. Every midweek, in around-the-clock marathons, he'd give his practicing its due—then he'd escape in order to be with Ginevra for the weekend.

They were instant soul mates: They both loved the mountains and the sea, dawn and dusk, Tolstoy and Twain, snow and sand, hiking and skiing, Gothic cathedrals and medieval castles, sidewalk cafes and old bookstores. But they were not clones: in art, she loved Georges de la Tour and Caravaggio whereas his patron saints were Dürer and Hieronymus Bosch; in music, he preferred Mozart and Prokofiev whereas she reveled in Chopin and Liszt.

He knew the day he met her that, for him, there would never be another woman. He was that rarity: a man who out of the whole world will choose but one—and if that one be denied him. . . .

But he wasn't denied. It was on the last day of her stay, just hours before she boarded her plane for home, that he asked her to climb with him the zig-zagging inner staircases of the bell tower of Votivkirche, that great neo-Gothic cathedral of Vienna, paling in comparison only with its legendary ancestor, St. Stephens.

Far up in the tower, breathing hard for more than one reason, his voice shook as he took both her hands captive . . . and looked through her honest eyes into her heart—his, he knew, even without asking. She never *did* actually say yes, for the adorable curl of her lips, coupled with the candle-lit road to Heaven in her eyes, was her undoing.

The rapture which followed comes only once in a lifetime—when it comes at all.

Then the scene changed, and he stiffened as if receiving a mortal blow, for but four months later, in that self-same bell tower, his world had come to an end. That terrible, terrible night when his nuptial dreams were slain by a violin.

❖   ❖   ❖

Ginevra drew her heavy coat tighter around her as the airport limousine disappeared into the night. Inside the Opera House she made her way to the ticket counter to ask for directions to her section.

From the other side of the doors she heard Bach's "Italian Concerto" being reborn. . . . She listened intently. She had not been mistaken after all: a change *had* taken place.

Leaning against a pillar, she let the distant notes wash over her while she took the scroll of her life and unrolled a third of it. How vividly she remembered that memorable fall. Michael's letters came as regularly as night following day: long letters most of the time, short messages when his hectic schedule precluded more. Her pattern was unvarying: she would walk up the mountain road to the mailbox, out of the day's mail search for that precious envelope, then carry it unopened on top of the rest of the mail back to the chalet, perched high on a promontory point 1600 feet above the Denver plain. Then she'd walk out onto the upper deck and seat herself. Off to her right were the Flatirons massed above the city of Boulder, front-center below was the skyline of Denver—at night a fairyland of twinkling lights—and to the left the mountains stair-stepped up to 14,255-foot Longs Peak and Rocky Mountain National Park. Then she'd listen for the pines— oh! those heavenly pines! They would be soughing their haunting song . . . and *then* she would open his letter.

So full of romance were her star-lit eyes that weeks passed before she realized there was a hairline crack in her heart—and Michael was the cause of it. She hadn't realized it during that idyllic summer as the two of them had spent so much time exploring Gothic cathedrals, gazing transfixed as light transformed stained glass into heart-stopping glory, sitting on transepts as organists opened their stops and called on their pipes to dare the red zone of reverberating sound.

She finally, in a long letter, asked him point-blank whether or not he believed in God. His response was a masterpiece of subterfuge and fence-straddling, for well he knew how central the Lord was to her. As women have ever since the dawn of time, she rationalized that if he just loved *her* enough—and surely he *did*—then of course he would come to love God as much as she.

So it was that she put her reservations and premonitions aside, and deflected her parents' concerns in that respect as well. Michael had decided he wanted to be married in the same cathedral where he had proposed to her, and as it was large enough to accommodate family as well as key figures of the music world, she had reluctantly acquiesced. Personally, she would have much rather been married in the small Boulder church high up on Mapleton Avenue. A Christmas wedding there, in the church she so loved . . . but it was not to be.

Deciding to make the best of it, she and her family drove down the mountain, took the freeway to Stapleton Airport, boarded the plane, and found their seats. As the big United jet roared off the runway, she looked out the window at Denver and her beloved Colorado receding below her. She wondered: Could Michael's European world ever really take its place?

It was cold that memorable Christmas Eve, and the snow lay several feet deep on Viennese streets. Ginevra, ever the romantic, shyly asked Michael if he would make a special pilgrimage with her.

"Where to?" queried Michael, "It's mighty cold outside."

"The bell tower of Votivkirche."

He grinned that boyish grin she loved. "I really *am* marrying a sentimentalist, aren't I? Oh well," he complained good-naturedly, "guess I'd better get used to it. Let's find our coats."

An unearthly quiet came over the great city as they once again climbed the winding staircases of Votivkirche. She caught her breath at the beauty of it all when they at last reached their eyrie and looked down at the frosted rooftops and streets below. Michael, however, much preferred the vision *she* represented, in her flame-colored dress and sable coat.

Then it was . . . faintly and far away . . . that they heard it. They never did trace its origin exactly. It might have wafted its way up the tower from below or it might have come from an apartment across the way. Ordinarily, in the cacophony of the city, they could not possibly have heard it, but tonight, with snow deadening the street sounds, they could distinctly pick up every note. Whoever the violinist was . . . was a master.

Ginevra listened, transfixed. Michael, noting her tear-stained cheeks, shattered the moment with an ill-timed laugh. "Why, you old crybaby, it's nothing but a song! I've heard it somewhere before. . . . I don't remember who wrote it, but it's certainly nothing to cry over."

He checked himself as he saw her recoil as if he had slashed her face with a whip. Her face blanched, and she struggled for control. After a long pause, she said in a toneless voice: "It's not a song—it's "Meditation" by Massenet."

"Well, that's fine with me," quipped Michael. "I'll just meditate about *you.*"

There was a long silence, and now, quite ill at ease, he shuffled his feet and tried to pass it all off as a joke.

But in that, he failed abysmally: "You . . . you don't hear it at all," she cried. "You just don't. . . . I never hear that melody without tears, or without soaring to heaven on the notes. Massenet *had* to have been a Christian! And, furthermore, whoever plays it like we just heard it played *has* to be a Christian too!"

"Oh, come now, Ginevra. Aren't you getting carried away by a simple little ditty? *Anyone* who really knows how to play the violin could play it just as well. . . . *I* certainly could—and I don't even believe in . . . in God—" He stopped, vainly trying to slam his lips on the words in time, but perversely they slipped out of their own accord.

Deep within the citadel of her innermost being, Ginevra felt her heart shudder as if seized by two powerful opposing forces. Then—where the hairline crack of her heart once was—there was an awful *"crack"*—and a yawning fault took its place.

The look of agony on her face brought him to his senses at last—but it was too late. She looked at him with glaciered cheeks and with eyes so frozen that he could barely discern the tiny flickering that had, only moments ago, almost overpowered him with the glow of a thousand love-lit candles.

She turned, slipped something which had once been on her finger into his coat pocket, and was gone. So quickly was the act done that at first he failed to realize she was no longer there. Then he called after her and ran blindly down the stairs. Ginevra, however, with the instinct of a wounded animal, found an unlocked stairwell door and hid inside until he had raced down the tower and into the street. Much later, she silently made her way out into a world made glad by midnight bells. But there was no Christmas gladness in *her* heart.

She determined to never see him again. Neither his calls nor his letters nor his telegrams would she answer; she wrote him only once: "Please do not *ever* try to contact me in any way again."

And he—his pride in shreds—never had.

❀　❀　❀

Never . . . would he forget that awful Christmas when—*alone*—he had to face the several thousand wedding guests and the importunate press with the news that it was all off. No, he could give them no reasons. And then he had fled.

Since he had planned on an extended honeymoon he had no more concerts scheduled until the next fall. That winter and spring he spent much time in solitude, moping and feeling sorry for himself. By late spring, he was stir-crazy, so he fled to the South Pacific, to Asia, to Africa, to South America—*anywhere* to get away from himself and his memories.

Somehow, by mid-summer, he began to regain control; he returned to Europe and quickly mastered his fall repertoire. That fall, most of his reviews were of the rave variety, for he dazzled with his virtuosity and technique.

For several years, his successes continued, and audiences filled concert halls wherever he performed. But there came a day when that was no longer true, when he realized that most dreaded of performing world truths: that it was all over—he had peaked. Here he was, his career hardly begun, and his star was already setting. But *why?*

Reviewers and concert-goers alike tried vainly to diagnose the ailment and prescribe medicinal cures, but nothing worked. More and more the tenor of the reviews began to sound like the following:

How sad it is that Devereaux—once thought to be the rising star of our age: the worthy successor to Horowitz—has been revealed as but human clay after all. It is as if he represents but a case of arrested development. Normally, as a pianist lives and ages, the roots sink deeper and the storm-battered trunk and branches develop seasoning and rugged strength. Not so with Devereaux. It's as if all growth ceased some time ago. Oh! No one can match him where it comes to razzle-dazzle and special effects, but one gets a bit tired of these when there is no offsetting depth.

❀　❀　❀

Like a baseball slugger in a prolonged batting slump, Michael tried everything: he dabbled in every philosophy or mysticism he came across. Like a drunken bee, he reeled from flower to flower without any real sense of direction.

And "Meditation" had gradually become an obsession with him. He just couldn't seem to get it out of his consciousness. He determined to prove to her that you didn't have to be religious in order to play it well. But as much as he tried, as much as he applied his vaunted techniques and interpretive virtuosity to it, it yet remained as flat, stale, and unmoving as three-hour-old coffee.

He even went to the trouble of researching the tune's origins, feeling confident that it, like much music concert performers play, would apparently have no religious connections whatsoever. In his research, he discovered that "Meditation" came from Massenet's opera *Thaïs*, which he knew had to do with a dissolute courtesan. Aha! He had her! But then, he dug deeper and discovered, to his chagrin, that although it was true that Thais had a dissolute sexual past, as was true with Mary Magdalene, she was redeemed—and "Meditation" represents the intermezzo bridge between the pagan past of the first two acts and the oneness with God in the third act.

So he had to acknowledge defeat here too.

As for Ginevra, she was never far from his thoughts. But not once would his pride permit him to ask anyone about her, her career, or whether or not she had ever married.

He just *existed* . . . and measured his life by concerts and hotel rooms.

❊   ❊   ❊

Ginevra too, after the long numbness and shock had at last weathered into a reluctant peace, belatedly realized that life had to go on . . . but just what should she do with her life?

It was during a freak spring blizzard which snowed her in that the answer came. She had been sitting in the conversation pit of the three-story-high massive moss rock fireplace, gazing dreamily into the fire, when suddenly, the mood came upon her to write. She reached for a piece of paper, picked up her Pilot pen, and began writing a poem. A poem about pain, disillusion, and heartbreak. The next day, she mailed it off to a magazine. Not long after, it was published.

She decided to do graduate work in the humanities and in education. She completed, along the way, a Masters, and later a

Ph.D.; in the process, becoming the world's foremost authority on the life and times of a woman writer of the American heartland. She also continued, as her busy schedule permitted, to write poems, essays, short stories, inspirational literature, and longer works of fiction.

So it was that Ginevra became a teacher: a teacher of writing, of literature — and life. Each class was a microcosm of life itself; in each class were souls crying out to be ministered to, to be appreciated, to be loved.

Because of her charm, vivacity, joie du vivre, and sense of humor, she became ever more popular and beloved with the passing of the years. She attracted suitors like children to a toy store. Yet, though some of these friendships got to the threshold of love, none of them got any further: it was as if not one of them could match what she had left behind in Vienna.

The good Lord it was who saw her through: who shored up her frailties and helped to mend the brokenness.

Meanwhile, she did find time to keep up with Michael's life and career. In doing so, she bought all his recordings and played them often. Yet, she was vaguely dissatisfied: she too noting the lack of growth — and wondered.

One balmy day in late November during the seventh year after the breakup, as she was walking down the ridge to her home, she stopped to listen to her two favorite sounds: the cascading creek cavorting its way down to the Front Range plain and the sibilant whispering of the pines. Leaning against a large rock, she looked up at that incredibly blue sky of the Colorado high country.

As always, her thoughts refused to stay in their neat little cages. She had tried all kinds of locks during those seven years, but not one of them worked. And now, when she had thought them safely locked in, here came all her truant thoughts; bounding up to her like a ragtag litter of exuberant puppies, overjoyed at finding her hiding place.

And every last one of the little mutts was yelping Michael's name.

What would *he* be doing this Christmas? It bothered her — had bothered her for almost seven years now — that her own judge had refused to acquit her for her Michael-related words and actions. Periodically, during these years, she had submitted her case to the judge in the courthouse of her mind; and every last time, after listening to the evidence, the judge had looked at her stern-faced. She would bang the gavel on the judicial bench and intone severely: "Insufficient evidence on which to absolve you. . . . Next case?"

She couldn't get out of her head an article she had read several months before—an article about Michael Devereaux. The writer, who had interviewed her subject in depth, had done her homework well: for the portrait of Michael rang true to Ginevra. The individual revealed in the character sketch was both the Michael Ginevra knew and a Michael she would rather not know. The interviewer pointed out that Michael was a rather bitter man for one so young in years. So skittish had the interviewee been when approached on the subject of women in his life, that the writer postulated that it was her personal conviction that somewhere along the way Devereaux had been terribly hurt by someone he loved deeply. . . . And here, Ginevra winced. The writer concluded her character portrait with a disturbing synthesis: "Devereaux, his concert career floundering, appears to be searching for answers. But he's not looking in the direction of God. Like many, if not most, Europeans of our time, he appears to be almost totally secular; thus he has nowhere but within himself upon which to draw strength and inspiration. Sadly, his inner wells appear to retain only shallow reservoirs from which to draw. . . . A pity."

A nagging thought returned to tug at her heart-strings: What had *she* done—what had she *ever* done—to show Michael a better way? . . . "But," she retorted, "I don't want him to become a Christian just for *me!*" But this time that oft-used cop-out didn't suffice. She kept seeing that stern-faced judge within. . . . In the long, long silence that followed was born a plan of action. If it worked, if he responded as she hoped he might, sooner or later, she would *know!* For inescapably, the secret would "out" through his music.

She determined to implement her plan of action that very day.

❖   ❖   ❖

Several weeks after Ginevra's decision, Michael had returned to his hotel after a concert, a particularly unsatisfactory one—and it seemed these days that there were more and more of this kind. Even the crowd had been smaller than any he could remember in years. He was increasingly convinced that his career and life were both failures—and that there was little reason to remain living. He went to bed and vainly tried to sleep. After an hour or two of thrashing around, he got up, turned on the light, and looked for the last packet of mail forwarded to him by his agent. There was something in it that intrigued him. Ah! Here it was.

A small registered package had arrived from New York. There was no return address, and he didn't recognize the handwriting on the mailer. Inside was a slim, evidently long-out-of-print book titled *The Other Wise Man* written by an author he had never heard of: Henry Van Dyke. . . . Well, it looked like a quick-read and he couldn't sleep anyhow . . .

A quick-read it was not. He found himself rereading certain passages several times. It was after 3 A.M. before he finally put it down. He was moved in spite of himself. Then, he retired, this time to sleep.

During that Christmas season, he reread it twice more—and each time he read it he wondered what had motivated that unknown person to send it.

Three months later came another registered packet from New York. It too was obviously a book and, to his joy, another old one. To his relief—for he had an intense fear of God and religion—it did not appear to be a religious book. The author and title were alike unknown to him: Myrtle Reed's *The Master's Violin*. The exquisite metallic lamination of this turn-of-the-century first edition quite took his breath away. *Someone* had spent some money on *this* gift! He read it that night, and it seemed, in some respects, that the joy and pain he vicariously experienced in the reading mirrored his own. And the violin! It brought back memories of that melody, that melody which just would not let him go, that melody which represented the high tide of his life.

It was mid-June, three months later, when the next registered package arrived from New York. This time, his hands were actually trembling as he opened the package. Another book by yet another author he'd never heard of: Harold Bell Wright. Kind of a strange title it had: *That Printer of Udel's*. But it was old and had a tipped-in cover: the combination was irresistible. He dropped everything and started to read.

He was not able to put it down. In it he saw depicted a portrait of Christian living unlike any he had ever seen before: a way of life which had to do not just with sterile doctrine but with a living, loving outreach to one's fellow man. He finished the book late that night. A month later, he read it again.

By late September, he had been watching his mail with great anticipation for some time. What would it be this time? Then it came: another book, first published in 1907, by the same author, with the intriguing title: *The Calling of Dan Matthews*. It made the same impact upon him its predecessor had. Nevertheless, Michael was no easy nut to crack: he continued to keep his jury sequestered — he was nowhere near ready for a verdict of any kind.

Early in December arrived his second Van Dyke: *The Mansion*, a lovely, lime-green, illustrated edition. This book spawned some exceedingly disturbing questions about his inner motivations. Of what value, really, was *his* life? When was the last time he had ever done anything for someone without expecting something in return? For such a small book, it certainly stirred up some difficult-to-answer questions!

March brought a book he had often talked about reading, but never had the temerity to tackle: Victor Hugo's forbidding *Les Misérables:* almost 1500 pages unabridged! He wondered: *Why!* Why such a literary classic following what he had been sent before? He didn't wonder long: the story of Jean Valjean was a story of redemption; the story of a man who climbed out of hell. It contained the first Christ-figure he could ever remember seeing in French literature. By now, he was beginning to look for fictional characters who exhibited, in some manner, Christian values.

At the end of the book was a brief note:

NO OTHER BOOK FOR SIX MONTHS. REVIEW.

He did . . . but he felt terribly abused, sorely missing the expected package in June.

By the time September's leaves began to fall, he was in a state of intense longing. Certainly, after *Les Misérables*, and after a half-year wait, it would have to be a blockbuster! To his amazement and disgust, it was a slim mass-market paperback with the thoroughly unappetizing title of *Mere Christianity*. The author he knew of but had never read: C. S. Lewis.

Swallowing his negative feelings with great difficulty, he gingerly tested with his toes . . . Lewis's Jordan River. As he stepped farther in, he was—quite literally—overwhelmed. Every argument he had ever thrown up as a barrier between him and God was systematically and thoroughly demolished. He had had no idea that God and Christianity were any more than an amalgamation of feelings—for the first time, he was able to conceptualize God with his *mind!*

Whoever was sending him the books was either feeling sorry for making him wait so long—or punishing him by literally burying him in print! He was kindly given two weeks to digest *Mere Christianity,* and then began the nonstop barrage of his soul: first came three shells in a row: Lewis's space trilogy: *Out of That Silent Planet, Perelandra,* and *That Hideous Strength.* At first, Michael, like so many other readers of these books, enjoyed the plot solely on the science fiction level. Then, he wryly observed to himself that Lewis had set him up: woven into the story was God and His plan of salvation!

The Trilogy was followed by Lewis's *Screwtape Letters.* How Michael laughed as he read this one! How incredibly wily is the Great Antagonist! And how slyly Lewis had reversed the roles in order to shake up all his simplistic assumptions about the battles between Good and Evil.

A week later: another shell—*The Four Loves.* In it, Michael found himself reevaluating almost all of his people-related friendships in life. That was but the beginning: Then Lewis challenged him to explore the possibilities of a friendship with the Eternal.

Two shells then came in succession: *Surprised By Joy* and *A Grief Observed.* At long last, he was able to learn more about Lewis the man. Not only that, but how Lewis, so late in life introduced to the joys of nuptial love, related to the untimely death of his bride. How Lewis, in his wracking grief, almost lost his way—almost turned away God Himself! Paralleling Lewis's searing loss of his beloved was Michael's loss of Ginevra: relived once again, it was bone-wrenching in its intensity. More so than Lewis's—for he had not Lewis's God to turn to in the darkest hour.

The final seven shells came in the form of what appeared to be, at first glance, a series of books for children: Lewis's *Chronicles of Narnia.* It took Michael some time to figure out why he'd been sent this series last—after such heavyweights! It was not until he was about half way through that he knew. By then, he had fully realized just how powerful a manifestation of the attributes of Christ Aslan the lion was. By the moving conclusion of *The Last Battle*, the fifteen shells from Lewis's howitzer had made mere rubble out of what was left of Michael's defense system.

Then came a beautiful edition of the Phillips Translation of the New Testament. On the fly leaf, in neat black calligraphy, was this line:

MAY THIS BOOK HELP TO MAKE
YOUR NEW YEAR TRULY NEW.

He read the New Testament with a receptive attitude, taking a month to complete it. One morning, following a concert the night before in Florence, he rose very early and walked to the Arno River to watch the sunrise. As he leaned against a lamppost, his thoughts (donning their accountant coats) did an audit of the past three years.

He was belatedly discovering that a life without God just wasn't worth living: in fact, *nothing*, he now concluded, had any lasting meaning divorced from a higher power. He looked around him, mentally scrutinizing the lives of family members, friends, and colleagues in the music world. He noted the devastating divorce statistics, the splintered homes, and the resulting flotsam of loneliness and despair. Without God, he now concluded, no human relationship was likely to last very long.

Nevertheless, even now that he was thoroughly convinced—in his mind—that God represented the only way out of his dead-end existence, he bull-headedly balked at crossing the line out of the Dark into the Light.

The day before Easter of that tenth year, there came another old book, an expensive English first edition of Francis Thompson's poems. Inside, on the end sheet, was this coda to their faceless three-year friendship:

> *Dear Michael,*
>
> *For almost three years now,*
> *you have never been out of my*
> *thoughts and prayers.*
> *I hope that these books have come*
> *to mean to you what they do to me.*
> *This is your last book.*

Please read "The Hound of Heaven."
The rest is up to you.

Your Friend

Immediately, he turned to the long poem, and immersed himself in Thompson's lines. Although some of the words were a bit antiquated and jarred a little, nevertheless he felt that the lines were written laser-straight to him, especially those near the poem's gripping conclusion—for Michael identified totally with Thompson's own epic flight from the pursuing celestial Hound:

Whom will you find to love ignoble thee

Save Me, save only Me?

All which I took from thee I did but take,

Not for thy harms,

But just that thou might'st seek it in My arms.

All which thy child's mistake

Fancies as lost, I have stored for thee at home.

Rise, clasp My hand, and come!

These lines broke him . . . and he fell to his knees.

※　　※　　※

It was the morning after, and Michael awakened to the first Easter of the rest of his life. Needing very much to be alone, he decided to head for the family chalet near Mt. Blanc. How fortunate, he mused, that the rest of the family was skiing at St. Moritz that week.

Two hours before he got there, it began to snow, but his Porsche, itself born during a bitterly cold German winter, growled its delight as it devoured the road to Chamonix. It was snowing even harder when he arrived at the chalet, where Michael was greeted with delight by Jacques and Marie, the caretakers.

Breakfast was served adjacent to a roaring fire in the great alpine fireplace. Afterwards, thoroughly satisfied, he leaned back in his favorite chair and looked out at the vista of falling snow.

He *felt*, he finally concluded, as if sometime in the night he had been reborn. It was as if all his life he had been carrying a staggeringly heavy backpack, a backpack into which some cruel overseer had dropped yet another five-pound brick *each* January 1 of his life, for as far back as he could remember. And now—

suddenly—he was *free!* What a paradoxical revelation that was: that the long-feared surrender to God resulted in—not the dreaded strait-jacketed servitude—but the most incredible euphoric freedom he had ever imagined!

Looking back at the years of his life, he now recognized that he had been fighting God every step of the way, but God, refusing to give up on him, had merely kept His distance. He went to his suitcase, reached for that already precious book of poems, returned to his seat by the fire, and turned again to that riveting first stanza:

> *I fled Him, down the nights and down the days;*
> *I fled Him, down the arches of the years;*
> *I fled Him, down the labyrinthine ways*
> *Of my own mind, and in the midst of tears*
> *I hid from Him, and under running laughter.*
> *Up vistaed hopes I sped;*
> *And shot, precipitated*
> *Adown Titanic glooms of chastened fears,*
> *From those strong Feet that followed, followed after.*
> *But with unhurrying chase,*
> *And unperturbed pace,*
> *Deliberate speed, majestic instancy,*
> *They beat—and a Voice beat*
> *More instant than the Feet—*
> *"All things betray thee, who betrayest Me!"*

❖   ❖   ❖

He turned away, unable, because of a blurring of his vision, to read on:

"How many *years* I have lost!" he sighed.

Years during which the frenetic pace of his life caused the Pursuing Hound to sadly drop back. Years during which he proudly strutted, wearing the tinsel crown of popularity. And then . . . that flimsy bit of ephemera was taken away and the long descent into the maelstrom had taken place. And it had been in his darkest hour, when he actually felt Ultimate Night reaching for him, that he plainly and distinctly heard his Pursuer again.

For almost three years now that Pursuer had drawn ever closer. There had been a strange meshing: the Voice in the crucifixion earthquake who spoke to Artaban, the Power that defied the Ally in the Dan Matthews story, the Force revealed through the pulsating strings of "Mine Cremona," the Presence which—through the Bishop's incredible act of forgiveness and compassion—saved the shackled life of Jean Valjean, the Angel who showed John Weightman's pitiful mansion to him, Malacandra of the Perelandra story, and Aslan in the Narnia series. As he read "The Hound of Heaven," all the foregoing lost their distinctiveness and merged into the pursuing Hound. They were one and the same!

❊   ❊   ❊

Michael resonated with a strange new power, a power he had never experienced before. It was as if, during the night, in his badly-crippled power station (a generating facility to which, over the years, one incoming line after another had been cut, until he was reduced to but one frail piece of frayed wire that alone kept him from blackout), a new cable, with the capacity to illuminate an entire world, had been snaked down the dusty stairs, and then: *plugged in.*

Then—from far back (even before his descent into hell), two images emerged out of the mists of time: one visual and one aural—the tear-stained face of the Only Woman . . . and the throbbing notes of "Meditation."

Tingling all over, he stood up and walked over to the grand piano always kept in the lodge for his practicing needs, lifted up the lid, seated himself on the bench, and looked up. Humbly, he asked the question: "Am I ready at last, Lord?"

Then he reached for the keys and began to play. As his fingers swept back and forth, something else occurred: for the first time in over nine years, he was able—without printed music—to replay in his mind every note, every intonation, he and Ginevra had heard in that far-off bell tower of Votivkirche. Not only that . . . but the sterility was gone! The current that had been turned on inside him leaped to his hands and fingers.

At *last* . . . he was ready.

❊   ❊   ❊

Michael immediately discarded the fall concert repertoire, chosen as it had been merely for showmanship reasons, and substituted a new musical menu for the old. Ever so carefully, as a master chef prepares a banquet for royalty, he selected his individual items. In fact, he agonized over them, for each number must not only mesh with all the others, but enhance as well, gradually building into a crescendo that would trumpet a musical vision of his new life.

Much more complicated was the matter of his new recording. How could he stop the process at such a late date? Not surprisingly, when he met with Polygram management and dropped his bombshell, they were furious. Only with much effort was he able to calm them down — and that on a premise they strongly doubted: that his replacement would be so much *better* that they would be more than compensated for double the expected production expense!

He walked out of their offices in a very subdued mood. If he had retained any illusions about how low his musical stock had sunk, that meeting would have graphically settled the question. If his new recording failed to sell well, he would almost certainly be dropped from the label.

Then, he memorized all the numbers before making his trial run recording; this way, he was able to give his undivided attention to interpretation before wrapping up the process. Only after he himself was thoroughly satisfied with the results did he have it recorded and then hand-carried by his agent to Deutsche Gramophone/Polygram management.

He didn't have to wait very long; only minutes after they played his pilot recording, Michael received a long-distance phone call from the president himself. Michael had known him for years and knew him to be a very tough *hombre* indeed. Recognizing full well that he and the company lived and died by the bottom line, he was used to making decisions for the most pragmatic of reasons. And recording artists feared him because he had a way of telling the unvarnished truth sans embellishments or grace-notes. And now he was on the line. Initially, almost speechless, he finally recovered and blurted out, "What has happened, Michael? For years now, your recordings have seemed — pardon my candidness, but you know blunt me — a bit tinny, fluffy, sometimes listless, and even a bit . . . uh . . . for want of a better word . . . 'peevish,' more or less as if you were irritably going through the motions again, but with little idea why. Now, here, on the other hand, comes a recording which sounded to us like you woke up one morning and decided to belatedly take control of your life and career; that there were new and exciting ways of interpreting music—interpreting with power . . . and beauty . . . and, I might add, Michael . . . a promise of depth and seasoning we quite frankly no longer believed was in you! *What has happened?*"

✣ ✣ ✣

That incredible summer passed in a blur of activity. The long ebb over at last, the incoming tidal forces of Michael's life now thundered up the beaches of the musical world. Deutsche Gramophone management and employees worked around the clock to process, release; and then market what they firmly believed would be the greatest recording of his career. Word leaked out even before it was released; consequently, there was a run on it when it hit the market. All of this translated into enthusiastic interest in his fall concert schedule.

Early in August, before the recording had been released, Michael phoned his New York agent, who could hardly contain himself about the new bookings which were flooding in for the North American tour, spring of the following year. Michael, after first swearing him to secrecy, told him that he was entrusting to his care the most delicate assignment of their long association—one which, if botched, would result in irreparable damage. The agent promised to fulfill his instructions to the letter.

He wanted of him three things: to trace the whereabouts of a certain lady (taking great pains to ensure that the lady in question would not be aware of the search process); to find out if the lady had married; to process a mailing (the contents of the mailing would be adjusted according to whether the lady had married or not).

✣ ✣ ✣

Meanwhile, Ginevra played the waiting game—a very *hard* game to play without great frustration. And for her, the frustration level had been steadily building for almost three years. *When* would she know?

Within a year after mailing her first book, she felt reasonably confident that he was reading what she had sent, but she had little data upon which to base her assumptions. During the second year, little snips of information relating to possible change in Devereaux appeared here and there. Nothing really significant, but enough to give her hope.

She had knelt down by her bed that memorable morning before she mailed Thompson's poems. In her heartfelt supplication, she voiced her conviction that, with this book, she had now done all that was in her power to do. The rest was up to Him. Then she drove down the mountain to the Boulder Post Office and sent it to her New York relayer—and returned home to wait.

It was several months before the Devereaux-related excitement in the music world began to build. Her heart beat a lilting "allegro" the day she first heard about the growing interest in Michael's new recording. She could hardly wait to get a copy.

Then came the day when, in her mailbox, there appeared a little yellow piece of paper indicating that a registered piece of mail was waiting for her in the post office. It turned out to be a *very large* package from an unknown source in New York.

Not until she had returned to her chalet did she open it. Initially, she was almost certain that one of her former students was playing a joke on her, for the box was disproportionately light. She quickly discovered the reason: it was jammed full with wadded-up paper. Her room was half full of paper before she discovered the strange-shaped box at the very bottom of the mailing carton. . . . *What* could it be? . . . *Whom* could it be from? . . . In this box, obviously packed with great care, were five items, each separated by a hard cardboard divider: a perfect flame-red rose in a sealed moisture-tight container, Michael's new Deutsche Gramophone recording, a publicity poster of a concert program which read as follows:

MICHAEL DEVEREAUX
FIRST CHRISTMAS EVE CONCERT
VIENNA OPERA HOUSE

(followed by the other data giving exact time and date), a round-trip airline ticket to Vienna, and at the very bottom, in an exquisite gold box—a front section ticket to the concert.

❈   ❈   ❈

Fearing lest someone in the standing section take her place before she could reach her seat, during the enthusiastic applause following Bach's "Italian Concerto," Ginevra asked an usher to escort her to her seat in the third row. Michael, who had turned to acknowledge the applause, caught the motion: the beautiful woman coming down the aisle. And she was wearing a flame-red rose. Even in Vienna, a city known for its beautiful women, she was a sight to pin dreams on.

How terribly grateful he was to the audience for continuing to clap, for that gave him time, precious time in which to restore his badly damaged equilibrium. It was passing strange, mused Michael. For years now, both his greatest dream and his greatest nightmare were one and the same: that Ginevra would actually show up for one of his concerts. The nightmare had to do with deep-seated fear that her presence in the audience would inevitably destroy his concentration, and with it the concert itself. And now, *here* she was! If he ever needed a higher power, he needed it now. Briefly, he bowed his head. When he raised it, he felt again this new sense of serenity, peace, and command.

Leaving the baroque world of Bach, he now turned to César Franck; being a composer of romantic music, but with baroque connections, Michael had felt him to be a perfect bridge from Bach to Martin and Prokofiev. As he began to play Franck's "Prelude: Chorale et Fugue," he settled down to making this the greatest concert of his career. He had sometimes envied the great ones their announced conviction that, for each, the greatest concert was always the very next one on the schedule—they *never* took a free ride on their laurels. Only this season it had been that he had joined the masters, belatedly recognizing that the greatest thanks he could ever give his Maker would be to extend his powers to the limits every time he performed, regardless of how large or how small the crowd.

The Opera House audience had quickly recognized the almost mind-boggling change in attitude. The last time he had played here, reviewers had unkindly but accurately declared him washed up. So desperate for success of any kind had he become that he openly pandered to what few people still came. It was really pathetic: He would edge out onto the platform like an abused puppy, cringing lest he be kicked again. Not surprisingly, what he apparently expected, he got.

Now, there was never any question as to who was in control. On the second, he would stride purposefully onto the stage, with a pleasant look on his face, and gracefully bow. He would often change his attire between sections: adding a visual extra to the auditory. His attire was always impeccable: newly cleaned and pressed, and he was neither over- nor underdressed for the occasion.

But neither was he proud, recognizing just how fragile is the line between success and failure—and how terribly difficult it is to stay at the top once you get there. Nor did he anymore grovel or play to the galleries. The attitude he now projected was, quite simply: *I'm so pleased you honored me by coming out tonight. I have prepared long and hard for this occasion; consequently, it is both my intent and my expectation that we shall share the greatest musical hour and a half of our lifetimes.*

Ginevra felt herself becoming part of a living, breathing island in time. Every concert performed well is that: kind of a magic moment during which outside life temporarily ceases to be. Great music, after all, is outside of time and thus not subject to its rules. Thus it was that Ginevra, like the Viennese audience, lost all sense of identity, as Devereaux's playing became all the reality they were to know for some time.

These weren't just notes pried from a reluctant piano they were hearing: this was life itself, life with all its frustrations and complexities.

With such power and conviction did César Franck speak from the grave that they stood applauding for three minutes at the end of the first half. In fact, disregarding Opera House protocol, a number of the younger members of the audience swarmed onto the stage and surrounded Michael before he could get backstage. The new Michael stopped, and with a pleasant look on his face all the while, autographed every last program that was shoved at him. Nay—more than that: as one of these autograph seekers, jubilant of face, came back to Ginevra's row, she saw him proudly showing the program to his parents. Michael had taken the trouble to learn each person's name so he could inscribe each one personally!

Michael's tux was wringing wet. As for the gleaming black Boersendorfer, with such super-human energy had Michael attacked it that it begged for the soothing balm of a piano tuner's ministrations; hence it was wheeled out for a badly needed rest. In its place was the monarch of the city's Steinway grands. Michael had specifically requested this living nine feet of history. No one knew for sure just how old it was, but it had for years been the pride and joy of Horowitz. Rubinstein would play here on no other, and it was even rumored that the great Paderewski performed on it. Michael, like all real artists, deeply loved his favorite instruments. Like the fabled Velveteen Rabbit, when an instrument such as this Steinway has brought so much happiness, fulfillment, meaning, and love into life . . . well, over the years, it ceases to be just a piano and approaches personhood. Thus it was that Michael, before it was wheeled in, had a heart-to-heart chat with it.

A stagehand, watching the scene, didn't even lift an eyebrow— concert musicians were *all* a loony bunch.

❖   ❖   ❖

Only after a great deal of soul-searching had Michael decided to open the second half of his concert with Swiss-born Frank Martin's "Eight Preludes." He had long appreciated and loved Martin's fresh approach to music, his lyrical euphonies. Martin reminded Michael of the American composer Howard Hanson. He often had a difficult time choosing which one to include in a given repertoire; but this season, it was Martin's turn.

More and more sure of himself, Michael only gained in power as he retold Martin's story; by the time he finished the Preludes, he owned Vienna. The deafening applause rolled on and on. And nobody appeared willing to ever sit down.

Finally, the house quiet once again, a microphone was brought out, and Michael stepped up to speak.

"Ladies and gentlemen," he began, "I have a substitution to make. As you know, I am scheduled to perform Prokofiev's 'Sonata #6 in A Major, Opus 82' as my concluding number, but I hope you will not be *too* disappointed"—and here he smiled his boyish grin—"if I substitute a piece that I composed, a piece that has never before been performed in public."

He paused, then continued: "Ten years ago tonight, in this fair city, this piece of music was born, but it was not completed until late this spring. I have been saving it for tonight." And here, he dared to glance in the direction of Ginevra.

"The title is . . . 'Variations on a Theme by Massenet.'"

❖   ❖   ❖

Nothing in Michael's composing experience had been more difficult than deciding what to do with "Meditation." And the difficulties did not fall away with his conversion. He still had some tough decisions to face: Should his variations consist merely as creative side-trips from that one melodic base? By doing so, he knew he could dazzle. Should the variations be limited to musical proof that he and his Maker were now friends? With neither was he satisfied.

Of all the epiphanies he had ever experienced, none could compare with the one which was born to him one "God's in His Heaven / All's right with the world" spring morning: He realized that he could create a counterpart to what Massenet had done with the "Meditation" intermezzo—a fusion of earthly love with the divine. Belatedly, he recognized a great truth: God does not come to us in the abstract—He comes to us through flesh and blood. We do not initially fall in love with God as a principle; rather, we first fall in love with human beings whose lives radiate friendship with the divine. It is only *then* that we seek out God on our own.

Ginevra was such a prototype—that is why he had fallen in love with her. And he had little doubt in his mind but that it was she who had choreographed his conversion. No one else had he ever known who would have cared enough to institute and carry out such a flawless plan of action. Besides, some of the book choices made him mighty suspicious.

Michael had also recognized what all true artists do sooner or later: that their greatest work must come from within, from known experience. If he was to endow his variations with power akin to the original, they must emanate from the joys and sorrows that made him what he was . . . and since she and God were inextricably woven together in Michael's multi-hued bolt of life, then woven together they must remain throughout the composition.

It would not be acceptable for her to distance herself and pretend she could judge what he had become dispassionately. No, Ginevra must enter into the world he had composed . . . and decide at the other end whether or not she would stay.

❖   ❖   ❖

In Ginevra's mind, everything seemed to harken back to that cold night in the tower of Votivkirche, for it was there that two lives, only hours from oneness, had seen the cable of their intertwining selves unravel in only seconds.

Furthermore, there was more than God holding them apart. More than her romanticism as compared to his realism. That far-off exchange of words had highlighted for her some significant problems which, left unresolved, would preclude marriage even if Michael *had* been converted. Let's see: How could she conceptualize them?

Essentially, it all came down to these. Michael had laughed at and ridiculed her deepest-felt feelings. Had made light of her tears. Had shown a complete absence of empathy. Worse yet, he exhibited a clear-cut absence of the one most crucial character trait in the universe: *kindness*. Also, at no time since she had known him had she ever seen him admit in any way that he was wrong about anything—and compounding the problem, he had refused to disclose his true identity to her:

There had been a locked door halfway down to his heart.

There had been another locked door halfway up to his soul.

As far as she knew, both doors were still closed. But if they ever were to be unlocked . . . "Meditation" would be the key.

✻   ✻   ✻

As-soft-as-a-mother's-touch pianissimo, Michael begins to play. So softly that there appear to be no breaks at all between the notes, but rather a continuous skein of melodic sound. And, for the first time in Michael's career, there is a flowing oneness with the piano: impossible to tell where flesh, blood, and breath end and where wood, ivory, and metal join.

Ginevra cannot help but feel tense in spite of blurred fingers weaving dreams around her. Deep down, she knows that what occurs during *this* piece of music will have a profound effect upon the rest of her life. And the rest of Michael's life.

But she didn't travel so many thousands of miles just to be a referee or a critic. If their two worlds are ever to be one, she must leave her safe seat in the audience and step into the world of Michael's composition. Strangely enough—and living proof that it is the "small" things in life that are often the most significant— Michael's exhibition of kindness to the young people who blocked his exit during intermission strongly predisposes her in his favor.

How beautifully his arpeggios flow, cascading as serenely as alpine brooks singing their way down to the sea. All nature appears to be at peace. As Michael plays, she can envision the birds' wake-up calls, the falling rain and drifting snow, the sighing of her dear pines, and the endless journey of the stars. The world is a beautiful place . . . and love is in the air.

Suddenly, she stiffens: certainly those are bells she is hearing. Yes: Christmas bells, flooding the universe with joy. She listens intently as their pealing grows ever louder—then *that theme!* It begins to mesh with the bells, but only for an instant. Right in the middle of it, there is an ominous shift from major to minor key, and from harmony to dissonance. And the bells! In that self-same instant, the pealing joy ceases and is replaced by tolling sorrow. How uncannily perfect is Michael's capture of that moment—that moment when all the joy in their world went sour.

The dissonance and tolling eventually give way to a classical music potpourri. Here and there she recognizes snatches of well-known themes, some of them from piano concertos. But the notes are clipped off short and played perfunctorily: more or less as if the pianist doesn't much care how they sound as long as they all get played in record time. Several times, the Theme tries to edge in, but each time it is rudely repulsed.

Now it is that Dvorak's "New World Symphony" thunders in. Aha! At last: some resolution! Some affirmation! Not so. It quickly becomes apparent that this paean to a brave new world is, ironically, in steady retreat instead of advancing to triumph. Almost—it seems to her—as if it were a retrograde "Bolero": its theme progressively diminishing in power instead of increasing. Once again, "Meditation" seeks entry; once again, it is unceremoniously disposed of.

By now, Ginevra is deciphering Michael's musical code quite well: vividly revealed has been the progressive deterioration of Michael both as a person and as a pianist. From the moment in the cathedral tower when the bells began to toll, every variation that followed has dealt with the stages of his fall.

Then, clouds close in, thunder rumbles in the east, lightning strikes short-circuit the sky, and the rain falls—torrents of it. Darkness sweeps in, and with it all the hells loose on this turbulent planet. Ginevra shivers as Michael stays in minor keys, mourning all the sadness and pain in the universe.

The winds gradually increase to hurricane strength. Far ahead of her—for she is exposed to the elements too—she sees Michael, almost out of sight in the gloom, retreating from the storm. She follows, and attempts to call to him, but to no avail. The tempest swallows the words before they can be formed. Then the black clouds close in . . . and she loses sight of him altogether.

As the hurricane reaches ultimate strength, major keys are in full flight from the minors (Ginevra discovered some time back that Michael is equating majors with the forces of Light, and minors with the forces of Darkness). It does not seem possible that any force on earth could save Michael from destruction.

It is now, in the darkest midnight, when the few majors left are making their last stand. She senses that, for Michael, the end is near. Now, when she has all but conceded victory to the Dark Power, she again hears the strains of Thais' Theme! How can such a frail thing possibly survive when leagued against the legions of Darkness? But, almost unbelievably, it does.

At this instant, Ginevra chances to look with wide-open eyes at—not Michael the pianist but Michael the man. He has clearly forgotten all about the world, the concert audience, even *her*. In his total identification with the struggle for his soul, he is playing for only two people: himself—the penitent sinner—and God. And his face? Well, never afterwards could she really explain, but one thing was absolutely certain: there before her . . . was Michael's naked soul.

With Michael's surrender, the tide turns at last: The storm rages on, but the enemy is now unmistakably in retreat. Dissonance and minors contest every step of the battlefield, trying vainly to hold off the invading Light. Then victorious majors begin sweeping the field.

Ginevra discovers in all this a great truth: it is minors that reveal the full beauty of majors. Had she not heard "Meditation" sobbing on the ropes of a minor key, she would never have realized the limitless power of God. It is the minor key that gives texture and beauty to the major; and it is dissonance that, by contrast, reveals the glory of harmony. . . . It is sorrow that brings our wandering feet back to God.

Finally, with the mists beginning to dissipate and the sun to break through, the Theme reappears, but alone for the first time. Now it is that Ginevra feels the full upward pull of the music, for

"Meditation" soars heavenward with such passion, pathos, and power that gravity is powerless to restrain it.

And Ginevra . . . her choice made . . . reaches up,
and with Michael,
climbs the stairs of Heaven to God.

❖   ❖   ❖

HOW THIS THIRD STORY CAME TO BE

By the time November of 1991 rolled around, I had already signed the contract for Christmas in My Heart 3, *so I took this third story more seriously than any that had come before. While I had asked for God's counsel in the previous two stories, it was not to the extent I did with this third story. I began by asking God for the plot—not after the fact, but up front. How far I had come since that first story when I was hoping God would grant me writer's block! The Lord came through: convicting me that I should write a story on the musical world. The setting would be split between two places I knew and loved: the city of Vienna, Austria, and the Rocky Mountains west of Boulder, Colorado. The catalyst was that great neo-Gothic cathedral on Vienna's Strand, Votivekirche, where my daughter Michelle had heard her Uncle Romayne perform only months before I wrote the story.*

When I began the story, I had no idea where the Lord would take it. In fact, it scared me because the story kept growing and growing—growing in both length and complexity. Several times it ground to a complete halt. Each time I prayed, "Lord, I feel it is Your will that this story be written, but Joe Wheeler has hit a brick wall. If it is to continue, You will have to take it from here." And each time, back came a celestial FAX with specific instructions—and the story moved on.

One of the unexpected dimensions had to do with a subject I had often thought about, written about, but never before articulated in fiction: that thin dividing line between success and failure. In fact, not long before, I had written an essay titled "The Wheel of Fortune." In it, I drew from ten years of observations (1974-1984) while I was directing a concert/stage (Community Lyceum) series in Texas. Into my mind came the memory of prima donas who flaunted much and performed just as little as they could get away with; who short-changed their audiences because, being famous, they could get away with it. In contrast, I thought of artists such as Victor Borge, Jerome Hines, the Sons of the Pioneers, Allen Funt, the U.S. Marine Band, Mel Blanc,

Roger Williams, Norman Luboff and his choir, Don Cooper, Stan Midgley, Ann Landers, and others, who gave and never ceased giving. I remembered how Ann Landers stayed hour after hour at a packed reception (after she had spoken), counseling with each of the four hundred or so who stood in line, as though each of them was a VIP to her. I thought of the pianist Roger Williams who, when I asked him which concert he considered to be his greatest, instantly responded, "Tonight's!" Whose tux would be wringing wet before intermission — we'd have to re-tune the piano before he could go on, because of the intensity of his playing. Who'd play encores until the proverbial cows came home, if the audience asked for them by their continued applause. All the great ones, I realized in retrospect, were both self-assured and humble. All this went into the story. So, too, did my favorite inspirational writers, and Francis Thompson's great epic poem, "The Hound of Heaven."

But even though I knew music fairly well, the story ran away from me, for it passed way beyond the known into the unknown. That's where I pulled in a remarkable young woman, Ingrid Vargas, a double-major in English and Concert Performance. Ingrid agreed to "help me" — what an understatement that turned out to be! Night after night, we'd talk on the phone for hours at a time, wrestling with lines and seeking not just "a good word" but "the perfect word" for each line in question. Ingrid would sometimes spend an hour on just one line! I learned a lot from her. How well I remember one night when she said, "Dr. Wheeler, I want all your earlier drafts back." I did a double-take and sputtered, "Why? . . . We're now in the seventh draft, and supposedly it's getting better." Instantly she shot back, "Dr. Wheeler, it's true the story is getting better technically — but it's also losing something in each draft."

"What's that?" I asked in disbelief.

She laughed, "Well, it's this way. . . . You, my dear prof, are an utter romantic, and thus your earliest drafts tend to excess in that respect, but your later drafts, in losing that romanticism, veer into sterility. I want the power of those earlier drafts back!"

Then we came to where we went beyond even Ingrid's knowledge of concert performance and programming. She decided to take the story to her professor at Georgetown University School of Music, a concert performer himself, figuring that since he'd been forced to put together seasonal concert menus, he could help us there, and he did.

Now we come to the theme that holds the story together. For as far back as I can remember, I have been haunted by "Meditation" — every time I hear it, I cry. It has moved me as has no other piece of music in my lifetime. It was *while listening to Zamfir's pan flute rendition of it that the initial dream for this story was born, some time before I decided to actually write such a story.*

For a long time, I had wanted to articulate in story form a music-related narrative much like this one, but lacked the vehicle, the glue that would hold the story together. All this Massenet's "Meditation" provided.

After having sketched out the story line, I let it germinate. I decided not to rush it. Ingrid Vargas agreed to do some research on the origins of "Meditation." I'll admit I was mightily apprehensive: What if the piece proved—as was more than likely—to have no religious tie-ins at all? Worse yet, what if it had roots in the opposite camp?

I'll never forget the day Ms. Vargas came bursting into my office, in great excitement, exclaiming, "Dr. Wheeler, you were right!" When she finally calmed down, she showed me the results of her research: that the piece was composed as an intermezzo bridge between the secular and spiritual realms of our lives, between the dissolute life of the pagan courtesan in the first part of the opera Thais and the redeemed sinner in the second part.

No story I have ever helped to write took longer to complete than this one. One professional writer wrote me declaring that while he admired my other stories, there was something very different about "Meditation." He found himself reading slower and slower because he was so fascinated by the perfect choice of words. A dear friend, Virginia Fagal (herself a concert violinist), wrote me saying, "Joe, that is a wonderful story that you and God wrote."

❧   ❧   ❧

Being my third story, it was not slated to appear in our first—and only (we had no expectation of ever doing a second collection) — Christmas in My Heart *collection. But, as I was proofing the manuscript galleys, I told my editor, Penny Estes Wheeler, that I had a growing conviction that she should read my just completed third Christmas story before she signed off on the book. Reluctantly—for the book had already been typeset and was complete— she agreed. After reading it, she phoned me, struggling with tears, saying, "Joe, 'Meditation' has got to be in the book. So it ended up displacing "The Bells of Christmas Eve." It was later reprinted in Doubleday's third* Christmas in My Heart *hardback treasury, in 1998, as well as in Focus on the Family/Tyndale House's* Great Stories Remembered III. *No other story I have ever helped to write elicits the volume of mail this story does. From 1992 till now, heartfelt responses to it have continued to pour in. It would be worth having lived just to have written this one story. I'm convinced, beyond a shadow of a doubt, that it was a divinely ordained story.*

DEDICATION

This story is dedicated to my dearly beloved brother Romayne, who himself is a living embodiment of all that is finest in the concert piano profession, and who lived in—and loved—Vienna for almost a third of a century. As for Votivekirche, Romayne performed in it every summer for many years. Not too long ago, our daughter Michelle climbed its soaring bell tower with her Uncle Romayne, that selfsame bell tower from which Ginevra and Michael hear the far-off strains of "Meditation."

The
THIRD ROSE

The human heart defies description or analysis. What inner force attracts one person to another no psychologist has ever been able to tell us. The same is true of why such attraction comes and goes rather than remaining a constant.

The story of "The Third Rose" is one that has haunted me ever since I first heard it a number of years ago. It is the story of two men, John and Walter, and the woman they both loved, Margaret—many years ago . . . once upon a war-time Christmas.

❖　　❖　　❖

Long years apart—can make no
Breach a second cannot fill—
The absence of the Witch does not
Invalidate the spell—
The embers of a Thousand Years
Uncovered by the Hand
That fondled them when they were Fire
Will stir and understand—

Emily Dickinson

❖　　❖　　❖

The surf was up at Point Arago on the Oregon coast. . . . The surf was up all over the world.

It was December 17, 1941.

Only ten days before, the Japanese had bombed Pearl Harbor. No American, child or adult, living then could possibly ever forget the static-plagued radio and the breaking voice of Edward R. Murrow, the broadcast sounds of anti-aircraft guns, bombs, and explosions; sirens wailing up and down the auditory register like roller coasters on an eternal circular track; the heart-stopping whine of dive bombers plummeting full-throttle at sitting duck targets below; and the pain-wracked voice of FDR announcing to millions clustered around radios that this was a date "which will live in infamy . . ." and, shortly afterwards, that we were at war.

Forever after, these searing sounds, coupled with newsreel footage, newspaper and magazine illustrations depicting the carnage and sinking battleships, would separate the world which had been before from the world which came after.

It was a somber Christmas that year.

* * *

To all appearances, Margaret saw nothing . . . but woman's eyes are not man's eyes (merely seeing or not seeing); thus, filtered through those deceptively demure eyelashes was every nuance of the charade at the window. Two young men leaning against the window sill; one, she had known for years; the other, she had first met only hours before. They were both looking at her, while pretending not to. John, with eyes luminous, tender, and possessive; Walter, conceding nothing, with eyes that challenged as clearly as if he had ripped off his knightly gage and hurled it to the floor, only inches from her feet. Daring her to pick it up.

This can't really be happening . . . this can't really be happening . . . this can't really be happening, she kept repeating to herself; *it must be just a dream.* But it wasn't a dream; it was real—the realest thing that had ever happened to her.

But . . . how could it have happened? she demanded of the faithless doorkeeper of her heart. . . . For it was all but settled: she and John. Six years it had been; six years of thoughtful attentiveness, steadfast devotion, and empathetic understanding. John was the kindest boy, the kindest man, she had ever known. The only one of her many suitors through the years who was more concerned with her inner journey than his own; encouraging her to follow her dreams, wherever they led, no matter how long the road.

How paradoxical, she mused, that out of all this world such a man could be. No one else had ever been intrepid enough to embark on such a long and arduous quest: searching behind the lovely facade for the shy little spirit huddled deep within . . . in a chamber only she had ever seen. His "Holy Grail," he termed it when she laughingly declared it didn't exist.

Margaret was both grateful and frightened by this quest: on one hand, she was deeply moved that he cared enough to make such a long and possibly unrewarding journey; on the other hand, she was not at all sure that she wanted to know this much about her inner self—and even, in a rather perverse way, resented his forcing her to unlock doors she wasn't sure she wanted unlocked. After all, women of her day were still "whither thou goest, I will go"; few indeed staked out career claims in the male-dominated world of 1941 America. She had no way of knowing—so many thousands of women would enter the workforce during the next four years—that by the time the veterans returned to reclaim their jobs, it would prove impossible to ever stuff women back into their claustrophobic boxes.

She had known for months that he was closing in—and she both dreaded and yearned for his coming. And then . . . he stumbled on the cobwebby secret passage to her soul's innermost chamber. Wearily, he cleared a path to her door, paused to regain his breath, then—ever so gently—knocked.

For so long had this vault been hers alone that she trembled like an aspen during a storm at the soft knock. When he softly knocked again, she pushed open the massive steel door . . . a fraction of an inch.

And there he stood, demanding nothing—asking nothing; not knowing even then if he would be turned away.

It was this very absence of force which decided her: she leaned all her weight into the door . . . and welcomed him in.

❀   ❀   ❀

To John and Margaret, poetry was meat and drink, the medium by which their intertwining souls could soar, their minds could expand, and their hearts could open wide.

Longfellow provided patriotism and the homely virtues; Wordsworth, the continuity of life; Tennyson its romance; Dickinson, the cosmic view; from Arnold, a sense of restraint; from Frost a perception of choices; and from Robinson, empathy—but it was Yeats who unrolled for them Life's long carpet, from beginning to end.

Paradoxically, however, in all this, John's own self-awareness lagged far behind; in fact, it took almost six years for him to wake up to his true condition. For Margaret, that knowledge had come much earlier; thanks to her intuition (God's kindest and cruelest gift to woman), she knew that he loved her—and that some day soon he would tell her so.

It came unexpectedly, on a balmy November day on Bandon Beach. One of those rare, absolutely perfect, days Life parts with so grudgingly. Serenely, Autumn held her ground, staring fixedly out to sea; while northward, beyond the mountains, Winter kept shaking his watch, scowling at the delay.

Hand in hand, John led Margaret away from the sea's edge to their favorite sand dune, and enthroned her there. Self-consciously, he opened a well-worn book and turned to a certain page. Then, his face aglow with more than he knew, he recited, without once looking at the page, Yeats' haunting "When You Are Old." It seemed to her both bizarre and oddly touching, in the morning of her beauty, to be the recipient of such lines as these:

> "When you are old and gray and full of sleep,
> And nodding by the fire, take down this book,
> And slowly read, and dream of the soft look
> Your eyes had once, and of their shadows deep;
>
> "How many loved your moments of glad grace,
> And loved your beauty with love false or true,
> But one man loved the pilgrim soul in you
> And loved the sorrows of your changing face;
>
> "And bending down beside the glowing bars,
> Murmur, a little sadly, how Love fled
> And paced upon the mountains overhead
> And hid his face among a crowd of stars."

"Pilgrim" was ever after his pet name for her—and the sea-framed image of her long dark tresses blowing westward in the wind were etched for all time on his heart.

The moment was that rarity: a twin epiphany—for her, a bittersweet revelation of the ephemeral nature of beauty, love, and life; and for him . . . the first realization that he was in love with her. As he reached those memorable seventh and eighth lines, a wave of scarlet flooded his face. Both instinctively knew, in that moment, that something had come to an end, something had begun—and nothing would ever be the same.

❖   ❖   ❖

Yesterday, as she and John had walked hand-in-hand, barefoot on the beach, her heart had met his more than halfway. Both were children of the sea, never happier than when freed from chores, school, work, and family, to wander at will down their sandy heaven, feeling themselves a symbiotic part of the eternal romance of sand and sea.

She knew then, without a shadow of a doubt, that sometime this Christmas he would ask that crucial question that determines earthly destiny more than any other—and her love-lit sea-blue eyes telegraphed what her answer would be.

Yet . . . she had stumbled once on a slippery rock, and he had opportunistically taken her in his arms. That almost certainly would have precipitated the moment had she let nature take its course; but, for some strange inexplicable reason, she had gently disengaged. Something within her warned, *Not yet*.

But all that was yesterday. . . . *Yesterday? . . . Only Yesterday? . . .* But the world had changed last night!

Last September, her sister Beatrice had written her about a young man who had just transferred to the parochial college she attended in Northern California. He was a senior theology major and so irresistible that most of the girls on campus melted at the sight of him. Apparently, he had every talent and gift the good Lord could give: his wit was rapier-sharp, his smile would cause a nun to repent her vows, he could sing like Sankey and preach like Moody—when he was through with an audience, dry eyes were a vanished species. For good measure, Walter had a wickedly irresistible sense of humor and the kind of looks and physique Michelangelo would have traveled far to capture in Carrara marble.

"But so far," rhapsodized Beatrice, "this paragon has not succumbed to the open invitations in the admiring eyes of so many campus beauties. The question everyone is asking is, 'Who in the world is he *waiting* for?'"

Beatrice, already signed, sealed, and delivered to Anthony, Walter's best friend, had become personally acquainted with the "Campus Dreamboat" (so designated by no less than the campus newspaper). On an October picnic at the Old Mill in the Napa Valley, Walter made the mistake of wandering over to where Beatrice sat enshrined, in a stone cleft, by the towering water wheel. To the music of the slumbering water cascading listlessly into the amber pond, they got to know each other better. For Beatrice, an incurable matchmaker, to have passed up such an opportunity as this would have been grossly out of character. On the spur of this autumn moment, she entered another candidate into the lists: her sister Margaret. Why she did such a thing, she was never afterwards able to explain to her husband, for both of them dearly loved John and had, for some time, accepted him as their brother-in-law-to-be.

❖   ❖   ❖

Whatever the reason for her mischief, once started, she fired every cannon on her ship. She described her sister's beauty, vivacious personality, irresistible smile, pixie-ish sense of humor, figure, bookwormishness, poise, wanderlust, and—for good measure—her close walk with the Lord.

When she had fired her last shell, Walter laughed as he hadn't in months, causing everyone within earshot to wonder what in the world had happened to *him?* "What a set-up!" he finally managed to say. "No woman could be *that* perfect!" Nevertheless, the damage was done: he now *had* to find out for himself, harassing the not overly reluctant Beatrice until she finally broke down and invited him home with them for Christmas. He accepted, on condition that he provide the transportation.

Along the way, in his sporty new Buick, he pumped both Beatrice and Anthony for additional tidbits of information. Anthony, having had second and third thoughts by this time, was beginning to regret the whole thing as he conceptualized what effect bringing "Dreamboat" home with them was likely to have on the all-but-engaged Margaret and John. To him, bringing Walter home was tantamount to giving a lion free rein in a hen house.

By now, even Beatrice was realizing the fuller implications of what she had done, the forces she was setting in motion. If she could have recaptured those more-enticing-than-she-had-planned-on words at the Old Mill, she would have—but it was too late. This particular lion had never in his life taken no for an answer if he really wanted something. Perhaps . . . oh pray God perhaps . . . he wouldn't be any more impressed with her than he was with the coeds back on campus.

Beatrice, sitting between the two young men in the front, mused, *John is the type of man most women in their thirties would choose to marry and father their children—but not, not women in their late teens and early twenties. . . . What have I done!* she cried out to herself.

Anthony, knowing even before he opened his mouth that his warnings would have no more effect than a water hose against a volcano, told Walter that his sister-in-law was as good as engaged to a young man the whole family loved. This line of reasoning was just a tad short of being inspired as he should have known that Walter, being Walter, would only be more intrigued: he only valued more the things he was told he couldn't have.

At last they crossed the state line into Oregon, steamed up and over the Siskiyou Pass, and began their long descent to Coos Bay. Even though war had been declared, towns they passed through had a festive air about them. It would be, after all, a Christmas to remember when the boys were gone—many, never to return.

❈   ❈   ❈

Reaching the coastal road at last, they turned north towards Coos Bay; finally, they could see, way up there on the hill, the large three-story home dominating everything between the forest and the coastal highway: *Home.* Walter turned off onto a long gravel road, then circled up and around to the back of the house, then cut the engine.

Anthony and Beatrice went in first, and were promptly engulfed by the family. Belatedly they remembered their driver, still waiting in the anteroom, and went after him.

Walter was escorted into the homey living room in a state of intense anticipation. Never before in his life had his anticipations been so high. Four of Beatrice's five sisters were in the room waiting for them. Mama, the only other person in the know, had sent Margaret off for a walk—knowing John would follow—as soon as her eagle eye had spied Walter's car turning into the long driveway. She too loved John—almost, in fact, as much as Papa did.

Walter, not in on Mama's diversionary tactics, kept searching for the sister who would answer to the description. As each sister—Daphne, Christina, Melissa, and Jasmine—was introduced—each attractive in her own way, his spirits rose and fell.

Thirty of the longest minutes in Walter's lifetime later, Margaret and John slipped back into the house. Beatrice, having reached the long delayed moment of truth, stumblingly went through the introductions—hoping against hope that Walter would be a good boy and let her off the hook. Instead, there occurred what she had most feared: an explosion of awareness generated by the two.

All Margaret did was smile. But that five-letter word hardly did justice to a weapon which had already bewitched the entire male population of the county. Papa (who certainly ought to have known, since it had been used with such unfailing success on him) had summed it up best: "That deadly smile of hers is both impish and demure; how in God's green earth can mortal man resist a combination like that?"

Walter broke no records in that respect: he was poleaxed, not even having the saving grace to hide his condition. The rest of that eventful evening passed in sort of a roseate haze for the principals: they spoke occasionally to each other in mere words . . . but almost continually with their eyes.

Rhetorically, Margaret asked herself, *Why is there a veil over my response to John, to the open love-light in his eyes, to that tenderness which only hours ago represented all that I most wanted in life?*

John, so attuned to her every vibration or nuance, sensed the difference almost immediately. Already he sensed a withdrawing of her inner spirit (that Pilgrim he had searched for so many years, before finding)—and he was deeply troubled.

Later that night, John trudged up the creaking stairs to the attic aerie where he always slept when visiting Margaret. Despondently, he reviewed the day's events and asked himself what he could have said or done differently to change the outcome. As he wearily lay down on the cot by the window, he felt he had somehow been battered black and blue during the evening. He looked out through the window, as he always did at night, down to the coastal highways where ghostly headlights in the fog searched for passage to somewhere. Always before, this bed had represented home (for once he had come to know Margaret, it had been inconceivable that home could ever be anywhere but next to her). But now, he had a chilling sense of being evicted: that he was going to be thrown out onto that foggy highway himself . . . to begin another search for he knew not what. Certainly he could not even imagine another woman.

※   ※   ※

As for Walter, he had gone to bed almost in a state of shock. Well he knew how unutterably dear Margaret was to John. In fact, "dear" was the ultimate understatement. She was his whole world, and every time he looked at her, his undiluted love was unmistakable. But, Walter also knew that were John the dearest male friend he had ever known, he could not possibly have surrendered the field short of the altar. Dimly he began to realize that love is the most powerful force on earth. When it comes in full strength, nothing (no person, no matter how close a friend) can stand in the way—the drama *has* to be played out.

Margaret, too, found sleep very elusive. Her sisters had given her a hard time, for they loved John like the brother they had lost so many years before. Heretofore they had assumed the certainty of his brother-in-law-hood. Nevertheless, they knew their sister well enough to realize that this complete stranger, in one short evening, had pulverized her once almost impregnable defense system. Margaret, loving John deeply, was furious with herself for her patent inability to hold Walter at bay; she was equally angry with Walter for wrecking what should have been the happiest Christmas of her lifetime.

For most of that interminable night, she wrestled with her terrible dilemma. Face it: she loved them both—but in totally different ways.

The next morning, all three were slow in reappearing—and when they did, the night's toll was painfully obvious.

※   ※   ※

The stand-off continued day after day, with most of the rounds seemingly won by John, for Margaret respected his right to be first in her company. But the victory was somewhat hollow, for John felt himself now only partly in possession of her love. When they were alone, he felt he had two-thirds of her; but when Walter was in the room it was an entirely different story. He could feel the aerial shock waves as the inner spirits of Walter and Margaret challenged each other, communed with each other, longed for each other.

It was the twenty-fourth of December when it finally came: the denouement. Long into the previous night, Walter tossed and turned, unable to find sleep. He candidly took stock of the situation and concluded that things didn't look very good for him: here he was, nearing the time when he'd have to return to college—and he was getting nowhere. Should he leave without a decision in his favor, he felt confident that the combined forces of family preference and John's residence in that part of the state would eventually break down the last of Margaret's resistance. Only with a bold stroke did he have a fighting chance. But all his life he would be known for such risk-taking; it was his willingness to seize the moment and take control that would make him a millionaire before he was thirty.

At breakfast, John was sitting next to Margaret as usual, and beginning to feel that the tide was at last beginning to shift in his favor. Somehow, Margaret's smile promised more than it had yesterday. Perhaps . . . all was not lost after all.

Across the table, Walter was reaching the same conclusions. There was not a moment to lose. As they got up from the table, his voice cut through the babble of voices and moving chairs: "Margaret, could I speak with you for a moment?" All action and speech froze in midair.

He led Margaret into the front parlor, her face changing color as she walked. *It's coming!* she couldn't help thinking. But she had underestimated Walter—he was not about to accept any front parlor odds if he could help it.

Within two minutes he pulled off what proved to be the greatest selling job of his long and illustrious career—he persuaded her that she owed him a few minutes alone with her. Since they both loved the sea, and since it was such an absolutely perfect morning, and since he was leaving so soon—as he had hoped, her face blanched as he spoke these words—surely she would grant him this one small favor: take a short ride to the beach with him. Smilingly, she allowed that perhaps it might be arranged.

Walter went out to spruce up the car and warm the engine. From inside he overheard loud voices: Papa was apparently most unhappy about something. More time passed. More voices. This time it was Mama, apparently trying to mediate. Almost he felt he had lost . . . then she came flying out of the house . . . her face flushed. Signs of recent tears confirmed his suspicion that her exit had not been an easy one. The car was already rolling as she lightly slipped aboard.

When Margaret had informed John that she would be gone a short while with Walter—wasn't it sweet of him to take her for a ride to the beach in his shiny new Buick?—John was under no illusions as to the mettle of his antagonist. In 1941 America, it just wasn't done for another guy to take another's steady (especially an all but affianced one!) off in an automobile alone. Not in conservative Christian families, it wasn't.

If Walter could pull this off in two minutes . . . then just give him sole possession for a few hours, especially with this particular woman—and at the beach, for good measure . . . short of a miracle, the game was lost. And, worst of all, he wasn't even being permitted to be on the scene; all he could do was worry and fear the worst.

The hours inched their way on crippled feet across that fateful day. Everything in the sprawling three-story home stalled to a virtual halt as family members tried to avoid meeting each other's eyes—*especially* John's, so brimming with misery (he always *did* wear his heart in his eyes). The morning hours passed, and afternoon came. Papa kept looking at his watch and muttering things. Mama kept out of range whenever possible.

Late in the afternoon, as evening shadows fell, the one-two slam of car doors ricocheted through the silent house. Faces froze during the interminable period it took for Margaret and Walter to climb the long set of outside stairs, open the front door, and walk through the front parlor into the inner one. And then: the verdict.

Every eye was riveted on the couple—every eye but John's. Heaven and hell were no further away than one glance at Margaret . . . so he preferred to remain suspended between.

Her voice had bells in it; bells of joy which no cloud of words could ever counter. Bells which tolled the death of all his dreams . . . for what was the use of anything without Margaret there to share it with him?

Across the room, Papa's face had hardened into cold gray stone— for, in his heart, he had long ago adopted John as the son he had always longed for, since his own had died such an untimely death. And Mama's face ignited with waves of burning pain, for she too had long loved John—with all the intensity of a sonless mother. The five sisters just sat there . . . for the first time in living memory . . . all silent at once.

Walter, in the egocentricity of youth, thought only of his own rapture, scarcely giving a second thought to the one he had displaced.

❊   ❊   ❊

As Margaret read in the faces of those around her the full impact of her decision, the bells ceased to ring in her voice. Well she knew how John must be feeling. She could read it in the anguish etched in his face, the abject slump of his body, and the unspoken thoughts that always arced between them—even without words. She knew all this but could do nothing about. it, for the very reasons Beatrice had feared: her standards of evaluation were those of the young—they who worship power, success, charisma, physical prowess, looks, and passion.

Walter had it all. John, on the other hand, was unfortunate enough to embody traits women don't appreciate until the traumas of the years reshuffle their priorities. His were the gifts of tenderness, empathy, understanding, introspection, sensitivity, serenity, and imagination.

Through swollen eyelids that never-to-be-forgotten Christmas Eve, John watched paradise recede from him. Margaret still went through the motions, still attempted to include him in—but both knew it was a sham. The heart, that unpredictable instrument, had shifted its center of gravity 180 degrees. One moment, John represented the perceived future; another moment, he did not. There were no ragged edges: it was a clean break.

On Margaret's face was that inward glow which illuminates a woman's face during that ever-so-short blooming period we label, for want of a better term, "falling in love."

It was the last night John ever spent in that house.

In the morning, on her bureau was a single long-stemmed red rose, and leaning against the stem, an envelope. It was the first thing Margaret saw when she awoke from a troubled sleep. Quickly, she slipped out of bed with a radiant smile spreading across her sleepy face—then stopped in dismay, her hands flying to her ghost-white cheeks. The writing was John's—not Walter's.

Even before she opened it she knew it was the end of something that only days before had embodied her fondest dreams. The note was short. The shortest one he had ever written her.

Dec. 25, 1941

My dearest Margaret,

It is clearly over.

Yet . . . if you should change your mind, just send me a red rose, signing the card "Pilgrim," and I shall come to you if it be in my power to do so.

I shall always love you.

John

Margaret's sisters woke to the sound of weeping, the most tempestuous sobbing they had ever heard from their sunny sister. When asked what it was all about, she could only point mutely to the note and rose. Each read it, looked at her pensively, and quietly left the room. This was *her* battle, *her* decision, and she would have to live with the consequences for the rest of her life.

      ❖   ❖   ❖

Margaret and Walter were married the first day of May.

The years swept by on winged feet. Margaret and Walter were about as happy as husband and wife ever are on this troubled planet. Walter had the Midas touch: everything he touched turned to gold. During the war years, he made a fortune; in after years, he merely augmented it.

If ever a man lived life in the fast lane, it was Walter. Living with him, Margaret soon discovered, was a perpetual adventure, for he lived with Falsattafian gusto. Fast cars, fast boats, and fast planes — he was ever on the move, always making deals that were even more lucrative than those that went before.

He tried everything: preacher, teacher, auctioneer, real estate salesman, politician, entrepreneur, and all-around tycoon . . . filling each role with incredible energy, joie de vivre, and robust laughter.

And Margaret was his Guinevere, the mistress of his splendid homes, villas, and mountain resorts. With Walter she was able to satisfy her yearning for travel — and that always in luxury, always first class.

They had everything money could buy — yet somehow both retained the common touch, selflessly giving to those less fortunate than they. In spite of many temptations, he remained faithful to her — and to the Lord, who remained paramount in their lives.

Only one child survived — and so excruciating was that second delivery that he swore never to inflict another pregnancy upon her.

Never once did Walter give her cause to regret having chosen him instead of John. John, who seemingly had dropped off the planet. In all their long years together, never once did they hear whether or not John had survived the war.

But John *did* make it through; rather perversely, fate brought him safely through battles he hoped to die in. Gradually, over time, he rediscovered his lost love of life and literature. And just before the Battle of Guadalcanal, he invited God back into his life.

After the war was over, he took stock of his options and determined that he would not permit the loss of Margaret to destroy his life. Taking advantage of the G.I. Bill, he went back to college and earned a degree in architecture. Increasingly lonely, he began to search for someone to spend the rest of his life with. Several years later, he found her. And she was everything he had hoped she would be.

Three children came their way . . . and life was good.

❊   ❊   ❊

It seemed impossible that *anything* could slow the juggernaut of Walter's life and far-flung involvements and enterprises—but it happened nevertheless. Three days after their forty-third wedding anniversary, he was diagnosed as having cancer—both terminal and fast-moving.

Five weeks later, on a spring afternoon, he asked Margaret to push his bed over to the large picture window that overlooked San Francisco Bay and the Golden Gate Bridge. The sun was setting, gilding the blue into bronze, and a sleek ocean liner (one they had traveled on several times) had just cleared the bridge and was heading out to sea. He sighed audibly, and she knew what he was thinking.

Life is such an overconscientious accountant, mused Margaret to herself: *when one is given the world on a silver platter . . . the reckoning tends to come earlier. Here is Walter, at the very height of his powers—and suddenly . . . it's all over. Why . . . oh why, God?*

She sensed that he had turned and was looking at her. The look in his dear hazel eyes was more than she could handle: the look that told her that, after all the long years, she was still . . . *everything.*

He took her hands in his . . . she could feel him trembling—from way down deep inside. "Don't cry, dear," he said in his now rather ragged voice, as he searched for the Kleenex box. "Don't cry. We've had it all. I've been lucky—far luckier than most—in that most all of my dreams have come true. There isn't much I wanted to do . . . that I haven't. . . . Don't let them give me one of those idiotic sentimental funerals when I go—or let Diane do it either. By the way, where *is* she?"

"Went down to Safeway for some groceries, dear. She'll be right back."

"Oh. . . . Dear . . . *promise* me there will be no funeral. Just cremate what little there is left of me"—he looked down ruefully at his emaciated body, comparing it to what had been—"and have it carried out to sea, way out beyond the Golden Gate, and dropped overboard. So when you wish to think of me, just walk down to the shore, as you so love to do . . . and listen to 'em coming in. I'll be out there somewhere—my spirit will . . . in whatever form the good Lord packages it. . . ."

Softly she answered, "I *promise*."

He paused so long she thought he had dropped off to sleep. But no, he had only been thinking—about her. There was that tender look again in his eyes . . . that remained in full strength even while his body was savaged by wave after wave of pain. "Any regrets, dear," he finally asked, as the pain temporarily receded, "any regrets at all?"

"None!" she responded instantly. "Oh, Walter, if I had it to do all over again . . ." and her eyes—her still impish eyes—twinkled wickedly through tears. She could see his face visibly relax . . . and a smile struggled against the only force he had never been able to outwit.

Those were his last words . . . and he died with that smile on his face.

And she was alone.

❖   ❖   ❖

Several long years passed . . . and life began to regain its savor. To take her mind off her loss, she resumed her volunteer stints at the local hospital. She also resumed her traveling to the far corners of the earth. Often she would book passage with her sister Melissa, just to have someone with her to keep the loneliness in check.

❖   ❖   ❖

Then it happened. . . . At a family celebration in a distant California city, she happened to sit behind a man who looked vaguely familiar.

Then he turned and spoke to the woman at his side—and she *knew!* Her stupefied "John!" escaped her before she could check it, causing him to turn around and look at her. He knew her instantly. He introduced his wife, Phyllis; and Margaret introduced her daughter Diana. They spoke only briefly, Margaret finding herself strangely tongue-tied. Then John turned around and faced the front again. The program went on without her—for all she could see in her blurred vision was that dear face now hidden from her. For the first time in forty-seven years she knew he was alive. *Alive!*

As long as Walter had been alive, so dominant was he that the force field of energy that he generated blotted out thoughts of all who were not part of his personal galaxy. Hence, during all those rushing years, rarely had the pace of life slowed down enough for much introspection. But now, with that dynamo quiet, cold, and silent, memories flooded back upon her, compounded with forty-seven years of interest: as if a towering dam had buckled under irresistible pressure and unleashed with a vengeance the no longer placid waters imprisoned behind. In such torrents did they engulf her that she stood to her feet, dazed, and left the family celebration without being able to explain her untimely exit to anyone, even her astonished daughter. The only rational thought that filtered through this deluge brought her anything but peace: *After all these years . . . the fire still burns!*

She returned to her life, only now she was lonelier than ever. Hungry again, but not hungry for Walter. That part of her life had come and gone like a gigantic meteor, utterly all-consuming, igniting the sky with its radiance. When such a shooting star burns out, no one who has lived with it for long could possibly desire a second ride: flesh and blood can handle such an experience only once in life.

She was reminded of Elijah: and after the whirlwind came the still, the small, the quiet, voice.

So it was that, after all these sonic years, she yearned . . . she longed . . . for John. But now . . . it was too late. Too late.

Now she used travel—not as the joy it had always been before . . . but as an escape—an escape from memories of John. She now rarely came home, but could be found instead in Nepal, in Bali, in the Australian Outback, in Patagonia, in Dubrovnik on the Dalmatian Coast, in the foggy Aleutians, in the Bay Islands . . . always moving on in a vain effort to forget.

One humid, tropical afternoon, as she fanned herself on the hotel balcony in Papeete, Tahiti, the "maitre d" brought her a letter on a tray. It was from her daughter.

November 12, 1991

Dear Mother,
Your grandchildren are growing up
without you. Wouldn't you like to be there
for them before it's too late?
By the way, just heard that the wife of
your old sweetheart died of cancer. A year
ago, I believe.
Much love,

Diana

Two days later, she was home.

But now it was even worse, for there was no longer any human barrier separating her from John. But would he, after all these years, still be interested in her? Would he so resent her rejection of him that he'd refuse to have anything more to do with her? After almost half a century, could he possibly still care for her in the old way? Furthermore, if he *did* still care, why hadn't he written her?

The weeks passed, and her composure continued to unravel strand by strand; she was rapidly degenerating into a nervous wreck. True, she had, by some diligent sleuthing, managed to secure his address. But she was of the old school, not the new one, thus she did not dare take the initiative herself. She called her daughter and asked for advice. Instead, she was invited to come visit that weekend.

That Saturday evening, looking out at the multicolored Christmas lights decorating houses and yards across the way, listening to carols on radio and CDs, her thoughts wafted back once again to that wonderful/terrible Christmas of '41. Mama—long since dead; the same with Papa. Now it was just the six sisters left—and the oldest would almost certainly not make another Christmas.

Suddenly, the voice of her daughter broke into her reveries: "Mother, I've been wracking my brain, trying to think of some way you could contact your John without violating the quaint ol' code your generation was plagued with. Why today—" and she chuckled diabolically— "today, your granddaughter would most likely have abducted him by now."

She had to laugh at her mother's crimson face. "Why, Mother, you can still blush! It's been a long time since I've seen anyone blush. Today, we are shocked so often, and at such a young age, and we are bombarded with so much sexual innuendo, that we are shock-proof. No one blushes anymore."

She went on. "Mother, didn't he leave any ragged edges—any open ends you could take advantage of? Or was it a surgical cut—" She stopped suddenly as her mother's hands flew to her face. "Mother, what *is* it?"

"Oh, I just remembered . . . no, it was anything but a surgical cut. How could I have possibly forgotten! He . . . he . . . uh . . . left me a rose the morning he left, Christmas morning. What a present! I cried like I never had before, or have since. A rose . . . and . . . a note."

"Go on. Go on!" commanded Diana.

❊   ❊   ❊

Her mother paused, and a dreamy look came into her eyes as she was swept back through the years. Diana thought to herself, *It must have been that look that captured those two so very different hearts. Mother is still beautiful—imagine—just imagine what she must have been like then. And all woman.*

"My dearest Margaret." Here Margaret's eyes filled with tears, and she could go no further. After some time, she regained her composure. "I had just . . . uh . . . jilted him . . . and he . . . he . . . still . . . called . . . me . . . 'dearest.' I'd never thought of that before."

Diana waited.

Finally, her mother was able to proceed. "My dearest Margaret.... It is . . . uh . . . clearly over." She paused, a stricken look in her eyes: "Oh it was, it *was*," she wailed, "but it's not, oh pray God it's *not!*"

After a while, she continued: "Yet . . . if you should change your mind . . . just send me a . . . a red rose . . . signing the card 'Pilgrim.' . . . ." She paused, and explained, "That was his pet name for me. At home . . . I still have that book of Yeats poems. When I moved into my small seashore home after Walter died, it was one of the few things I just couldn't bear to part with. I . . . I mean *we* . . . used to eat, drink, and sleep poetry. But through the years . . . uh . . . well, as you know, your father never liked poetry very much . . . and so he discouraged me from reading it—so I didn't. But I could now. . . . I *can* now!"

Diana pounced: "Mother! You never told me. But, of course, I never asked. . . . But, come to think of it, *you* were Dad's queen, weren't you? Just as I was his princess. But you were the crown jewel of his kingdom. But . . . but . . . before Dad died, I never really knew you as a person . . . like me . . . with drives . . . and dreams . . . of your own."

Her mother didn't answer. She didn't have to.

"Mother, tell me more about that pet name he had for you, 'Pilgrim.' That, in a strangely beautiful way, seems to fit you. But how did he tie it into—what did you say the writer's name was?"

"Yeats." And again that tender softness came back into her eyes. *The look of a Raphael Madonna,* Diana thought to herself. *That's not a look one sees much today.*

"Pilgrim." Her mother's mouth curved adorably as she formed the word. "He said I was his pilgrim. We both memorized the poem."

"Can you, after all these years, still remember any of the lines?"

"Let's see." She paused, wrinkling her forehead. Finally, in exasperation, she sighed: "I just can't seem to remember. I do remember that Yeats begins by telling his beloved that when she is old—oh! I am old now, aren't I! . . . When she is old and thinking back to when she wasn't, when she was still . . ."

"Beautiful?"

"Yes. Beautiful. . . . Wait! I do remember that one middle stanza. The one that told him he was in love with me."

"Well, let's hear it quickly . . . before you forget."

"I won't forget. . . ."

> "How many loved your moments of glad grace,
> And loved your beauty with love false or true,
> But one man loved the pilgrim soul in you
> And loved the sorrows of your changing face."

As she came to the last words of the stanza, Margaret broke down completely, her tears falling unchecked like silver rain.

Diana just sat there, quietly, a pensive look on her face. This was a mother she'd never known before. Where had she been all these years?

At last, the tears spent, her mother looked up, saying, as she dabbed her eyes, "You must think I'm such a silly fool."

"No," responded Diana slowly. "Never have I loved—or admired—you more. . . . Was that all of it?"

"All of what—oh, you mean the letter?"

"Of *course.*"

"Not quite. Come to think of it: a rather big 'quite.'"

"Oh?"

"Yes. Let's see, where did I leave off?"

"Pilgrim. I believe you said, 'Pilgrim soul.'"

"Oh, yes. 'Just send me a red rose, signing the card "Pilgrim" . . . and I shall return to you if it be . . .'" and here she paused for control . . . "'if it be . . . in my power to do so.'"

"Was that all?"

"No. A thousand times *No!* He ended with these six words. . . . 'I shall always love you. . . . John.'"

"Do you think he really meant them?"

"*Yes!* Meant them then. Yes. But the big question is . . . is . . ."

"Whether or not he still does today?"

In an almost inaudible whisper, her mother answered, "Yes."

❧   ❧   ❧

It was the twenty-first day of December.

John stood in the front room of his modest split-level home in the Oregon highlands, gazing absent-mindedly out at the falling snow and snow-flocked pines. Christmas alone. . . . He just didn't know how he could handle it again. Oh, of course, the children had invited him home to be with their families, but somehow he just couldn't seem to get in the mood for that kind of Christmas.

Well, to be truthful, it was more than that.

The past. He was living more and more in the past these days, it seemed. Phyllis was already part of the past that could no longer be changed. She had come into his life when he needed her most . . . and stayed until her life forces failed her, as sooner or later they do for all of us. But she was gone, never to return. And as Frost's persona put it in his poem "Out, Out—"

"Little—less—nothing—and that ended it.

No more to build on there."

"No more to build on there." In fact, he asked himself, was there anything or anyone to build on at all? Was his life over?

The raucous ring—really, he *must* change that thing!—of the doorbell jerked him out of his dream world. Who could be calling on a day like this? He certainly wasn't in the mood for company, he growled to himself, as he pulled open the door.

A florist delivery boy was standing there, the snow already frosting his blond head.

After signing for the slim package, John closed the door in relief. At least he would not be forced to leave his journey into the past in order to talk about things that mattered less and less to him. . . . Oh, the package. Wonder who it could be from. As for the "what," older people don't get very excited about that, for they have everything already, and are far more concerned about having to part with something they already have than they are anxious to receive something new.

He opened it. In the narrow box was one of the loveliest red roses he had ever seen. He lifted it out of the box with arthritic hands, and inhaled its fragrance. Then, wondering whom it could be from, poked around in the green tissue paper until he found a small, white envelope. He opened it.

His eyes widened in disbelief as he read the message on the card. It consisted of but one word:

PILGRIM

On the back of the card there was no name — but there was an address and phone number.

❅　❅　❅

It was the twenty-third day of December.

Margaret's heart was racing like a cold engine on a frosty morning. Two entire days had passed — and she had heard nothing. Had she been a silly old ninny to imagine John would still be interested in her? An old woman with precious few good years left.

She leaned against her bedroom window and gazed idly out at a sight she never tired of: the booming surf off Point Lobos. One of Walter's last gifts to her had been this little hideaway overlooking one of the grandest views on this planet. Since no more land was available on this stretch of Seventeen Mile Drive, she knew he'd probably bought off half of the California Legislature, and paid a king's ransom for it to boot. Wisely, she had asked no questions, just accepted it as his Taj Mahal, the ultimate gift to the woman he adored.

She leaned against the window and spoke with God. Always, she had maintained a child-like faith in Him. And her prayers were rarely formal things; rather, they were as casual as if she were merely chatting with a friend in the room. This one was typical in that respect:

"Oh, God, have I done it again? Did I move too quickly . . . before I had Your blessing? But oh, Lord, I am so lonely . . . and John was so good to me all those years ago when I was young. But that's what worries me, God. Will he still think I'm pretty today? What do You think, God?"

She looked out the window again and noticed that the fog was coming in—and the gulls were protesting.

She jumped as the telephone shattered the stillness. It was the gateman. "Sorry to disturb you, Ma'am, but a package just came for you. The man who delivered it declared it urgent; said it *had* to get to you today. Shall I bring it up?"

Within minutes, he was at her door with it (on the long box was the engraved imprint of her favorite Carmel florist). The gateman thanked, the door shut with almost impolite haste, and the box opened with shaking fingers, she beheld three perfect red roses. But she refused to pick them up until she found out whom they were from and what the message was.

Her normally nimble fingers had trouble finding the small envelope; then, ever so carefully, she opened it—*almost,* she quipped to herself, *as if I thought a bomb would explode when I opened it.*

On a small sheet of stationery were these words:

Dearest Pilgrim,

Second Rose received; am returning. First Rose long since dead; am sending replacement. Third Rose to present my case—*and* Emily:

"Where Roses would not dare to go,
What Heart would risk the way—
And so I send my Crimson Scouts
To sound the Enemy—"

If they are persuasive enough, I'll see you at Bandon Beach, Dec. 25, 9:00 A.M., in vicinity of Yeats Sand Dune.

Until then—

Your John

❊   ❊   ❊

It was Christmas morning on Bandon Beach.

At 9:00 on the second, a tall, graceful woman descended the stairs leading down to the beach. The roses of youth were in her cheeks, and pinned to her breast was a corsage of three crimson roses.

At the bottom of the stairs, she kicked off her shoes.

After rounding the huge rock, she saw him, standing by a sand dune that looked vaguely familiar.

When she got close enough to read his eyes—
   and see his open arms—
      she broke into a run.

Pilgrim had come home.

❦   ❦   ❦

"Long years apart—can make no
Breach a second cannot fill—
The absence of the Witch does not
Invalidate the spell.
"The embers of a Thousand Years
Uncovered by the Hand
That fondled them when they were Fire
Will stir and understand."

BIBLIOGRAPHY

"Long Years Apart —,"
   Emily Dickinson. Written ca. 1876.
"Where Roses Would Not Dare to Go,"
   Emily Dickinson. Written ca. 1883.
"When You Are Old," William Butler Yeats,
   "The Rose", 1893.

HOW THIS FOURTH STORY CAME TO BE

This particular story had a gestation period of eight years. In 1985, at a golden wedding anniversary program, a tall, attractive woman left the proceedings early, causing a bit of a stir, for she was a close relative of the couple being honored. I was there, and wondered. Some time later, I heard the story.

Such an impact did the story have on me that almost immediately I wanted to retell it. But I waited, for a number of reasons. First and foremost, because the female protagonist was a member of my own extended family and had always preserved her privacy. Another reason for waiting was that the story was still being written in real life.

Finally, late in 1993, I decided that its time had come. I'm often asked whether certain stories are true or not. I have a tough time answering that question where this story is concerned, for about 90 percent of it is actual, and the other 10 percent is to give the real-life protagonist wiggle-room should people ask her if she is the prototype of the story.

I knew both "Margaret" and "Walter" intimately; in fact, they were the closest thing I knew to a fairy godmother and fairy godfather during my growing-up years. "Walter" was larger than life, a man who towered over most other mere mortals. How shocked I was later on to discover that he was a mortal after all—and was dying of cancer. His untimely passing cast a dark cloud over all of our lives. And I had always assumed he was the one love of "Margaret's" life. That golden wedding walkout revealed the truth: the reason "Margaret" (a widow now) walked out was that she suddenly realized why the man sitting in front of her looked strangely familiar: he was the "John" of this story, sitting there with his wife. They hadn't seen each other since that long-ago parting (even their children were all grown now, and had children of their own); yet, seeing him so close, and yet so far, was more than "Margaret" could handle. The old feelings swept back and engulfed her. She just couldn't handle it. So she walked out with her startled daughter. Some years later, "John's" wife died, and there followed, a year or so later, a coming together, a marriage, a second chance at love.

So I wrote their story, using several of my favorite poets as thought syntheses. After the story had been completed and gone through the usual gauntlet of readers (including students in my writing classes), I sent "The Third Rose" couple a copy of the story, and trembled. How would they take it? I needn't have worried: I got a long-distance phone call with a ragged voice on the other end—she had to speak between tears. She said, "Joe, this is the most wonderful thing that has ever happened to me! It's like you've been with me all down through the years!"

I sent them—then living in central Oregon—three stunningly beautiful rose bushes, each with blooms of a different shade of red and gold. They planted them just below their front window, so that they could watch them every day. Every day they considered to be an unmerited gift from God.

Since this is a true-life story, sadly, I'm forced to add that, not long ago, "John" too faced that ultimate enemy, and lost. But not before they had the opportunity to share a number of years of joy and love.

Oh what heartbreak when she lost "John!" She left Oregon for another state, to start over again all alone. Well, not quite alone—outside her windows are three rose bushes, reminding her daily of a great love that will not die—ever.

❖   ❖   ❖

The story was first published in Review & Herald Publishing Association's Christmas in My Heart 3 *in 1994, and was republished in Focus on the Family/Tyndale House's* Great Stories Remembered II *in 1998.*

The story-related mail has been most intriguing. Amazing how many people assume either they or someone they know are the real-life prototypes for the story! Some are quite broken up to discover that they aren't. But what has surprised me most has been the number of people who write in sharing similar stories: of men and women who marry, then years later (after the death of the spouse) find again that earlier love. Others write in this vein: how lucky could a woman get! To land both of one's dearest loves in life — well, one can't get much luckier than that!"

LUTHER

as told by
Michelle Wheeler Culmore

Nine Christmases ago, our daughter Michelle came home from New England with a story. A story of a goose named Luther. A goose she could not get out of her head.

Or her heart.

This is her story . . . told, as far as possible, in her own words.

❖   ❖   ❖

Actually, it was a miracle that I ever met Luther, for he had been bought earlier in the fall to fatten up for Thanksgiving dinner. But something happened along the way to give him a Hezekiah reprieve: they fell in love with him — to have eaten him would have been like eating one of the family!

So, partly at least, to get him out of temptation's way, he was delivered to the theatre to begin his dramatic career.

A senior fashion major, I was interning in a New England public theater, cutting my teeth — and other body parts — on costume design and repair.

Having always yearned to be in New England in the fall — *and* in the winter — the opportunity seemed almost too good to be true. When I arrived, it was to the lazy, hazy days of late summer when the heat slows life down to a cat-like slouch. But before long, the cooler winds of autumn swept down from Canada, and all nature came alive again.

Soon it was "peak," as the natives label it, and all across New England the leaves turned to scarlet, orange, amber, and gold. Their reflection, in the sky blue of the lakes and rivers, took one's breath away. And spearing through the rainbow of colors were the soaring spires of blinding white churches, legacy of those intrepid Puritans, three and three-quarters centuries ago.

And then came Luther.

They sent him to stay at the theatre for the remainder of the fall season. He came with his snow white feathers in a small cage with some plain, dried food and a water dish. Because no one knew what else to do with him, he was hauled down to the theatre basement with the unwarranted assumption that the stage manager, Torsten, would somehow take care of him.

The theatre basement was one of the places I hated the most. It was very, *very*, V-E-R-Y dirty, damp, dark, and unorganized. I can't even *begin* to describe how dirty it was. Sort of a dumping ground for the theatre: stage supplies, props, tools, trash, and remnants of the theatre itself were strewn all over. And, like most New England buildings, it had been there a long, long time. It was even said that there was a resident ghost. If true, it surely slept a lot, because no one I knew had ever seen it. Nor did I.

The basement was under the theatre itself (duh), but was not paved or floored. It was essentially gravel, rocks, loose rusty nails, cement chunks, and who knows what else. One never went down there without heavy shoes on. When I remembered—and could find one—I'd wear a mask. Heaven only knows what toxic chemicals (asbestos, etc.) were staining the air—and it was grossly filthy to boot. Every time I went down, within an hour or so, I'd get a headache, feel like I was coming down with a cold, and get a runny nose. And the grime in the air would rain down on body and clothes; in no time at all, you were filthy—inside and out.

I have to give Torsten credit, however. He did his best to fix it up during those rare occasions when he had spare time. As foul as it was, it was said to be an improvement on his predecessor's subterranean junkyard, one strata down.

Needless to say, imagine what all this did to the beautiful, clean goose—stuck down there for more than a month! In no time at all, he had lost his shimmering white beauty and had turned an ugly, grimy gray. And his health obviously suffered as well.

As if these conditions and the intermittent darkness were not enough, there were the kids—all 150 of them—streaming downstairs in hordes in order to get measured for their "Christmas Carol" costuming. They needed that many because there were two children casts and a month-long run; out of the 150, they hoped 50 a night would actually show up.

Unfortunately, we could only process them a few at a time—and that left them with time on their hands. To no one's surprise, they didn't wait well. In fact, it was bedlam! Just the memory of it gives me a headache.

Worse yet, it didn't take them long to discover Luther. They took turns playing with him, teasing him, taunting him, mistreating him. Amazingly, not once did he use that sharp beak of his to strike back—he just took it.

The staff wasn't much help either. Quite frankly, they were ticked that this unexpected responsibility had been thrust upon them, a not unsurprising response given the fact that they were all overworked and underpaid—if paid at all.

So . . . Luther quacked and crapped (green, by the way) all the time—most likely because he was in goose hell and yearned to get out.

I suppose he became attached to me because I was the one around the most, and consequently paid the most attention to him. I ended up being the one that fed and watered him most of the time. At that time, we were in the concluding days of *Othello* and frantically— simultaneously, of course!—preparing for *A Christmas Carol*.

Luther detested his cage and used his canny mind to the fullest in figuring out ways to ditch it. As a result, he got out often. And when he didn't get out on his own, the kids *helped!* During one of these escapes, he cut one of his webbed feet on a rusty nail. Fortunately, Tracey (one of the actresses) had previously worked for a veterinarian. She was the only one other than me, and later on, Jay, (head costumer and actor) sympathetic to Luther's plight.

We dug up some first aid stuff and tried to clean up his poor foot—no easy task when the grimy sink appears to never have been washed itself. There was nothing clean down there to ever set such a precedent! Then, we put him in the shower (disgustingly dirty, too, but the "cleanest" alternative around), and Tracey—costume, stage makeup and all—got in with him. I locked the bathroom door (to keep kids and others out) and joined her in the cleaning process.

Unfortunately, she forgot she was supposed to go on stage when she was "called," nor was I there to help with last-minute costume changes and alterations, etc. The play went on without us (luckily for her, in that scene she was only an extra). But later on, the director added a scene not in the script when he tracked us down after the curtain call.

Anyway, we used soap and shampoo to clean Luther up, feather by feather, layer by layer. He adjusted to this tripartite shower with such nonchalance one would have thought such strange doings were part of his normal routine. We were a little apprehensive about what effect shampoo might have on the natural oil in his feathers, but concluded that few alternatives were worse than his current state. We then toweled him off (a process that gradually revealed light-gray feathers), cleaned, disinfected, and wrapped up his foot as best we could, taped it, and he was free to try and walk. He was very cheerful about it all—except for the dubious looks he gave our bandaging artistry—and began cleaning his feathers.

The next morning, he was white again.

And so Luther and I became friends.

Once he got to know me, he adored my petting him. He was most inquisitive, always wanting to know what was going on. Had he been a cat, he would have been purring on my lap; being a goose, he took second best and enthroned himself on the floor beneath my sewing machine.

And he was *very* vocal—I'd love to have a transcript decoding his end of our long talks together.

The bandage kept coming off—or was snipped off, we never knew which—but we tried to monitor his recovery as best we could. He'd get dirty again and again and again. I tried to keep him with me as much as possible, but it was difficult—and more than a little annoying—as what went in one end promptly came out the other—in a steady stream. He never seemed to feel the need to wait for a "more convenient season." Consequently I was continually cleaning up behind him, feeling much like a circus lady with a shovel in the wake of an elephant. Disgusting! Nevertheless, the process didn't seem to humiliate *him!* He followed me around everywhere I went in those downstairs catacombs, quacking indignantly as if to say, "Hey! Where do you think you're going? Wait up!"

As the *Christmas Carol* marathon began gathering speed and my work accelerated at an ever faster pace, I moved my ironing board, sewing machine, etc. over to the theatre basement and into the backstage makeup room. Luther thought he had died and gone to heaven when I moved him in too, to keep me company. Maintaining sideways eye-contact (goose-fashion), he quacked away with his stories hour after hour, only stopping once in a while to take a nap.

Then, as we neared zero hour, I worked there with Luther virtually around the clock, till I was hard-pressed to avoid falling asleep at my sewing machine. Every once in a while, I'd shake myself awake again, only to look down and see Luther eyeing me with puzzled concern and quacking solace.

Opening night came at last, but by this time I was almost too tired to care. Everyone else, however, was illuminated by that inner excitement that always accompanies first-night performances. Rumor had it that a big-time city critic was going to be there, which added an extra edge to the excitement.

Soon, I could hear the crowd upstairs. The milling around. The voices. And then, the clapping. And, after all the work I had done, I wasn't even able to sit back in the auditorium and enjoy seeing my handiwork. Here I was, still sewing, still altering, still helping to salvage or repair garments, during and after each scene. Before the winter street scenes, it was a mad house putting mittens, hats, coats, and mufflers on all the fidgety children before their entrances on-stage. As an added treat, just before the biggest scene, one frightened little girl, overwhelmed by stage fright, threw up on half a dozen costumes we had spent so much time mending, cleaning, and ironing. This created an even madder rush to find more costumes to replace them.

And then it was finally time for the big street scene, when Dickens' London was reproduced in all its vitality and diversity: with fifty children—all behaving now, wide-eyed and innocent—with several pet dogs and a pet ferret (one previous year, there had been a horse!) The entire cast was on stage at the same time . . . and Luther.

So it was that long before Tiny Tim's piping, "God bless us. Every one!" would bring that beloved story full circle, Luther had celebrated his acting debut by waddling across the stage. Noting how frightened he looked, Jay leaned down and picked him up. Tenderly cradling his feathered (white again) body in his arms, and feeling the tom-tom of his fast-beating heart. From that refuge, Luther contentedly looked out over the delighted audience, and quacked out a soft "hello."

Sadly, I was not able to stay for the rest of the run. In all my last-minute packing and bequeathing of responsibilities, however, one worry remained constant: *After I am gone, what will happen to poor Luther?* We moved his cage to a far corner of the basement (actually, into Torsten's office). There was thus a cement floor and a door we could shut to (1) try and keep the kids from tormenting him, and (2) keep his lonely squawks from disturbing the audience. This room was much, much better than the first. But there he was, left alone. I felt terribly guilty every time I shut that door and heard him entreating me to come back.

As the last moments of my tenure at the theatre trickled down like sand in the hourglass of my life, Luther began squawking nonstop. Actually, "squawking" is a totally inadequate word for what I heard. There is no one word in the dictionary that can begin to capture it; the closest I can come to is that it was halfway between an outraged squawk and a heartbroken sob. There is absolutely no question in my mind: he *knew!* Even though Jay promised to take care of him, I knew it would never be the same. It was heart-wrenching. It was terrible!

All the way back to Maryland . . . I could hear him cry: "Why, why did you forsake me? *Why?*"

I *still* hear him . . . in sleepless nights . . . in restless days. How this one little goose—nothing but soiled, once-white feathers, two inquisitive eyes, a quacking story that never quite got told, and a heart as big as all New England—could make such a difference in this hectic life I live, I guess I'll never understand. It just has.

That Christmas, Jay, bless him!—knowing I'm such a sentimental ol' fool—sent me a present. It was small, and my fingers shook a little as I opened it. It was a lovely ceramic ornament. One side was flat. But the other—the other side featured, in relief, a white bird. A goose. Luther.

❖   ❖   ❖

HOW THIS FIFTH STORY
CAME TO BE

It was autumn in New England nine years ago. Our daughter Michelle (a fashion and French major at Andrews University) decided to do her fashion internship in a Massachusetts public theater. It was tough work for her—mighty tough—and she had very little leisure time.

When she came home for Christmas, she slept around the clock.

After she caught up on sleep, she began telling us about her experiences. It had been a world such as she had never known: a world of rootless men and women whose love of the stage kept them ever on the move. A profession that paid poorly, if at all, but which they loved anyway.

But of all the experiences she shared with us, the story that never failed to bring tears was the story of a goose named "Luther." The poignancy of the story had to do with the undeniable fact that Luther had adopted Michelle—had bonded in ways she is still sorting out in her mind and heart.

A year passed, and still, huddled in Michelle's heart and adamantly refusing to go away, was Luther: a story without an end.

Seasons passed, and it was now July of 1994. Since Luther yet reigned in our daughter's heart, I finally concluded that any handful of feathers with that kind of staying power deserved to be remembered, so I asked her if she'd mind writing out the story. She agreed. I tried, in its retelling, to preserve the natural rhythm of Michelle's original narrative. It is told simply, naturally, just as she remembers it.

She remembers it still. Through Luther, she has gained new insights into why God placed each creature on this planet; creatures large and small, each with a role to play.

❖   ❖   ❖

The story was first published in Review and Herald Publishing Association's trade paper Christmas in My Heart 4 *in 1995, and again in 1999 in Doubleday/Random House's fourth* Christmas in My Heart *hardback treasury.*

Hans and the
TRADING GAME

It is not known who invented the Christmas Trading Game, where it came from, or when. Even in our family, the same questions remain unanswered. All we know is the game wasn't—and then it was.

Unquestionably, it has changed Christmas for us. In fact, in a very special way it has come to define our Christmases, each game representing a frozen-in-time snapshot of who we were during that magical hour.

On that level playing field there is no generation gap, for the acquisitive instinct has no expiration date. It is said that one can learn more about a person in one hour of play than in a year of work. The children of our family can testify to the truth of that, for every year at Christmas they have seen us shed our adult masks and become children again. It is only in looking back, however, that we see our frailties revealed in bold relief, there for all the family to see. The difference between our rhetoric and who we really were. Who we really *are*.

But . . . come along and see for yourself.

❊   ❊   ❊

It is Christmas Eve . . . and the house is swarming with cousins, uncles, aunts, and two sets of grandparents. For days now they have been coming, and the house feels it. The once near spotless house — cleaned, dusted, waxed, vacuumed — had been a showpiece only three days ago. *Had* been. Now, look at it! Instead of rooms, there are paths.

And under Greg's bed, glaring with baleful eyes at any childish face that peers in at him, is snow-white Moby Dick. He's certainly not purring now, surrounded as he is by nasty children with sticky hands, syrupy voices, and less than angelic intentions.

The kitchen is a boisterous place, where scolding aunts and grandmothers fight a losing battle: trying to keep cousins, uncles, and grandfathers from emptying the cookie jar before dinner is announced. Only the strident clanging of the dinner bell saves the last cowering cookie.

There is a stampede for the long Spanish trestle table, groaning under the weight of platters, bowls, casseroles, china, silverware, and enough food to carry Valley Forge through an entire winter. Grandma Barbara (who remembers holidays, not by who was there or by what was done, but by the exact menu of what people actually ate) pans the festive table with her inner lens, recording every dish for posterity. Her inner computers can print out, on an instant's notice, every holiday menu for the past sixty-five years.

Everyone seated at last, hands are held; each is made welcome; the blessing is said; and — at Indy 500 speed — the tonnage on the table is transferred to the seats of the high-backed Spanish chairs. The demolition job is accompanied by much laughter, stories, family gossip, admonitions fired at erring children, and a steady counterpoint of outrageous puns.

In order to understand the story, we must first be introduced to the characters. Grandpa Lawrence and Grandma Barbara had flown into Dallas from Portland yesterday. Grandpa Derwood and Grandma Vera lived only three miles away in what locals label "the Castle" (because of its turreted tower). From far off Vienna had come Uncle Romayne, luckily between concert engagements. Only two hours ago the blue Ford pickup with California plates had turned into the driveway, carrying Uncle Elmer, Aunt Marjorie, Cousin Hans, and Cousin Shawn. Missing from the circle are Uncle Gary, Aunt Marla, Cousins Richie and Sonya (missionaries in Kenya), and Uncle Kirby and Aunt Molly (missionaries in

Rwanda). Present, however, are their children, Cousins David, Byron, and Nikyla. This leaves only the hosts, Uncle Joe, Aunt Connie, Greg, and Michelle.

All told, there are sixteen.

The completion of the meal and the imminence of kitchen KP unleashes mysterious vibes that occasion a modern-day miracle: an instantaneous vanishing of every last male in the house. The girl cousins, a hair slower at the starting gate, are caught at the very last instant, only milliseconds from freedom. Trying vainly to avoid tears, eight-year-old Michelle howls her indignation at this unequal distribution of blessings. She calms down only when assured that the boys' turn will come. But for now, her succinct summation of events so far is, "I hate boys!"

Several hours later, the kitchen finally clean, the men and boys magically reappear and sheepishly peer into the kitchen. Uncle Elmer shamelessly asks if there is anything he can do to help—then flees the room, vainly attempting to outrun a projectile originating in the vicinity of Aunt Marjorie. Somewhere during the hilarity that follows, the last cookie mysteriously disappears; the chipmunky cheeks of Cousin Hans reveal where.

Not long after, the house quiets down some, and the migration to the vicinity of the gloriously decorated tree begins. Each individual establishes territorial rights to specific acreage—and waits for the Christmas story to begin. Some minutes later, Grandma Barbara puts on her spectacles and begins reading "David's Star of Bethlehem," a story she has never yet managed to get through dry-eyed. She finishes with her record still intact. However, rather strange honking and nose-blowing by cousins David, Byron, and Greg attest to the fact that Grandma's well documented inability to get through that story without histrionics has nothing to do with age or gender.

In the quiet moment that follows, Grandma Vera articulates what many are thinking: wishing that the circle were complete.

Three-year-old Shawn is the first to hear it—the Christmas carol being played on the harmonica outside. He runs to the window, wide-eyed. "Santa Claus!" he squeals. "Look, Mommy . . . Santa Claus!"

Suddenly, the front door is flung wide, and Santa harmonicas his way into the room. The carol continues as Santa Claus (who everyone knows is really Grandpa Lawrence, but nobody will spoil the illusion by saying so) plays on. But the last vestiges of even that feeble illusion are now rudely torn away with Shawn's high-pitched discovery: "Mommy! Mommy! . . . It's *not* Santa—it's *Gwampa!*

When a measure of equilibrium is restored, Santa asks Aunt Connie to bring in the big brown bag. Once the bag is in his hands, Santa proceeds to "search" for a helper—but that is a sham, for Hans has already locked up that starring role by the use of these tender words: "Last year, that twerp Michelle got to do it, so it's *my* turn this year!" (Hans has sulked all year about this injustice).

After the bag is vigorously shaken so that all the numbers are mixed up, Hans begins his rounds. He first takes the bag to Grandma Barbara. She reaches into the bag, feels around some, pulls out a piece of paper, unfolds it, gives it one lightning-quick glance, and poker facedly refolds it. Only the tell-tale look of triumph in her eyes gives her away.

Next is Grandma Vera. She, too, almost achieves Sphynxhood— only a slightly droopy left lip gives her away.

Greg is third, and he radically changes the tone of the event with an exuberant shout: "All right!" Clearly, he's either first or last.

Grandpa Derwood takes one look at his number, and his renowned rubber face is magically transformed into his patented sour persimmon look—a middle number must be his.

Eventually, Hans gets the bag to every person in the room, and everyone by now has inspected that excitement-laden number which will dictate the role each will take in the drama of the evening. Hans and Grandpa Lawrence now each draw a number. Hans' quivering lips tell Grandpa the whole story: the number is most certainly not a high one.

Uncle Joe now stands up to give the annual instructions about how the game is played, a process the cousins deeply resent, for they already know the rules inside out. Nineteen-year-old David feels the weight of his seniority, hence his man-of-the-world, I've-seen-and-heard-this-all-before look, seasoned with touches of noblesse oblige. Byron (two years younger than his brother David) is somewhat less successful at achieving a look of sophisticated boredom; for he is excited and can't seem to keep from showing it. Fifteen-year-old Greg valiantly attempts to mirror David's world-weariness, but wrecks the effect by his being unable to keep his thoughts and eyes away from the presents under the tree. Fourteen-year-old Nikyla, exhausted from the long flight from Nairobi, is too overwhelmed by jet lag to even be sure what world she's in. Michelle, being only eight, still retains most of her illusions; hence she makes no attempt to hide her excitement. Six-year-old Hans is all business; staring with mad lust at the beribboned treasures. Little Shawn, at three, is too young to know what the game is really about. However, sensing that an opportunity to rip paper to shreds appears imminent, he can hardly wait.

The adults, sophisticated and full of years though they may appear on the outside, deep within, even they have to keep stuffing their unruly excitement back into their Jack-in-the-box canisters.

Meanwhile, Uncle Joe continues to explain how the game is played, just to ensure a minimum of misunderstandings and hurt feelings. The person who drew number one will select a package under the tree, unwrap it, and take temporary custody of it. Next, the person who drew number two may either open another present *or* snatch away the present now held by number one. If number two takes number one's package, it will be number one's turn again. Now there will only be one option: open another package as the rules preclude immediate retaking of a package that has just been taken from you.

After *all* packages have been opened, the process will be repeated twice more. The secret to landing a desired gift is this: if you have been able to secure possession of it three times, it's yours.

Heads nod impatiently to each portion of the annual spiel, each listening with all the rapt attention of a frequent flyer listening to his one hundredth pre-take-off emergency exit charade. *Get on with it!* is the unspoken but heartfelt plea.

So on with it we go.

ROUND ONE

Uncle Joe bellows out, "Number one!" There is a long silence. Then, confirming suspicions, Grandma Barbara reluctantly vacates her soft easy chair, walks over to the tree, and slowly inspects this package and then that, lifting some, and shaking some; with each delaying tactic torquing up the frustration level of the younger participants.

Finally, little Shawn voices the feelings of his peers with his importunate "Huwee, Gamma! Huwee!"

With only a little tell-tale twitch of the mouth giving away the secret that she'd been deliberately delaying the game just to see what kind of a rise she'd get, she picks up a medium-sized package, takes it back to her seat, checks to see if Moby Dick has reclaimed his favorite chair, and is reassured to see him owlishly watching the action from the safety of Greg's lap bastion—and so she deigns to sit down.

All eyes are riveted on her as she fluffs an adjacent pillow, searches for the most comfortable seating angle, smiles conspiratorially at Grandpa Lawrence, pushes back some ostensibly stray hair, clears her throat several times . . . and begins what promises to be a long search for her lap robe.

By this time, Byron, grinding his teeth in a medium-boil rage, dashes over to her, retrieves the lap robe from its in-plain-sight position, and ungraciously heaves it into her lap. Impolite snickers ripple around the room.

Not by an eyelash does Grandma Barbara acknowledge the sideshow. With exasperating slowness, she carefully unwraps the package so that not an inch of paper will tear. By this time, every time Shawn launches another "Huwee, Gamma!" more voices join the chorus (some sounding—perish the thought!—suspiciously low in register). At long last, the paper all neatly folded for reuse, the bow gently placed in a box, she opens the package and pulls out a tall, white flower-bedecked juice pumper. "Oohs" and "ahs" testify to the likelihood that the pumper will travel soon.

"Number two!"

David uncoils his long length, brushes off some invisible lint, tucks in a part of his shirt that doesn't need tucking in, takes a swipe at Moby Dick, barely avoids being tripped by Byron, and saunters over to the tree. While there, he decides that perhaps someone ought to find out whether or not the Christmas tree needles are still fresh. It would be such a shame if they were getting a tad dry. Conscientiously, he checks a number so as to get an honest count: Let's see, some dry ones here, some dry ones there; some not so dry ones here, some not so dry ones. . .

The hardest couch pillow in the house whangs into his back. Whoever threw it is a real Cy Young candidate, for it smoked as it came over the plate. Thanks in part to the persuasive logic of the pillow, David concludes that the needles are in surprisingly good shape. While in the area, he decides that it might not be a bad idea to check out a present or two. Not wanting to be unduly hasty, he fondles every last package, some of them several times. At last, a pleased smirk on his face, he returns to his seat with what he *knows* is a certified winner. Forgetting his ennui, he rips it open, only to discover, set in fold after fold of tissue paper, three padded pink coat hangers. His audience, noting his glassy-eyed stare of disbelief, looks closer, then dissolves in snickers, chortles, and guffaws.

"Number three!"

Aunt Marj rises quickly, walks over to Grandma Barbara, and asks for the pumper.

"*What* pumper?" responds Grandma Barbara, vainly trying to hide the evidence behind her.

"*This* pumper!" rejoins Aunt Marj, reaching around behind the chair and snaking out the "nonexistent" subject of the conversation.

"Oh *that* pumper!" exclaims Grandma, finally bowing to the inevitable, but not before patting it on its nozzle and promising to reclaim it soon.

Audible groans are heard as the significance of Grandma Barbara's pumperloss sinks in, for everyone remembers — *vividly* remembers — the eternity she took to process the first present. But this time she surprises everyone. She strides over to David, who *implores* her to take the pink coat hangers: "You *need* these coat hangers!" But Grandma concludes that, deep down in his heart of hearts, David really cherishes the satin-covered threesome; hence she edges around to the back of the tree and picks up one of the larger packages.

Always adept at working the family grapevine, even before leaving Oregon for the flight to Texas, she had her suspicions. Now she is going to find out if her premonitions were correct. This time, she wastes no time in husking the box. In fact, she even lets Shawn rip the paper off, to his obvious delight. And her face — as she sees what is underneath the tissue paper — is transfigured. She gasps as she tenderly lifts out of the box Aunt Connie's yearlong labor of love: a hand-sewn "Grandma's Fan" quilt.

Everybody swarms around her, trying to see it, trying to touch it. After a while, Greg and Uncle Elmer stretch it out so it can be seen in its full glory. It is a long time before the game can be resumed.

"Number four!"

There is a long pause. Suddenly, Michelle, who had been scratching Moby Dick's head, awakens to reality and springs to her feet. Her first stop is David's hanger stand; she sadistically torments him, pretending to be interested in them just to crank up his hopes, then walks over to Aunt Marj and her pumper, strokes it a bit, then eases over to Grandma Barbara who has been sensing trouble with a capital T coming. Like a she bear defending her cub, she roars her determination to keep the precious quilt — at all costs. But Michelle is determined too. From watching the long evolution of the quilt, she knows how many hours of work went into it. Young as she is, she already has maternal instincts of her own. The little bear wins and carries the precious quilt back to her coterie of admirers.

Grandma Barbara wearily gets up again, glances briefly at David, whose philanthropic spirit is so obvious. Such generosity is so rare in our youth these days. But Grandma has promises to keep; she relieves Aunt Marj of the trusteeship of the pumper.

Aunty Marj, an opportunist to the bone, studiously ignores David's outstretched pink things and moves over to her just-beginning-to-relax niece. The quilt is demanded, and battle is joined: the two growl and snarl at each other for some time, but in the end, the little bear loses.

Again, Michelle goes a'hunting, grinning slyly as she takes stock of David's eager attempts to adopt out his triplets. She looks longer at the pumper, then walks over to the tree, rummages around a bit, picks up a big but rather light package, and goes back to her seat. In less time than it takes to tell, she has unwrapped a large, oh-so-soft-and-cuddly cinnamon teddy bear. Michelle hugs it to her breast as the younger set mob her and the older set wish that it was socially acceptable to keep collecting teddy bears all life long.

"Number five!"

Nikyla shakes off her jet lag and gets to her feet. She loves her brother David dearly — but not dearly enough to relieve him of the Pepto Bismol-colored coat hangers. She pats the pumper. . . . She moves over to Aunt Marj. The quilt has disappeared. When asked for it, Aunt Marj sings the second stanza of that popular refrain: *"What* quilt?" Nikyla might be torn between two continents, but she isn't dumb: *"You* know what quilt! The *quilt,* please!" The resurrected quilt walks away.

So it comes to pass that Aunt Marj, muttering darkly, eases into motion once again. She looks over at David, but he is becoming more subdued as the truth is gradually being revealed to him: No one else wants the miserable hangers either. So David is reduced to deciding just what it is that he would do to the person who *put* those pink things under the tree.

Aunt Marj pauses at the pumper, again at the teddy bear, looks longingly back at the quilt, and then walks over to the tree. She pokes here, and pokes there; shakes this, and shakes that. Finally, she picks up a likely looking package and heads back to her seat. To her utter disgust, she unearths a Henry Aaron baseball mitt. Cheers ring out from sports fans all around the room.

"Number six!"

This time it's Grandpa Derwood's turn. Characteristically, he plays the moment and the audience for all they are worth. He first heads for David, and a five-watt glimmer of hope lights up the boy's eyes. Perhaps Grandpa is crazy enough to like padded pink coat hangers. Grandpa is crazy—but not *that* crazy. He does, however, commiserate by patting his grandson on the shoulder and reminding him that, in each life, some rain must fall. Without losing a beat, David retorts that *some* he could handle.

Grandpa next sidles up to Michelle and asks if he can hold Teddy. Michelle dies a hundred deaths while Grandpa hugs Teddy, tells everyone in the room how he was deprived of a teddy bear when he was young. In fact, he has always felt teddy bear deprived, and here is a heaven-sent opportunity to help make his dreams come true. Then, noting the look of absolute misery on her face, he hands Teddy back to her and moves on to his next victim—Grandma Barbara, ensconced with the pumper.

Grandpa lets her know that it's bloomin' hot working in Texas construction projects. Yes indeed: *mighty* hot! How often he has *longed* for a pumper. How he's lived this long without one, he'll never know. It was so good of Barbara to have saved it for him. . . . Then, having tormented *her* long enough, he stalks his next prey: Nikyla. Nikyla tries to bury the quilt somewhere, but it's too big. Now it is that Grandpa shows how great an actor was lost when he took up the hammer instead of the stage. He strokes the quilt; he fondles it; he announces that quilts are the very essence of all real meaning in life and that one can never have too many of them. Furthermore, he has always had a weakness for "Grandma's Fan" quilts. . . . Perhaps—and here he leers at his audience to see if they are hanging on to every word (they are)—it's because he's married to a grandma.

Grandma Vera beams. *How good of him—he's going to bring the quilt to her!* But if there is one thing Grandma Vera ought to have learned by now, it is that Grandpa Derwood was "born" cantankerous and unpredictable. He will zig when everyone else, including his wife, expects him to zag. . . . He heads toward the tree. The limelight is just too precious a thing to surrender, even for a quilt.

He rummages around under the tree, weighing each package on his inner scales. He *knows* what's in a few of them; in fact, he knows which one he wants to end up with, But, this is the most fun he's had in a long time, so he's not in any great hurry to let anyone else get up on the stage. Finally, he stumbles on a package that is suspiciously light. Years of such doings have taught him a great truth: light packages often pack a surprisingly big wallop. That truism proves to be an ever so slight understatement. In spite of his crust, Grandpa is a gentleman of the old school—hence he is totally unprepared for the ultra skimpy and sheer Fredericks of Hollywood negligee that greets his unbelieving eyes. He just stares at it in a sort of frozen horror— sort of like there was a cobra in the box.

By this time, everyone realizes that anything capable of holding its own with Grandpa has got to be mighty interesting indeed. So they crowd around and look into the little box. . . . All self-control comes to an end. *Everyone*—young, middle aged, old—laughs until it hurts; and they can't quit even then, so they laugh some more. By now Grandpa is holding it by the northernmost 10,000th of the strap—holding it out like it is a poisonous snake out to get him.

Finally, when people are so weak they don't feel they could ever laugh again, if they lived a hundred years, Grandpa Derwood realizes he's in danger of losing his audience. Always lightning-quick on the uptake, he swings the deadly critter over towards

Grandma Vera, causing her to blush beet red. Years of being married to him tells her he's up to no good, not when he sports that naughty little boy grin. Now, seemingly recovering from his deadly fear of the thing, Grandpa begins to see unexpected possibilities; perhaps Grandma might want this after all. In fact, it might be rather exciting to see Grandma *try* to get in it. By this time, his audience is moaning, beating their breasts, turning purple, begging him to sit down and let them live. Grandpa, loath to give up on a roll, here makes the mistake of looking back at his wife—what he sees tells him that this scene ain't got no mo' lines in it.

Just at this instant—providentially—the doorbell rings. . . . Greg answers the door, and in walks Michelle's playmate, Jeannine from across the street. So inseparable are the two girls that both mothers are convinced that they must have conceived twins—and since the food bills for two are offset by the food bills for none, nobody complains. When Jeannine sees the house full of people, she attempts to retreat; but Michelle tackles her halfway to the door and brings her back. Of *course* she will stay for the rest of the game! . . . Meanwhile, Aunt Connie has the unenviable job of trying to find another trading gift to put under the tree. She finds nothing at all. Finally, out of sheer desperation, she settles on something that is *far* from the kind of gift she sought . . . but at least it's something. She wraps it, places it under the tree, and—after consulting with Greg, gives Jeannine a number. And thus is lit the fuse that will change the course of the game.

"Number seven!"

"Number seven . . . who has number seven?" Suddenly, Uncle Elmer decides he'd better re-check Shawn's number. Sure enough, it's his. He informs Shawn that it's his turn, but Shawn is afraid to go up to the tree all by himself. Not with so many crazy people around. So Uncle Elmer takes his hand and steers him in the direction of Cousin David. But Shawn is less gracious than the others: not having yet learned to be devious, he curls his lip and spits out: "Yucky pink coat hangers!" Having put his cousin out of commission, Shawn moves on to the pumper, which he spares, not having any interest in it. As for the quilt, "Snertainly *not!* Who wants a dumb quilt?" . . . The negligee? "What's it for?" . . . But the teddy bear—now that's more like it! Without even asking Michelle if he can hold it, he snatches it out of her arms and runs back to his mother, shouting: "Mommy! Mommy! Look what I got—a *Teddy!*"

So a much persecuted Michelle rises once more, feeling sorely abused and picked on. This time, she ignores all the opened gifts and heads straight for the tree. There is a package—a *big* package—that she strongly suspects her brother of wanting. She'll just get to it first. Aha! Here it is. True enough: Greg's smoldering eyes verify that her suspicions are well-founded. Inside is a top-of-the-line HO narrow gauge train system. All the kids, as well as most of the adults (all of the male adults, that is), gather around the open box.

"Number eight!"

This time, Santa himself gets up and makes the rounds. He looks at the train system; looks at the teddy bear; looks at the coat hangers. David doesn't even bother to look up. Shawn's deadly salvo has blown out his last five watts of hope. Then, Grandpa Lawrence makes the mistake of passing within range of Grandpa Derwood, who has been uncharacteristically silent ever since Grandma Vera's eye-lashing. But one thing you can say for Grandpa Derwood: he's resilient.

"Hey, Larry, here's *just* the thing for you! You can, uh, be sure that Barbara has wanted one of these things for a long time! Come to think of it, it's really amazing that the two of you have gone this long without getting one. Why Vera and I"—and here he makes another mistake: he locks in on eye contact with his wife and promptly sputters to an untimely halt.

Grandpa Lawrence never does find out what "Vera and I" do with such night attire. He stops by the pumper, strokes it, and moves on. He pauses in front of Aunt Marj and murmurs platitudes about the great game of baseball, and how good it is to see women taking up the sport; then sensing that he's rapidly wearing out his welcome, he moves on to the quilt. Nikyla looks up at him with worried eyes, as well she should, for Grandma Barbara has let it be known that it's his Christian duty to bring back that quilt. Having joked for years about his having the last word in the marriage, his "Yes, dear" does little to refute that assertion. He annexes the quilt from Nikyla and carries it to "headquarters."

Nikyla gets up again and more or less perfunctorily makes the rounds of the opened gifts. She turns scarlet only once, when she strays too near Grandpa Derwood and the skimpy nightgown.

David, Byron, and Greg, sensing a wonderful opportunity to embarrass her, do so, shouting out: "Put it on! You're *just* right for it!"

She flees to the tree. After looking over the remaining presents for a while, she strains as she picks up a *large*, strangely shaped box, one that makes weird sounds when it's shaken. After lugging it back to her seat, she begins the ordeal of actually opening it. When she finally *does* get it unwrapped, it still takes her a while to figure out what the upside-down marimba-looking object really is. Since she can't figure it out, everyone else gathers around, and the mystery is finally explained: it is the wackiest—and by far the largest!—piggy bank anyone has ever seen. For the first time, David feels that his pink coat hangers may have a rival.

"Number nine!"

Byron, so tall and gangly he bumps into everything in sight, at last enters the game. He takes one look at the Rube Goldberg piggy bank contraption and launches a horse laugh, which endears him to his sister not a whit. The Henry Aaron baseball mitt really tempts him, but not quite enough. Almost, he takes the train system away from Michelle. He really doesn't know what he'd do with a quilt. The negligee? He soon learns the lesson others have learned before him: It's a mistake to wander within range when Grandpa Derwood has both barrels loaded, for the old man cackles: "Just the thing for you, my boy! Fits you to a T! Put it on and model it for the good folk!"

The cousins, delighted to see the irrepressible Byron discomfited for once, join the chorus: "Put it on, Byron! Put it on!" So shaken is he that Byron gallops past the teddy bear, the pumper, and the much extolled coat hangers, to the comparative safety of the tree.

It takes a long time to regain his composure—and he deliberately delays his final choice until his face fades back into an off-white. Ah! Here's a package that offers some real possibilities: not too big, not too small, not too heavy, not too light—absolutely *perfect!* And he bears it in triumph back to his seat. The cousins crowd around him as he eagerly opens his treasure, and they—all except one—are convulsed as they see his forehead wrinkle up in total disbelief:

"What in the *world!* What is this dumb thing, anyhow?"

David, delighted at having more company, consoles him with this explanation: "Looks sorta like a rhinoceros."

Greg, who has read "Billy Brad and the Big Lie" several times too often, chortles: "Nosserness . . . an . . . an . . . a great big nosserness comes up on the porch, an, an, an he hooks the door down, and he eats my poor mama's cake . . ." and then, unable to continue, rolls on the floor in delight.

Byron, utterly failing to see the humor, and ungracious to the last, grouses, "What a dumb gift — just a stupid wooden rhino from Africa! We've a room full of these dust-catchers! Who in the world's trying to foist off on us another of . . ."

He stops, as Nikyla runs from the room in tears.

Grandma Vera breaks in: *"Now* you've done it! Nikyla hand-carried that all the way from Rwanda. She thought it would be a real prize for someone. Don't you think you owe your sister an apology?"

Byron, who is at heart a great big marshmallow, gets up immediately and goes in search of his sister. . . . It is some time before they return (he, sheepish and she, with tear-stained cheeks) so that the game can resume.

"Number ten!"

Uncle Elmer, with a sighed "At last!" puts Shawn down and starts on his rounds. He stays in Byron's vicinity a long time, praising the rhino's wonderful qualities, trying to win back a smidgeon of a smile to Nikyla's face, but she refuses to be consoled. Halfway to the piggy bank, Uncle Elmer wheels, walks back, and asks Byron for the rhinoceros. For the first time, a glimmer of a smile sneaks into Nikyla's eyes.

A subdued Byron now gets up, scans the other eight presents, and once again heads for the tree. The mood has radically changed in the room, for each one is now acutely aware that behind every present under the tree are feelings — easily wounded feelings. And Byron, who dearly loves his sister, wonders just what he'll have to do to make amends for his thoughtless response. It's just that, with parents and other relatives in Africa, it's really hard to get very excited about yet another African wood carving, since that's about all missionaries bring home.

This time, he decides he'll avoid hurting anyone else's feelings but his own; so he picks up a familiar-looking package, takes it back to his seat, and opens up his own gift: a deluxe edition of Monopoly. As he had hoped when he bought it, all over the room can be heard music to his ears: "I want that!", "I'd sure like to have one like that!", and "Boy, just wait until *my* next turn!"

"Number eleven!"

"It's me. . . . It's finally me!" shrieks Hans, leaping to his feet; so eager is he to get a present of his own, he can hardly keep his feet from dancing. He studies the Monopoly game, but Byron's fierce glare scares him off. He checks out the rhino, but not for very long. He *certainly* doesn't want that crazy piggy bank that takes up half a room. The Hank Aaron mitt would be great to own—so would the train system . . . and so he passes from item to item, not really excited about any of them: what he *really* wants is something all the cousins want for themselves. So he heads for the tree. He spends some time studying each package for its possibilities. Finally, he finds one that looks promising—and it's heavy enough to be a toy. He lugs the heavy package to his seat and feverishly rips the paper off. But alas!

"It's not a gift for kids at all—it's a dumb *power drill!* Oh! Oh!" He struggles to hold back the tears. The adult males grin understandingly at each other. Hans won't be left with the drill.

"Number twelve!"

Grandma Vera, by now weary of sitting so long, welcomes the opportunity to stand up. And having done so, she's in no hurry to sit back down. The power drill? Ha! Derwood will get that for himself—if he wants another one. Monopoly? Nope. Now if it had been a color set of double nine dominoes—that would be different. The rhinoceros? Not when there's already a house full of African artifacts. She moves on from opened present to opened present, pausing at each, finally arriving in the vicinity of the quilt. *Hmmm. Lawrence and Barbara are guarding that quilt like two protective dragons—they certainly aren't going to give it up without a fight. Funny, isn't it, how when you get old it's so hard to find gifts that you really want. Except for quilts. At any age, you'll almost kill for a hand-sewn quilt.*

She doesn't have to kill for it, but prying it loose from Lawrence and Barbara comes close.

Having lost the quilt, Grandpa Lawrence has to go on the prowl again. The quilt temporarily off limits, he's on his own this time. Thinking back to Nikyla's rhinoceros, he too decides to go to the tree instead of again looking over the presents, although that power drill is something he could really use. He settles on a package that looks and weighs like a sweater. A large one. It *is!* And a nice color too.

"Number thirteen!"

Aunt Connie rises quickly to her feet and strides over to Grandma Vera, now protectively hovering over the embattled quilt. Having *made* the thing, it seems only fitting that she retrieve it.

"But," sputters her mother, "it would look so *be-yootiful* in that upstairs bedroom!"

Deaf to all pleas, Aunt Connie takes her quilt back.

Grandma Vera gets up, muttering louder this time. Words such as "ungrateful daughter" can be distinctly heard. Just in case they failed to register the first time, she says them again, this time in the immediate vicinity of the traveling quilt. If she can't reacquire the quilt, she might as well go to the tree. Here it is: a rather intriguing package, both weight and size wise. She takes it back to her seat and unwraps it. Oh good! Romayne's latest record! And his latest book of poetry too!

"Number fourteen!"

Uncle Romayne leaps out of his chair, then slows down to a sloth-like pace. He looks intently at each gift—and each temporary guardian. Except for the quilt, there's nothing he feels strongly about, but Aunt Connie just took possession of it, and she doesn't look like she'll give it up without a fight. So, he heads for the tree. There are now only four presents left. Fortunately, however, there is a *big* package, a *heavy* package, that no one has chosen yet. This is almost too good to be true!

It is indeed: it is a very large and very heavy yellow Tonka dump truck. Seeing his shock, laughter sweeps back into the room—and Nikyla, who is sitting closest to him, is laughing hardest of all!

The Nosserness wound has healed.

"Number fifteen!"

At last, it's Uncle Joe's turn. Feeling it's time to speed up the game, he bypasses the large arena of opened packages and walks straight to the tree, looks at each of the remaining presents, then chooses the largest one. It is a popcorn popper. Underwhelmed, and muttering to himself about what happens to greedy people, he glares at the poor popper.

"Number sixteen!"

Slowly, Jeannine stands up. What a family this is—and what a wait! There are only two packages left, and, like Uncle Joe, she picks the largest one. Oh no! Not a dumb *book!* . . . Uncle Joe tries in vain to console her, telling her it is a First Edition of Zane Grey's *Nevada.* Her heartfelt response: *Who cares!* All this time for a lousy book! She could cry—and does.

"Number seventeen!"

Greg stands up. There is now only one present left. He has waited a long time for this moment, and he is distinctly in no hurry to end it. Naw, doesn't want the pumper. Coat hangers?

"Hi there, David. See you still got your heirlooms!" And Greg quickly gets out of range.

Nope, no teddy bear, no negligee. . . . Ah! The *train system!* Of course! The train system changes hands, and Michelle is once more on the loose. Noting that the quilt is temporarily in family custody, she turns to the one small present left under the tree. This is small, the smallest of the last three, so it's *got* to be good! She opens it. . . . Talcum powder—bath talcum powder with a fluffy puff. "Talcum powder! Is somebody playing a joke?" she shrieks.

And so the wild card fuse flares into flame.

R O U N D   T W O

"Number One!"

Now the serious part of the game begins: the battle for long-term possession of gifts . . . and, joy of joys, the opportunity to pass on to others certain "very special" items. Grandma Barbara swaps the pumper for the quilt, which Aunt Connie grudgingly parts with.

Each number is called again, and the presents change hands, each transaction punctuated with hilarity or groans. The quilt especially keeps traveling almost continuously, as do, for radically different reasons, the huge piggy bank, the skimpy negligee, the pink clothes hangers, the nosserness, and the forlorn talcum powder.

When number six is called, Grandpa Derwood, negligee in hand, steps back into the limelight. There is a morbid fascination in watching Grandpa's efforts to find a good home for the postage-stamp-size nightie. After inspecting each gift at his disposal, he decides he really needs the sweater Grandpa Lawrence has been guarding. Perhaps Preacher Lawrence will have better luck getting his wife to see the nightie's possibilities than he has. Preacher Lawrence's jaw drops two feet; and Grandma Barbara almost swallows her teeth. The house rocks.

Eventually, things settle down again, and Preacher Lawrence casts about for a way of escape. Unfortunately for poor Hans, Grandpa catches sight of the power drill on his lap and, with the desperation of a drowning sailor seizing a life raft, he lunges for the drill.

So now it's poor Hans' turn to hold the skimpy nightie. The bedlam that occurred before is nothing compared to what happens now. The look of absolute disbelief on poor Hans' face is more than anyone can handle.

After some time, relative quiet is achieved, and the game proceeds, with the precious quilt almost always on the go. But round two has one last dramatic scene left. It was sidesplitting enough to see poor, bewildered Hans standing there with the nightgown, turning beet red; but even that pales in comparison to Uncle Romayne—the perennial bachelor wedded only to his music—standing there like Bambi on ice, paralyzed with terror, holding the deadly nightie's northernmost end.

ROUND THREE

When "number one" is called out, the room becomes the quietest it has been all evening as the moment of final truth arrives. This is *it!* Everyone looks down at the current holding, glances around at the others, and calculates odds. Grandma Barbara impressively stands up with her baseball mitt and looks for someone who needs it more than she does. But then the wheels turn in her head, and a smile as big as Texas spreads across her face as she walks over to Greg, hands him the baseball mitt—and takes permanent possession of the Grandma's Fan quilt. The whole family applauds. Grandma wipes away tears of joy, drops the quilt in Grandpa Lawrence's lap, and runs over into Aunt Connie's arms. It is the most moving moment of the night . . . so far.

Eventually, things settle down so the game can go on.

The final fate of the quilt decided, the playing out of the remainder, for a time at least, is seen as anticlimactic. The stakes are now not necessarily to win but rather to not get stuck with one of *"those."*

So it is that the piggy bank, the pink coat hangers, the negligee, the nosserness, and the talcum powder circle around with each holder feeling like a musical chairs game player faced with fewer and fewer chairs on which to land.

In the process, Nikyla ends up with her own gift.

"Number eight!"

Grandpa Lawrence stands for his last time and begins walking over to relieve Grandpa Derwood of the power drill—but, just before reaching it, he chances to look at Nikyla's face. What he sees there brings him to a frozen halt. He looks down at the Nosserness, and his brow can be seen to wrinkle slightly. Well he knows how fragile is a child's self-esteem. Rejecting the power drill, he leans down and trades the Monopoly game to Nikyla for the nosserness.

Hans has had the misfortune to lose the teddy bear. In place of it he is left with the "coveted" talcum powder.

"Number fourteen!"

The negligee—where will *it* end?

Uncle Romayne and the negligee—*stand!* What will he *do* with it? . . . He holds the slithery object out, *far* out, as he walks over to Uncle Elmer and makes a present of it to him, then retreats with Uncle Elmer's sweater in its place. Now it's Aunt Marj's turn to turn deep red—for she is one of the only two who *could* wear it, and wear it very well. Now, Uncle Elmer begins to blush too. And everyone half laughs, half cries, and half claps—all at the same time. . . . All except Hans—he keeps looking down at the talcum powder, and wiping his eyes.

CONCLUSION

The game is all but over, and Greg, with his "number seventeen" last choice, is king of the mountain. Nothing in his entire fifteen years of life can possibly compare with it, for not only does he have his cousins and Jeannine at his mercy, he has most of those authority figures, the adults, as well.

The once raucous din has ceased; in its place is near total silence. Everyone, it seems, has simultaneously realized that the drama has not yet been played out.

Greg looks first at Grandma Barbara, smiling beatifically with her hard-fought-for and already cherished quilt. Then, Shawn, playing on the floor with his big yellow Tonka truck. He notes how happy Mother appears with the brightly-colored pumper. Uncle Romayne, safe at last from the onslaught of the skimpy nightgown, has gratefully sunk back into an easy chair, holding onto the sweater. And Greg smiles as his eyes meet Aunt Marjorie's, who has impishly slung the nighty back into Uncle Elmer's lap. His sister Michelle's eyes are wistful as she holds the first edition of *Nevada* in her lap, solaced by the $50 bill Dad had hidden inside — she had whispered her discovery to her brother just moments ago.

Quicksilver expressions flicker across Greg's face. For some unaccountable reason, that story Grandma read earlier in the evening has thrust itself into his consciousness. That little David — destitute, an orphan, forsaken by those who might have loved and cared for him. Why, even his books were stolen from him, and his good clothes hidden so he could not perform in a Christmas program.

Greg shakes his head. *Why are these images clouding this ultimate moment?* Suddenly it seems as if a thick fog has lifted from his mind. It's as if he'd been almost blind, seeing only indistinct forms passing back and forth in the mist — and now the mist has dissipated, the sun has come out; and he can clearly *see!*

It's all changed now. Somewhere during this evening, he has stepped out of childhood into a different world.

With new eyes, he again looks at his family, ringed in a circle formation as if seen through a fish-eye lens. He sees Nikyla. For the first time, he *really* sees her. Sees the dread in her eyes, so certain is she that he will take away her Monopoly game. And Byron. How utterly miserable he is, stuck with that atrocious bank. And he knows there's no chance on earth that he'll be relieved of it.

Then Greg looks at David. Where is that aura of bored man of the world now? Now that he *knows* there's no possible hope that anyone will trade him for those infamous coat hangers that he just reinherited.

Let's see: what to choose? The HO gauge train? The power drill? Michelle's book and fifty bucks? Uncle Romayne's record and book? Or keep the Henry Aaron mitt in his hand?

A slight movement to his left catches his eye. Poor little Hans, his childish cheeks red and wet from the tears — the tears that have flowed for the last quarter of an hour. The look of hopeless dejection. The can of talcum power discarded at his feet now that he knows there's no possible hope of trading it.

The eyes of the family have followed Greg's and have riveted on the tableau. Staring through his new lens at them, Greg sees things never conceptualized before. Barring an act on his part, how will the story play out? Grandma Vera's lips are quivering a little. Much as she yearns for the teddy bear she never had, she yearns even more to bring a smile back to Hans' cheeks. Should he end the game with the talcum powder, unquestionably, she'll console him by giving up her teddy bear.

Grandpa Lawrence. Why in the world did he take that dumb nossernus? He has another just like it at home. Oh! . . . Oh! So *that's* why he did it—so Nikyla's gift should not be put down, discarded as of little worth . . . *Oh, Grandpa!* A lump surfaces in his throat, and a mist clouds his eyes.

For some strange reason he is seeing the forlorn orphan David there, with shoulders trembling, instead of Hans. David's lips quivering, instead of Hans'. He makes one last attempt to temporize: *What's Hans to me? Other people are also ending up with things they don't want.* But it's futile, for his heart retorts, *That argument won't wash—they aren't five years old.*

Then, it's as if he'd always known it would come to this. He doesn't dare look at the other gifts calling to him. Instead, he walks over to Hans, leans down and picks up the talcum powder, and drops the Henry Aaron mitt into his lap.

❖   ❖   ❖

HOW THIS SIXTH STORY CAME TO BE

Christmas of 1994 was over. Our family had gone out to Oregon to spend Christmas with my folks in Coquille. We played the now beloved "Trading Game," and pigged out to wonderful cooking. I observed in my journal how good it was to see Dad and Mom still self-sufficient in their own home. I didn't then realize how little time they had left—before Dad's strokes would change forever how they lived.

But I must have had a premonition, for several weeks later I was impressed to write a Christmas story very different from any I had ever written before—a story about a game. It was anything but easy to make work.

My mind went back, back through the Christmases that gave structure to the years: "What year are you referring to?" "Oh, the Christmas we . . ." But I couldn't remember when it was when we played our first Trading Game—so it had to be a long time back. All I knew was that, somewhere along the line, the Trading Game had become the one activity that defined our Christmases.

Finally I concluded that the only way to make this particular story work would be to gather up all our most memorable Trading Game incidents and throw them into one story. I wrote every family member who was present at these annual celebrations and asked them to write down their favorite Trading Game-related memories, then send them to me.

The letters started coming in, and kept coming. A number of the incidents I had long since forgotten. After they were all in, I started writing the story, synthesizing into one game all our most memorable Trading Games, telling the story in sequence to the usual pace of the game. But the story was too episodic to work, so it ground to a halt.

Then came the epiphany: use one of the game's contestants as the protagonist so that there could be some cohesion. I froze one particular Christmas in time for the story, and then checked to see how old each of the cousins would have been that particular Christmas. I used actual names in the story, and tried to retain personality traits in the telling. Grandpa Derwood, for instance, is just as funny in real life as he is in the story.

Remembering the anguish when some of the younger ones got stuck with an unwanted gift, I decided to use little Hans as that brokenhearted child. And I used our son, Greg, as the last player who could alter the course of the game. This gave the story its needed suspense.

At the end, it all came together.

❈   ❈   ❈

The story was first published in Review & Herald Publishing Association's trade paperback Christmas in My Heart 5 *in 1996. Since then, many a letter testifies to the fact that readers everywhere, previously unfamiliar with the game, have begun adding it to their family Christmas celebrations. Some readers have even written stories based on "Hans and the Trading Game."*

But to the Wheeler, Leininger, and Palmer families featured, the story has a special significance, for it catches in these few pages "ourselves as we once were," portrayed honestly without rose-tinted glasses, with our frailties spread out for all the world to see. And two of those depicted—Grandma Vera and Grandpa Lawrence—are no longer with us, making its reading even more poignant to the rest of us who can only remember them as they once were—as they lived within the pages of this story.

Pandora's BOOKS

I t was just another bookstore—well, another used book store. And what could possibly happen in a bookstore that would be worth remembering?

PROLOGUE

Later it would be remembered as "the year with no spring." It came as a surprise after a bitterly cold winter, complete with record snowfall, frequent ice storms, traffic gridlock on the Washington, D.C. Beltway, closed airports, and snow days—longed for by children and teachers alike.

At first, people assumed it to be a fluke: *surely* the geese couldn't possibly be flying north already! Why, the iced-over Potomac and Severn Rivers were only now beginning to break up. But the honking geese kept coming, attuned to their planet's moods in ways humans will never understand.

Surely the cherry blossoms down on the Tidal Basin couldn't possibly be blooming this early! And the daffodils too? . . . But they were—and those who delayed but a day missed Jefferson's lagoon at its loveliest, for unseasonably warm air, coupled with sudden wind, stripped the blossoms from the unbelieving trees.

Azaleas and dogwood were next—way too early, as well. Usually, the multi-hued azalea, along with dogwood of pink and white, ravish the senses for weeks every spring, but not so this year; they came and went in only days. By early April, the thermometer had already climbed to one hundred, and now schools began to close because of the heat instead of the cold.

Once entrenched, the heat dug in. And the mercury kept climbing. Even the spring rains failed to come; and farmers shook their heads, trembling in their mortgages. Plants dried up; lawns turned brown, in spite of frequent watering; and centuries-old trees dropped their already yellowish leaves in abject defeat.

Tourists stayed home, making sizzling Washington a veritable ghost town. For the first time in recent memory, one could park anywhere one went—no waiting, no endless circling.

And for those Washingtonians who did not have air-conditioning in home, office, and cars, it was hell. One couldn't even escape by boat, for prolonged calms plagued the Chesapeake, interspersed by blasting gales of fierce, tinder-dry winds.

On television weather maps, the entire eastern seaboard turned brown in early April—and stayed brown, altering only to a deeper hue of brown. There was a morbid fascination in watching as heat record after heat record fell before that immovable front, seemingly set in concrete.

So . . . when the weather reporters trumpeted the glad news that, come Memorial Day weekend, the siege would at last be lifted and blessed coolness from Canada would flow in, most people greeted it as a second Armistice Day, a time to climb out of their bunkers and celebrate.

Traffic jams clogged roads everywhere, and Highway 50 became a parking lot from Washington to Ocean City. The euphoria ran so high, people didn't seem to mind at all. They got out of their cars and vans, set up their lawn chairs on the median, threw frisbees back and forth, and ate picnic lunches. One enterprising caravan of college students even found enough room between their cars to play a screwy sort of volleyball in the middle of the Chesapeake Bay Bridge!

But some people find happiness in places other than the beach. Places like book stores, used book stores—Pandora's book store.

❖   ❖   ❖

Oh, it feels so great to have a cool day again! mused Jennifer as she drove out onto Highway 50 with the top down for the first time in— well, it *seemed* a year. It felt good to just let her hair fly loose in the wind. As Annapolis loomed ahead of her, she veered off on Riva Road, and then headed south on Highway 2. Stick-um'd to her checkbook were Amy's directions.

"Oh Jen, you'll just *love* it," her closest friend had raved. "It's unlike any other bookstore you've ever seen!"

Jennifer, a veteran of hundreds of used bookstores, strongly doubted that, but not wanting to flatly contradict her friend, she merely mumbled a muffled, "Oh?"

Amy, noting the doubt written on her face (Jennifer never *had* been able to keep a secret, for her expressive face gave it away every time) merely grinned and looked wise: "Jus' you wyte, 'enry 'iggens, jus' you wyte!" she caroled.

In the months following that challenge, several other friends had rhapsodized about this one-of-a-kind bookstore, each report torquing up her curiosity another notch. Now, on this absolutely perfect late May day, she saw no reason to delay further; she would see this hyped-way-beyond-its-worth place for herself. After all, there were no other claims on her day. *More's the pity*, she told herself. And her truant memory wafted her backwards (without even asking permission) — backwards to a time when she *had* been needed, *had* been wanted, *had* been loved. Or, she qualified to herself, at least I *thought* he loved me.

It had been one of those childhood romances adults so often chuckle about. The proverbial boy next door. They played together day by day, inside one of their homes in bad weather, outside the rest of the time. When school started, they entered first grade together.

He carried her books, fought anyone who mistreated her, and at home they studied together. He was the first boy to hold her hand, the first she kissed. Their parents merely laughed in that condescending way adults have about young love and prophesied: "Puppy love *never* lasts. . . . Just watch! They'll each find someone else."

But they didn't find "somebody else." Not even when puberty messed them up inside, recontoured their bodies, redirected their thoughts. Each remained the other's all.

They even chose the same college — and studied together still. They went to concerts and art galleries together, hiked the mountains together, walked the beaches barefoot together, haunted bookstores together, went to parties together, and even attended church together.

So it had come as no surprise that spring break of their senior year, when walking among the dunes near Cape Hatteras, he asked her to marry him. And there was no hesitation in her joyous, "Yes, Bill."

That it somehow lacked passion, that there was little yearning for the other physically, didn't seem to matter. Hadn't their relationship stood the test of time? How much longer than twenty years would it take to *know*, for goodness sake!

So the date had been set, the wedding party chosen, the bridal and attendants' dresses made, the flowers ordered, the tuxes measured, the minister and chapel secured, the honeymoon destination booked, the apartment they would live in arranged for, the wedding invitations sent out.

And then—thirty-six hours before the wedding—her world had caved in on her. He had come over and asked if they could talk.

"Of course!" she had smiled, chalking up the tense look on his face to groom-jitters.

They sat down in their favorite swing on the back porch and looked out at the yard, already festive for the reception to be held there. Her smile faded quickly as she took in his haggard face, his eyes with dark circles around them. Premonition froze her into glacial immobility. Surely it couldn't be what she, deep down, sensed it would be. Not after all these years!

But it was. He could only stammer brokenly the chopped up words and phrases that would amputate two dreams that over a twenty-year period had grown within hours of becoming one. He had found someone whose presence—or absence—raised him to the skies or plunged him to the depths, someone who ignited his hormones to such an extent that life without her was unthinkable. Bill hadn't gone far before his face turned scarlet and he began to sputter.

In mercy, Jennifer broke in: "Don't say anything more, Bill," she cried in a strangely ragged voice. "You can't force love—not the real lifetime kind. I . . . I'd far rather know this now than later. . . ." She paused for control.

Bill could only sit there miserably, his head in his hands.

So it was up to her to finish this thing. She knew she would always love him; after all, he had been her best friend for almost as far back as she could remember. And there is no trap door to open and dump such things—for the memories remain *always* and cannot be so easily disposed of.

He couldn't bring himself to face her parents, so after a few more minutes they stood up; there was one last hug—and he walked away.

She salvaged a bit of her battered pride by calling off the wedding herself. That was the hardest thing she had ever done. Numbly, she phoned them all, but gave no reasons. They would know why soon enough, if they didn't know already.

And so her marital dreams had died.

A year passed, and another, and another, until six years separated her from that fateful parting that, like "no man's land," separated the girl from the woman. On one side, trust and unconditional acceptance; on the other, suspicion and reserve.

During that first two years, she turned down all the men who asked her out. But, gradually, as her bludgeoned self-esteem began to get up off the floor, she belatedly realized that life must go on, that she must not wall herself off from living. So she began to date again, but not very often. Nine months of the year, the children in her third-grade classroom were her world. During the other three, she took graduate work, traveled, wrote, visited art galleries, and attended plays, concerts, and operas—often alone, but frequently with dear friends such as Amy or with her brother James.

She sometimes wondered if she'd ever find the kind of mate Bill had found: the kind of magnetism that would call her even across the proverbial "crowded room." Would there ever be someone who would set her heart singing? Who would be the friend Bill had been, but who would also arouse a passionate yearning to be his physical, mental, social, and spiritual mate? Every once in a while, she would wonder, *Why is it so difficult to find "the one"? Is there something wrong with me?*

So the long hours, days, weeks, months, and years passed. She completed her Masters at Johns Hopkins, and she was invariably doing *something*, anything, to avoid admitting to herself that she was unutterably lonely.

None of her diversions worked.

Not one.

✼   ✼   ✼

Oh, she'd almost missed her road! She slammed on the brakes, almost getting rear-ended in the process, and turned left. "Three and seven-tenths miles," Amy had said. Sure enough, there loomed the sign: "PANDORA'S BOOKS."

Gotta be a story here somewhere, she smiled. Now she slowed and turned into an ancient-looking brick gateway. Just inside, another sign announced that this was a wildlife sanctuary. *Some bookstore!*

The road snaked its way through first-growth trees (according to report, one of the only such stands of timber left on the Chesapeake). Here and there azalea, rhododendron, and wild laurel bushes banked the road.

She slowed the Camaro to a crawl to give some deer time to get off the road. Birds seemed to be everywhere: cardinals, goldfinch, sparrows, even a couple of bluebirds—and high overhead, hawks and gulls. It seemed incongruous, this close to the Washington metroplex of six million people, to discover such solitude.

At last the road straightened out and dropped down into the strangest parking lot she'd ever seen. Following directions from a sign, she drove into another grove of trees, finally finding a pull-in without a vehicle in it. After putting the top up and locking the car, she found a path to the beach.

She sensed the water's edge before she could see it, and now she could plainly hear the *ca-ca-ca-ca*-ing of the gulls. Suddenly, there it was: blinding white clapboard, framed by the silver-flecked blue of the Chesapeake. No clouds overhead today, only seagulls; and on the water, like swans taking flight, sailboats, as far as the eye could see. She stopped, transfixed, and inwardly spoke these words to her best Friend.

Lord, thank You for this day—this almost-too-beautiful-to-be-true day.

She had always been more intense than any of her friends, more deeply affected by beauty.

Before going in, she added a rather strange postscript: *Lord, please let only good things happen to me today.* Then she opened the door and walked in.

Inside, classical music was playing softly, meshing wondrously with the lapping of the waves on the shore, the ca-ca-ca-ca-ing of the gulls, and the occasional raucous croak that could come only from the long throat of a great blue heron.

And ah, that one-of-a-kind fragrance of old books, which to book-lovers is the true wine of life. And not marred, as is sadly true of so many used book stores, with disorganization, overstocking, clutter, and grime. But this store was blessedly different. She set out to analyze it and find out why.

First of all, it was clean. Not antiseptically so—but just close enough. No grime besmirched the shelves, books, walls, windows, or floor. Second, although the store contained tens of thousands of books, there was no perception of clutter or of being engulfed by the sheer mass of it all. Why that was so was easy to see: Masses of books were broken up by old prints, paintings, sculpture, bric-a-brack, and flowers—*real* flowers. She could tell that by their fragrance. And the windows—today, *open* windows—to let in the outside world. Or just enough of it. And there were benches and soft chairs everywhere, graced by lamps of great beauty.

Quickly, she discovered that the artwork tied in perfectly with the genre displayed on the shelves. For instance, Remingtons and Russells dominated the walls of the western room, supplemented by dust jacket originals, magazine art, movie posters, lobby cards, and old photographs. The adolescent/youth section had as its focal center a wondrous display of Maxfield Parrish, with its piece-de-resistánce, the largest print she'd ever seen of his "Ecstasy." Blow-ups of dust-jackets, paperbacks, and magazine art graced the walls in just the right places.

And amazingly, different music played in every room. Softly. In the western room could be heard most of the old standard western artists, from The Sons of the Pioneers to Eddy Arnold. In the religion and philosophy room, she heard the great music of the church. Lilting, happy music children love flowed from the children's room.

But best of all was the literature and general fiction room. For one thing, it dominated the seaward side of the second story. And on walls where no direct sunlight would fade what hung there, she saw faithfully reproduced copies of old masters: Zurburan, Titian, Leonardo, Ribera, Caravaggio, De la Tour, and Rembrandt. A massive stone fireplace anchored the southeastern corner. Just to its right stood a nine-foot grand piano. On its shiny surface was flopped, in abandoned comfort, as beautiful a Himalayan as Jennifer had ever seen. Without even thinking, she crossed the room towards it and reached out her hand, allowing it to be sniffed before she ventured to scratch the cat's head and massage its ears. A loud purring told her that she had been accepted into the narrow circle that could induce purring.

Jennifer crossed to one of the open windows, leaned against the sill, and gazed out across the silver-flecked blue water. Then (ever so softly, floating out of the very walls it seemed), she heard those haunting first bars of Chopin's *Étude in E.* . . . It was just too much: Her intensely passionate nature could handle only so much circuit overload. She lost all track of time or reality.

❊   ❊   ❊

Coming up the stairs with a load of books for restocking, Arthur sighed. On this seemingly perfect day, he longed to be outside. But so did his employees, so he had let many of them go—reluctantly. As he heard *Étude in E,* he slowed his pace. No matter how often he heard it, that *Étude* got him every time. Something in its melody brought an ache, reminded him that he was alone—incomplete. Thus his normal defenses melted like wax when he stepped into the room which housed his classics and stopped, rooted to the floor, when he saw the figure staring out the window. Her sapphire blue dress draped long, loose, and Maxfield Parrish classical; her complexion cameo ivory; her long hair a copperish flame, her ankles and Teva-sandaled feet slim and graceful—a Pre-Raphaelite painting suddenly come to life there in the room. He hardly dared breathe lest he break her trance.

Subconsciously, he weighed the external pieces that added up to the totality. *No,* he concluded, *she is not beautiful, though she has classical features and classical form, but she's alive, as alive as any woman I've ever seen.* He watched, as the strains of *Étude in E* internalized in her heart and soul and overflowed into her face (that face that always mirrored her inner self in spite of all efforts to control it). A tear glistened in her eye, the color of which he could not see from that angle, and slowly made a pathway down her cheek. But in her reverie she did not even notice it. Strangely enough, even though he'd never seen her before, he yearned to wipe that tear away and find out what caused it—if it was the *Étude* . . . or if it was something more.

❈   ❈   ❈

Something woke her, told her she was no longer alone. She turned slightly and saw him standing there, photographing her with his blue-gray eyes. (Hers, he now discovered, were an amazingly burnished emerald green). Gradually, as the mists of her reverie dissipated, he came into full focus. He stood 6'2", dark brown hair salted with premature gray; trim, physically fit. Dressed well, in a button-up chambray shirt, khaki dockers, and slip-on loafers. In his mid-to-late thirties, she guessed.

But his face . . . , she felt instinctively that this man standing there knew pain, for it etched his face. Especially did she note it in the ever-so-slight droop of a mouth that seemed made for smiling. His eyes, she concluded, were wonderfully kind. (He was not photographing her with pin-up intentions, but with tenderness and concern; and for such ammunition, she had no defense. Until that moment, she had never needed any.)

Feeling a familiar softness rubbing against his leg, he looked down and smiled. She liked that smile, and wished to prolong its stay. Clearing her throat, she spoke just one word, "Yours?"

And his smile grew broader as he tenderly picked up the purring cat, cradled it in his muscular arms, and announced, "Pandora."

She laughed, a delightfully throaty laugh, and retorted, "So here's the *real* owner of all these books!"

He laughed too. "Yes, well it's a long story. . . . If you're not in a hurry, I'll tell you."

I'm not in a hurry, she decided. *Never in less of one—in all my life.*

So they sat down on opposite ends of a sofa, and he told her the saga of a Himalayan kitten who got into *everything!* (hence her name), and how she had wrapped her tiny little soul around his when things weren't going very well for him (Jennifer sensed that admittance to be a major understatement). So when certain developments had made possible this bookstore, in gratitude, he had named it in her honor.

And he smiled again. "It *is* her bookstore. . . . I'm sure she feels it is hers, perhaps more so than a human ever could. And our customers, well, the people who come here feel she is boss. Everyone asks about her, and no one ever wants to leave without paying his or her respects." He chuckled again. "I'm not so important; not many feel short-changed if they leave without seeing me."

She thought, but did not say, *I'm afraid—I'm very afraid . . . that I would.*

So interested did she become in the story of this wonderfully different bookstore that she kept at him until the entire story spilled out. Even—or perhaps *especially*—a brief account of the motivation for it: the failure of a relationship central in his life. He did not elaborate.

Other book lovers came and went, eyed the man, woman, and dozing cat on the couch, attempted to listen in, then reluctantly moved on. Three times, they suffered interruptions: once for a customer downstairs, once for a phone call, and once by refreshments brought up by the assistant manager. Noticing Jennifer's raised eyebrows, he explained that fresh-brewed coffee (straight and decaf) and herbal tea were always ready on both floors, as were bagels and cookies, cold sodas, and bottles of fruit juice.

"Yeah," he admitted, "coffee's one of my besetting sins . . . the jump-start that gets me going. Maybe it isn't very smart to mix coffee and snacks with books, but real book lovers rarely mistreat books. No one's wrecked a book yet because of it. But no smoking! I can't stand it, and—" he looked down at the sleeping cat on his lap— "neither can Pandora."

Suddenly, Jennifer looked at her watch and jumped to her feet: "I can't believe it. Where has the day gone? So sorry, but I gotta run. Thanks ever so much for everything, but I'm late for an appointment. But I'll be back! Bye-bye, Pandora." She stopped to give the cat one last scratch under the chin, then she was gone, without so much as revealing her name. *But then*, Arthur mused, *neither did I!*

With her departure, although there remained not a cloud in the sky, a partial eclipse darkened the sun. To Arthur, the day had lost its brightness. The droop came back to his lip, but not—not quite so pronounced as before.

❖   ❖   ❖

Jennifer stayed away for almost two weeks, but each day she felt the magnetic pull; then she'd recoil from her inner yearning to return: *How silly! How ridiculous to blow out of proportion a simple little conversation. He'd probably talk like that to anyone who came by and asked the same questions. After all, he's in the business to make customers and sell books.*

Finally, thoroughly confused by her inner turbulence, she went back—and he wasn't there! But books are books, and she soon lost herself among them. She wanted to ask about him but could find no reason that didn't seem transparently obvious. However, she did find the books in the vicinity of the checkout stands to be unusually interesting. She kept taking them off the shelves, one at a time, studying them intently, then returning them to the shelves, all without remembering anything about them. She blushed crimson when it suddenly came to her what she was doing. Scolding herself, *You foolish, foolish schoolgirl, you!* she sheepishly put the last book back on the shelf and moved towards the next room.

She had not waited in vain, however. While she was passing the first cash register, she heard someone ask the clerk where the boss was. She slowed her pace. The clerk's voice was low and pleasing to listen to: "Mr. Bond?"

"Yes, of course! Mr. Bond!"

"Oh, . . . uh, . . . he didn't tell me where he was going . . ."

Jennifer's sharp ears then picked up a whispered jab from the clerk at the next register: "But you surely wish he had, huh?"

Jennifer sneaked a look. The face of the first speaker flamed scarlet, her blush speaking volumes. *So that's the way the wind blows!* she thought. She appraised the girl carefully: young (at most mid-20's), statuesque with midnight black hair (undoubtedly Spanish), and strikingly beautiful. . . .

Even more confused than when she came in, Jennifer hurried out of the bookstore without even looking up Pandora. She was disturbed, angry, and more than a little jealous of this girl who got to work there all the time.

      ✵   ✵   ✵

The three-digit heat returned after the Memorial Day reprieve, and the steamy humidity slowed life to a gasping crawl. Since it was patently too hot to do other than wilt like an unwatered impatien outside, Jennifer returned again to Pandora's Books.

Looking for him, but not looking for him, she reconnoitered her way through the various rooms, restless as a child the last afternoon of school. Suddenly, she saw him sitting on an easy chair by the empty fireplace, a portable phone at his ear. And curled around the back of his neck like a fur stole (and just as limp) was Pandora.

Her eyes twinkling, she surreptitiously edged her way out of the room, assuming he'd not seen her. Eventually, she gravitated back to the children's room, in the center of which was a sunken playground; and apparently, there were *always* children playing there. . . . After browsing awhile, she found a book she had always wanted to read, but could never find: Alcott's *Flower Fables*. Sinking into a soft chair with a seraphic sigh of pure joy, she opened its covers.

But she was not to sink into another world so easily. Across from her, a sandy-haired little boy of about five was vainly trying to capture his mother's attention: "Mama, Mama . . . please, Mama, will you. . . ."

"Oh, don't bother me!" she snapped.

Undeterred, the little boy persisted: "But Mama, I found this pretty book, and uh . . . I wonder if you'd . . ."

"Oh, for goodness sake! Will you leave me alone!" she snarled.

At this, the boy recoiled, as if struck, and, lips quivering, backed away. After one last look at the unyielding face of his mother, engrossed in an Agatha Christie thriller, he turned and headed towards a raven-haired woman who was restocking books across the room. But his courage wavered as he approached the clerk. Would she rebuff him too?

By now, Jennifer had forgotten her book completely. *How will the Spanish beauty respond to a child's need?* she asked herself. She didn't have to wait long to find out, for the woman, on being tapped on the leg by little fingers, whirled around in surprise—but she did not smile. She'd been enduring a raging migraine that afternoon. Milliseconds later, her dark eyes scanned the room to see if anyone had seen. Satisfied that no one had—Jennifer was watching her through veiled eyes (a trick women have and men do not)—she brusquely turned her back to the child, and continued restocking the shelf.

The little boy didn't cry. He didn't say anything at all. He merely turned around and just stood there, the book still in his hand, lips trembling, and a tear finding its way down his cheek.

It was just too much! Mother or no mother, clerk or no clerk, Jennifer swiftly left her seat and swooped down like a protective hen; then slowed, knelt down, and spoke words kind and gentle, "Can *I* help, dear?" And she tenderly wiped away the tear.

But he had been hurt that afternoon—hurt terribly!—and was no longer as trusting as he'd been only minutes before. He just looked at her, eyes still puddling. She, respecting his space and his selfhood, didn't touch him again—only waited, with tenderness in her eyes. It was no contest. An instant later, vanquished by those soft eyes, he was in her arms, his eyes wet, his little shoulders heaving, but making not a sound.

Across the room, his mother continued reading.

When the little body had stopped shaking, and the tears had ceased to flow, Jennifer led him to a nearby couch, sat down, and drew him to her. Then she asked him about the book. As he slowly turned the pages and read some of the words, she helped him with the others and explained the illustrations. A look of joy transfigured his face, and excited comprehension filled his voice . . . if one had been there to see it. . . .

Arthur, who *had* entered the room just in time to catch the entire tableau—*had* seen it. But Jennifer did not see *him*, neither then nor when she took the boy across the room to find another book, his hand held trustingly in hers.

Withdrawing quietly from the scene, Arthur returned to his office, asked his secretary to field all his calls and inquiries, and shut the door. He walked over to the window and looked unseeingly out on the iron-gray bay.

❖   ❖   ❖

The next time, she came on a rainy afternoon. Evidently a lot of other people agreed with her that a bookstore was the best place to be on such a day. Long lines piled up behind the cash registers, and many people waited with questions. The clerks, she noticed, tried to be helpful and answered all questions politely and with the obvious willingness to go the second mile. They knew many customers by name.

Even the Spanish girl. From time to time, Jennifer saw the girl turn to see if a certain gentleman remained in his office. Then, when Mr. Bond finally *did* come out, the girl's cheeks flamed as she looked everywhere but in his direction. A number of people clustered around him, asking questions, and each one received that same warm smile and attitude of eager helpfulness.

Then the Spanish girl went up to her boss to ask a question. Jennifer didn't fail to notice both the smile he gave his lovely clerk and the rapt expression in the girl's eyes. *Hmm.*

She moved on to the American writers section, looking for some of her favorite authors. *Oh! what a selection of Harold Bell Wright! I've never seen this many in one place before!* She took down a dust-jacketed *Exit*. No sooner had she done so than she felt a presence behind her.

"Are you into Wright?" a familiar voice asked.

She turned, smiled *(I like her dimples,* Arthur observed to himself), and said, "Well, sort of. I've read five or six, but I've never seen this one — or, for that matter, a number of the others here. Rarely do I see more than a few of his books in any one place."

"Well, there's a reason for that . . . uh . . . Miss — it *is* Miss . . . ?

"Yes," and she found his steady gaze, kindly though it was, more than a bit disconcerting; "my last name is O'Riley."

"Mine," he grinned a little wickedly, is Bond. But not" — (obviously he had used this line many times before, she concluded) — "James . . . but Arthur."

"And I answer to Jennifer," she said, blushing.

Ignoring the opening, he returned to Wright, "Well, Miss O'Riley, Wright books are hard to get, and harder to keep in stock. . . . Might I ask which ones you've read?"

"Well, the first of his books I read when I was only seventeen. Read it one beautiful day on California's Feather River Canyon. I was visiting a favorite aunt and uncle at the time — will never forget it, for it changed my life."

"I'd guess it was one of his Social Gospel Trilogy," he broke in.

"Trilogy?" she asked. "There's a trilogy?" The one I read was *The Calling of Dan Matthews*, and it really changed my life."

"Oh?" he asked quizzically.

She stumbled a bit for words, finally stammering out, "I just don't know how to go on . . . and I don't know yet if . . . if . . . uh . . . "

"If I'm a Christian?" he finished for her.

"Yes."

"Well, I am. Why do you ask?"

"Oh, it's just that *The Calling of Dan Matthews* gave me a new vision of God, of His all-inclusiveness. I'm afraid I had been rather elitist before I read that book."

He laughed (conspiratorially, she thought), "I agree, Miss O'Riley. It hit me that way too. Only, I had read *That Printer of Udell's* first—by the way, it anchors the Trilogy—so I was somewhat prepared for his contention that Christ's entire earthly ministry was not about doctrine at all . . . but about—"

"Service," she broke in softly.

"Yes, service for others," he agreed.

They talked a long time about Wright that day, and after that about other authors of mutual interest as well. Some, they loved in common; others they did their best to convert the other to.

Arthur had always felt he could more than hold his own in any battle of wits, but he discovered that in Jennifer, he had met his match. One day, as they sparred back and forth on the historical romances of Rafael Sabatini (while each had favorites, both agreed on the one that stood out above all others, *Scaramouche*, that great tale of the French Revolution), he grimaced—*she never misses a trick . . . not a nuance escapes her!*

Not long after, during another visit, she found a copy of a book she'd searched for, for years: Gene Stratton Porter's *The Fire Bird*. She quickly found a quiet niche, settled down in an easy chair, turned up the lamp, and began leafing through the book. She held no illusions about buying it, though. Beautiful and rare, true—but the price was far too high for *her* budget.

Then she heard voices, one of which sounded very familiar. She pulled in her feet so as to be as inconspicuous as possible. When the voices drew nearer, she drew her legs under her, yoga style. Since the speakers sat down in the alcove just before hers, she couldn't help but overhear:

"I just don't know what I'm going to do, Mr. Bond!" quivered a woman's voice: "I really don't. Lately . . . I . . . I . . . just feel even the good Lord has forsaken me."

"*That*, Mrs. Henry, I can assure you is not true. The Lord *never* forsakes His children," he responded.

"Oh, but Mr. Bond, you just don't *know!* Or you wouldn't be so sure. My oldest son—you remember Chris! . . . Well, he's on drugs. Worse than that: he's become a pusher . . ." Her voice broke. "And Dana—I . . . I . . . I just found out she's pregnant. I just can't believe it. She grew up so faithful at attending church every week. . . . And the man, the man who . . . uh . . . uh . . . ."

"The father of the unborn baby?"

"Yes. He attends our church too."

"Oh. Are they planning to marry?"

"That's the worst part. He says it's all her fault for not taking precautions. Won't have anything more to do with her. And Dana's near desperate. I'm afraid she'll, she'll—" And again her voice broke.

Arthur's voice broke in, firmly and kindly. "Mrs. Henry, there's no time to lose. Is Dana home this afternoon?"

Answered in the affirmative, Arthur led Mrs. Henry out, and after explaining to the clerks that an emergency had come up, he and Mrs. Henry hurried through the heavy rain to their cars.

For a long time Jennifer just sat there, thinking. *Just what kind of bookstore—what kind of man—was this?*

Jennifer came back within the week, and shamelessly stayed within listening range of where he worked. She simply *had* to know, for sure, what manner of man this was. So many times before, she'd been disappointed, disillusioned—so why should this one prove to be any different?

She was, by turns, amazed, then moved, by what she overheard. Apparently, he possessed endless patience, for she never heard him lose his temper, no matter what the provocation. Even with bores, who insisted on talking on and on about themselves. She discovered that while most asked book-related questions, a surprisingly large number of these people felt overwhelmed by life and its problems. In Arthur, they found, perhaps not always solutions, but at least a listening, sympathetic ear. In used bookstores, she had discovered, there appears to be an implied assumption: one finds an ear, no matter how stupid, inane, or ridiculous the topic may be. In that respect, used bookstores function as courts of last resort: the last chance to be heard before outright despair sets in. But, in Arthur's case, it went far, far beyond mere listening—for he genuinely *cared!*

❋　❋　❋

At last came August, and with it pre-session. Vacation was over, for school would begin in a few weeks. So busy was she that it was almost Labor Day before she got back to Pandora's Books. Just as she was leaving, he came out of his office and smiled at her. On the confidence of that smile, she walked over to him and asked if he could spare a moment.

"Of *course!*" he replied, and steered her into a quieter room and seated her by an open window. The heat had finally broken, and the cool bay breeze felt like heaven.

During the small talk that followed, she became increasingly aware of how strongly she was affected by this man, this tangible synthesis of strength, wisdom, and kindness. She was more aware of being near him than she had ever been with any other man. Stumbling a bit over her words, she asked him if he ever spoke to students about books—not just singly but in the schoolroom itself.

"Often, Miss O'Riley."

For some unaccountable reason, she blushed.

Pandora chose this moment to demand attention, and he lifted her up into his arms, where she ecstatically began to purr and knead her claws into him.

"You see, Miss O'Riley," he continued, "they represent our future. There can be no higher priority than children."

She found herself inviting him to speak to her class, and he gladly accepted.

As she drove home, and her Camaro left a trail of greenish-yellow leaves dancing in her wake, she acknowledged to herself that she'd just, by that act, set forces in motion—forces that might breach almost any wall she'd built up through the years.

Apprehensive she was, a little. But she sang an old love song over and over all the way home—not realizing until her garage door opened on command, just what she'd been singing.

❧   ❧   ❧

He *came!* And the children loved him! He came with a big box of books and sat down on the floor with them, holding them enthralled by stories that came from those books . . . and the men and women who illustrated them. And he answered each of the many questions they asked. The ones he couldn't, he promised to answer the day their teacher brought them on a field trip to his wildlife sanctuary/bookstore, when they could meet Pandora.

Jennifer pulled back from her usual focal center to give him the opportunity to be in control. She needn't have bothered. She knew now that when he walked into a room, it was as if he was iridescent, for he attracted all eyes just as if he shone like the sun. Just as was true—though she didn't know it—of herself.

She watched his every move, listened to his every word, and watched the quicksilver moods as they cavorted on his face and danced in his blue-gray eyes—eyes with the impishness of the eternal child in them. Like the legendary Pied Piper of Hamlin, he so enthralled that the children would have followed him *anywhere.*

And he, though apparently he saw nothing but the children, never missed a nuance of her. The vision she made, leaning against the window, would hang in the galleries of his mind for all time: a Dante Gabriel Rossetti dream woman. Her long, bronze hair, ignited by the late morning sun, her emerald green dress, and her seize-the-day face, added up to far more than mere beauty.

Before he left, he let each child choose a favorite book—and left the rest for the room library. Then, after reminding them to come see Pandora soon, he was gone . . . and the halcyon day clouded over. But the sun came back out again when one curious little boy sneaked to the window and caught sight of Mr. Bond getting into his '57 Thunderbird. His awestruck "Wow!" brought the entire class to the window in seconds, and they all waved—and he, catching the motion at the window, waved back as the coral sand convertible sped out of sight.

But not out of memory.

But just to make sure, that afternoon a florist delivered a large autumn floral display, crowned by a couple of book-topped spears, and at the very top, a goldish-brown cat.

That night, he called. Did she want to go with him to the Kennedy Center to hear the Vienna Choir Boys? *Is the Pope Catholic?*

Not long after, his second call came, asking her to attend church service with him. After that, the telephone worked both ways. Concerts, the many galleries and exhibits of the Smithsonian, opera; rides to the seashore, to quaint restaurants in old inns; and hikes along mountain trails—all these brought roses to her cheeks and a glow into her eyes.

After Thanksgiving dinner at her folks', he told her to bundle up for a rather chilly ride. Always, it seemed with him, the top stayed firmly down—he reveled in the panoramic view. On and on the Bird sped, and as she nestled down, the excitement brimming over in her eyes and the way her sapphire blue paisley scarf set off her flaming mane of hair—well, it made it mighty difficult to keep his eyes on the road.

The population thinned out as the Bird's deep throat rumbled into old St. Mary's City.

Here, they stopped by the river for a while, ostensibly to watch the geese, but in reality, because he felt reflective.

"You know, Jennifer, I think it's time I told you a little more about my failed marriage."

"That's up to you, Arthur."

"Let's see, how do I start? . . . Well, I had known Marilyn for a number of years; we attended the same parochial high school, same college—even same church. . . . My folks were good friends with her folks—had been for many years. . . . We liked the same things, shared many of the same dreams."

She listened, gazing out at the river.

"Actually," Arthur laughed, a strangely undefinable laugh, "I don't think I ever actually proposed—we just drifted into it. All our friends, our families, our folks, took it for granted. So we married. We loved each other. *That,* I'm sure of. It was to be for life—at least it was for *me.*"

There was a long pause, as he searched for the right words.

"We were married about eighteen months. Then, one never-to-be-forgotten spring morning, after breakfast, she announced that marriage was 'a bore,' 'a drag,' and that she wanted to regain her freedom."

A pause, then in a flat voice, he continued. "So she divorced me, and found another—several anothers. That was about twelve years ago, but it seems like yesterday. . . . Oh, I floundered for a time; my self-esteem was at its all-time low." Then he brightened: "But God saw me through. I escaped to the New England coast—stayed there a long time, healing. It was there that the epiphany came to me: 'Pandora's Books'."

"Oh!" she breathed, half a sigh, half a paean.

"Yes, a dream bookstore—unlike any I had ever seen or heard about. . . . But the Lord showed me that mere business success would not be enough: I must also care for His sheep. *That* would be my ministry. And the frosting on the cake. . . ."

"Was Pandora," Jennifer finished.

"Yes, Pandora," he smiled as he started the engine, and again they were out on the highway, heading south.

I'm so glad he told me! she murmured to herself as the Bird gathered speed. *He didn't walk out on her! That's what I was afraid of. . . . He had to have been hurt more than I was, yet he didn't let it destroy him. There was closure—a long time ago. . . . And joyously, there's a clear road ahead! Oh Lord, thank You!* And her heart began to sing.

Then she lost all track of time as the Bird raced down the peninsula, churning up waves of gold, brown, orange, crimson, and green leaves in its wake. Suddenly, there ahead was only a narrow strip of land, banked by white-capped slate-blue below and white-winged gulls in cloudy sky above. The Bird nosed into a parking space at the end of the road: Route 5, dead end. Since it was both cold and blustery, they had it all to themselves.

For a few minutes they just sat there, watching and listening to the gulls. She wondered what he was thinking.

Leaning back, his hands behind his head, he finally broke into her reverie: "You know, Jennifer, this is what I miss most. Solitude. The solitude you can still find out west and up north. So many people live here that, after a while, one gets claustrophobic. At least I do. If anything ever moves me away from this bay, it will be that. Well, that and my beloved mountains. I miss them."

Suddenly, he shifted in his seat and laughed. "Am I ever the gabby one today! Enough about me. What about *you?* What is *your* story? Hasn't some armor-clad knight tried to gallop away with you?"

Shyly, she answered, "Y-e-e-s."

Well, what happened?" he demanded, an impish look in his eyes. "Fess up: I did my stint, now it's *your* turn."

So she told him . . . and took a while doing it.

When she finally finished, he sat in silence a while, then smiled, "I'm glad. Someday I may tell you why."

"Someday you may, huh?" she laughed, her eyes narrowing.

"You know, Jennifer, your voice has bells in it . . . your laugh, most of all. Even on the phone, I hear bells ringing when you speak. You radiate happiness."

She blushed, started to say something, then stopped.

"Go on," he chuckled. "Might as well get it out."

"Oh!" she said, trying to slow her racing heart. "It's just that I've been happy a lot lately . . . and . . . and"—refusing to meet his eyes—"*you're* to blame."

There! It was out, and her eyes fell, unable to meet his.

Silence thundered in her ears, and when at last she looked up, he was looking out to sea with an enigmatic look on his face. His body had tensed; his face was now rigid. She felt utterly humiliated by her admission.

Then he turned, placed his hand on hers butterfly-briefly, and said, "Well, it's getting late. What do you say to heading back?"

All the way back, she wallowed in misery: *Why did I wreck what had been so perfect? Why change gears when we were just beginning to gain momentum in the lower one?*

Once she caught him eyeing her pensively.

When he walked her to her door, they didn't banter as usual. He didn't ask her for another date, just said in a flat voice, "Thank you, Jennifer, for a perfect Thanksgiving!"

❖   ❖   ❖

That was a long, *long* night for Jennifer. To herself, she wailed, *Stupid me! I've blown it! I took a wonderful friendship, just beginning to bud, and wrecked it. Might just as well have demanded the full-blown rose! But that's just it: I'm in love with him. Been in love with him for a long time—just refused to admit it. He storms me in his quiet, gentle way. I . . . I . . . . I've never met anyone before who lights up every room he's in—at least for me. I know it's shameless: but here am I—in my 30s—having never known passion (wondering if I even had it in me!), and now, with this man, I yearn for him, long for him, desire him, with every inch of my body, heart, and soul!*

Her thoughts raced on. *Friendship alone is no longer enough—even if, as is all too obvious!—it is to him. My passionate heart cries for far more. I cannot be merely another in a long line of friendships—perhaps even romances—with him.*

If only, if only, though, I had waited, perhaps it would have come.

Oh, why, O Lord, did I do it! Oh, God . . . to find my soul's other half—after all these long years—and then to lose him because of my big, big mouth!

And she wept through that endless night.

When he called, as usual, to ask her to attend church with him, she turned him down in an icy voice, then cut the conversation short by saying, "I'm sorry . . . but gotta run—I'm late!" and hung up. Then she *was* miserable, for in reality she had nothing else to do at all, and an entire evening to mope about it.

❅ ❅ ❅

Jennifer had always loved the Christmas season, a time when being a child again became an accepted thing. With what joy she always greeted the wreathes and garlands, the multicolored lights on the neighborhood eaves and trees, the Advent candles, the Christmas trees seen through the windows, the Christmas carols played continuously by radio stations! This year, though, she just wished it would go away—even in her schoolroom. True, she decorated it in the usual way, drilled the children for the big Christmas program, and helped them make personalized gifts for those dearest to them. But it all seemed hollow, all a sham. Even God, she felt, irrationally, had somehow let her down: *Lord, how could You do this to me? How could You let me make such a fool of myself!*

She no longer kidded herself about what Arthur meant to her. Or that he could be but a passing fancy that would go away. No, for better or for worse, he'd be a deep-rooted part of her as long as she lived.

He did not call again. Several times—nay, a hundred times!—she felt the urge to call him and apologize for her curtness on the phone, but her lacerated pride just would not let her.

Her last papers had been corrected and the scores added up, gifts had been accepted from each of her students, and the big program—to which she'd once planned to invite Arthur—had gone off without a hitch . . . yet none of it meant anything to her. Nothing at all.

Finally, it was over for another fall.

❅ ❅ ❅

On a certain dismal, winter evening, she was sitting there in her undecorated townhouse, wallowing in misery and self-pity, wishing for him, *yearning* for him, and dreading Christmas week.

The phone rang.

She answered it, but no bells rang in her voice, just a subdued "hello?" Almost she hung up when she heard his voice on the other end, inwardly raging because his voice still possessed this power over her, giving her goose bumps. It just didn't seem fair! But there *was* something different in his voice, almost a pleading note. He had a big favor to ask of her, he said.

"A favor?" she snapped, and then could have choked her misbehaving other self for that snippiness.

Silence swirled around her. Then he continued, more haltingly this time. He had a big favor to ask, yes, but with a qualifier or two thrown in. First of all, he wanted her to share "The Messiah" with him at Washington's National Cathedral, and secondly, he wanted to show her something of extreme importance.

When the silence on the other end of the line continued, he gulped and added, "If you'll accept just this once, I'll promise not to ever bother you again."

Seeing no graceful way out of it, she grudgingly parted with an undernourished "yes."

There! Finished! That will end it. No ellipsis, no dash, no exclamation mark. Period! Period! Period! . . . But three periods would be an open-ended ellipsis! shouted an irrational thought from a far corner of her brain.

Her mind raced, her thoughts milling in chaotic confusion: *I shouldn't have said yes, that I'd go . . . but I'd hate to miss out on going! I don't think I can handle being close to him again—I'm so sure my face will give me away if my big mouth doesn't. Yet, how can I possibly give up this one last time—the last time we'll ever be together? Oh, it will tear my heart out to be close to him and not be able to touch him! Not to be able . . . Oh! Oh! Yet I don't want him to take anyone else there! Certainly—make that double certainly!—not that Spanish beauty! Oh! What am I gonna wear?*

The big evening (the *last* evening! she promised herself) finally came. She dressed carefully in her favorite blue gown, a Diane Fries she'd purchased, in a rare fit of recklessness from Nordstroms. She'd make it a swan song to remember. Then she put on her heavy black cashmere coat, bought on sale just before I Magnin closed.

The doorbell rang; her pulse quickened. She forced herself to walk very slowly to the door, lest she appear too eager. *Oh, I'm a despicable vixen!* she reprimanded her misbehaving other self.

When she opened it and saw him standing there, in spite of her well-planned intentions, sapphire stars sparkled in her eyes and her cheeks crimsoned. For he was so . . . so . . . so detestably dear.

At the curb, its motor purring, was a car she'd not seen before, a Mercedes 560, in color a suspiciously emerald sort of green.

"Wouldn't dare park the Bird in D.C." was his only explanation as he helped her in.

Outside the window, the white of the first snowfall of the year enveloped the world. Christmas CDs played softly through the sophisticated sound system, and she relaxed a little in spite of herself.

Neither one said much during the ride to the cathedral.

They had a tough time finding a parking space, but finally did, then joined the well-dressed throng filling the streets. Excitement flooded Jennifer's cheeks, and once or twice she trembled as Arthur's hand brushed hers.

Inside the world's sixth largest cathedral, all was Christmas, and Arthur moved, with Jennifer just behind him, toward the nave. He took her hand now to keep her close. Eventually they arrived at the spot where he felt the acoustics to be nearly perfect, and they found a pillar on which to lean, for the seats were all taken.

Then the organ found its voice, shaking the near-century-in-the-making building, and chills went up her spine. Pipe organs had that power over her. She sneaked a sideways glance at him and felt satisfied by the look of awe on his face. Then the orchestra, then the soloists, then the choirs, and then she lost all track of time as Handel transported her through the drama of the ages.

Through it all, she remained aware of him, but in a sort of haze. He left once and brought back two chairs. She sank down with a sigh of relief. After a couple of hours, unconsciously declaring a temporary truce, she took advantage of his tall frame next to her and leaned her head against him. She felt him tremble when a draft of cold air blew a strand of her flame-colored hair across his face.

Soaring upward, her soul drank deeply of the majesty of the mighty columns and graceful arches that portrayed the architectural yearning for the Eternal. The words and music and organ and choirs and soloists and cathedral battered her sensibilities into a pulp. It was too much of a sensory overload for mere flesh and blood. During the "Hallelujah Chorus," when she stood at his side, she again felt him tremble, and peeped sideways to find him wiping away tears. Since she was crying, too, she felt a renewed sense of kinship with him.

The crowd was unbelievably quiet as they found their way out, almost as if words seemed far too fragile to accommodate such divine freight.

On the slippery road again, neither spoke, and the sound system remained silent, as if anything else right now would be anticlimactic.

For this she inwardly thanked him, for his sensitivity and empathy. For not shattering the mood.

So surreal was it all that she didn't even notice they had passed her highway exit until the Mercedes veered off Highway 50 onto Riva Road. To her raised eyebrows, he merely smiled and said, "Remember, there's more yet to this promised evening."

As the traffic thinned out south of Annapolis, and the flocked evergreens flashed by, slowly, haltingly, he began to speak.

"Undoubtedly . . . you . . . you . . . uh wondered about my strange response to your—uh—to what you said about yourself . . . the last time we were together."

She stiffened: *How dare he bring up that utterly humiliating afternoon, when he rejected my stupid disclosure of my inner feelings. How dare he!*

But he ploughed on, not looking at her. "You see, Jen,"—he'd never called her by her family pet name before!—I was so wounded, so scarred, by the rejection I told you about . . . that I determined that never again," and here he struggled for control, then continued— "never again would I let a woman get that close to me."

He paused, and she hardly dared breathe.

"But it's been hard, Jen, because I'm still young . . . and lonely. It's been very hard."

Inadvertently, her lesser self got in another lick: "The beautiful black-haired girl who works for you?"

He almost hit a tree, but when he turned toward her, his face had relaxed just a little: "How did you know?"

"I have eyes. Any woman could have told you."

There was a long silence as he searched for the right words. Finally, as if he'd given up finding any better ones, the refrain again: "It's been hard." But he did not tell her that it was the Spanish beauty's lack of tenderness, her repulsing of the little crying boy, that had turned the tide of his life.

Neither did he tell her about the effect *she* had made on him that same day: a Raphael Madonna, tenderly holding a child.

After a time, he continued. "You see, Jen, I could not take such rejection twice in one lifetime. I'm afraid it would . . . uh . . . destroy me!" He paused again. "Marriage for me is for life—even if our society seems to disagree with me." Here, his words seemed sadly bitter to the wondering woman at his side. "And marriage without

God to cement it is dead-end! I don't see how any marriage can last a lifetime without a Higher Power to anchor in. All around me, I see marriage after marriage, live-in relationships galore, collapse, so few making it through. I have been afraid. I'm not ashamed to admit it, Jen: I've been terribly afraid to even consider marriage again!"

She remained silent. Numb.

"As for children and what divorce or separation does to them . . . there are simply no words in the dictionary terrible enough to fully describe what it does to them, to their feelings of self-worth. I see it every day. And I don't yet know what to do, what to say, to their anguish—anguish so intense it's long since wrung out all the tears they can cry."

And she, remembering those lonely, deep-scarred, wounded ones in her classes, could only nod her head.

"And then *you* came," he added, groping for the right words. "You scared me."

He caught her whispered, "Scared?"

"Yes. . . . Scared. For you were, well, what I never had, yet had always wanted. In a way, too good to be true. Jen, I never expected to find such a woman as you. So, when you told me last Thanksgiving that I . . . that I made you happy, like an absolute fool, I panicked! I had blocked such a future out of the realm of the possible for so many years that when it came, I just . . . just didn't know how—"

Suddenly, he slowed and turned down a familiar road, now a fairyland in snow. Her heart began to thud so loudly she felt certain he must overhear it. Then he turned down a road she'd never noticed before and made a long wide turn. Suddenly, directly ahead, in a blaze of holiday lights, stood Pandora's Books. It was so beautiful that her lips formed an *O*, and her hands flew to her face. She didn't see his relieved smile.

Inside, festive music played in every room, only all the same track this time. Christmas decorations were everywhere, as were lights and trees of various sizes.

"I've always loved Christmas—kinda never grew up," he said simply.

Unconsciously, she groped for his hand.

He showed her each room, and her delighted response and the restored bells in her voice were all he could have hoped for. Finally they came back to the office area, and he stepped briefly behind the counter where he must have flicked a switch; for suddenly silence shattered the mood, and she was alone with him in the big building.

He walked back to her, and she raised her emerald eyes to his, seeking to find something that had not been there before. Suddenly she heard music again—froze for a moment—and whispered, "Étude in E."

"Yes."

"Why, Arthur? I don't understand what you're trying to — "

Softly placing his finger on her lips, he whispered, "Listen!"

She listened. And, as she knew it would—it always had—it melted her. And, as she knew she would—she always had—she cried.

Fire blazed through her tears, and she accused, "How could you! You *know* how that étude affects me. I saw you watching me that day."

Know? Yes, he knew. *She's right*. It's come. . . . It's all come down to this question, this moment, he thought. *I hurt her terribly by my inexcusable fear of commitment. . . . And now I must answer. But one thing is certain: this is no time for halfhearted measures. Words . . . words can be such inadequate things! How can I make her know?*

Gathering her in his arms, he answered softly, "I just *had* to, dear . . . dearest."

Her wounded pride struggled to assert itself. *How dare he assume I'd forgive him this easily for the hell he put me through—how* dare *he!*

In the end, her pride lost. Gentle, he remained, but as immovable as Gibraltar. The étude was on his side too—it was two against one. She felt her resistance ebbing. Then she made the mistake of trying to read the expression on his face—not easy, considering the dim light in the room. But what she saw there closed forever all avenues of escape. It was love. Love undiluted, unqualified, undistilled, unreserved, undivided—he had cleared the deck of his heart of everything else but *her*.

Her struggles ceased, and all the lights of the world came on in her eyes as her arms stole up and closed behind his neck. Then it was, as the shackles of fear and regret fell clanging to the floor, that he started to tell her in mere words how much he loved her, but she, cutting his words off with her lips, showed him a better way. A far better way.

✳   ✳   ✳

Some time later, Arthur sensed a familiar presence at his ankles. Looking down, but not releasing Jennifer from the prison of his arms by so much as one link, he smiled and said, "Sorry, Pandora, you jealous ol' thing. From now on, you're just gonna have to *share!*"

✳   ✳   ✳

HOW THIS SEVENTH STORY CAME TO BE

It was the last week of January of 1997, and I stared out the windows of our Gray House high in the Colorado Rockies. Only four months before, we had taken the greatest leap of faith in our lifetimes: taken early retirement from our full-time jobs and moved from our beloved home on Maryland's Severn River to the top of Conifer Mountain, Colorado (with an average yearly snowfall of over sixteen feet), there to begin a full-time ministry of stories. I had reached the point where I had to make such a decision: either scale back on the story collections or move out of teaching (was close to cracking because of trying to do both).

The view from our deck was soul-filling that January morning. To the south, about fifty miles, was the Rampart Range; directly east were the skyscrapers of Denver; and eighty miles north were the snow-white peaks of Rocky Mountain National Park and Indian Peaks. After thirty-four years in the classroom (mostly college), here I was. Memories of the ten years in the Chesapeake Bay and Annapolis area flooded in on me, a world as lovely as that outside our windows. Pandora, our Himalayan cat, suddenly leaped onto my lap, seeking a head-scratching.

I thought back to when Pandora was a kitten and was a perpetual motion machine; when she'd leap onto my lap-board and try to bat my pen away, when she snagged everything that was snaggable in our house. I remembered how, as she got older, she still resented my writing and would plop herself down in the middle of the paper I was writing on and dare me to continue. I remembered how every night, within sixty seconds of our getting into bed, we'd wait for that soft four-point landing, the purr, the butting our heads for her scratching, and then the flop-down against us to sleep with us the rest of the night. I remembered how when we'd come back from a long trip, she'd not let us out of her sight for days on end, and would forget we were back and cry in the middle of the night. I remembered that as she got older, she'd sleep or loaf for twenty-three hours, fifty-nine minutes, and forty seconds of each day, and would race at Indy speed for twenty seconds up and down our two-level house.

As Pandora began to purr, I leaned back and asked God to give me the seventh Christmas story. Because I have always loved books (case in point, we had just moved over 100,000 books to Colorado), because I have always loved used book stores, because my thoughts were on the shimmering Chesapeake, because I was suffering classroom withdrawals (I missed my students!), and because Pandora helped to make our house a home, I took the plot the Lord gave me and . . . for the next few weeks, was—in my mind, at least—back on the Chesapeake.

In looking back, I'm convinced that I had been preparing to write this story all my life. Each of the thousands of used book stores I've known (many that I've loved) represent the gestation period. Part of the mix is the Haunted Bookstore in Annapolis, where Mike, the big tabby cat, undisputedly ruled its premises. Occasionally, he could even be found basking in the sun streaming into the front display window. Sadly, Mike and that wonderful bookstore no longer grace Maryland's capital city, owing to the escalating rent. And there is some of Christopher Morley's unforgettable book, The Haunted Bookshop, stirred in, as well. Actually, the story represents a synthesis of my own dream bookstore, had I the money and the time to make it happen.

"Étude in E" is considered by many to be the most beautiful étude ever composed. Chopin dedicated it to his dear friend, Franz Liszt, and it remained Chopin's personal favorite of all his études. Norman Luboff recorded it in perhaps as romantic a record as has ever been made, in his Reverie *album.*

Through Jennifer, I was able to vicariously return to the classroom I so missed. Ah the deeply wounded Jennifer and Arthur—each of us knows them personally, for they represent a far too large part of our love-'em-and-never-count-the-cost society. Many of them are, in fact, so seared by the act of desertion that they wall themselves off from the society of their peers, unwilling to risk loving again for fear of another rejection.

And Pandora. Oh how I hate to write these lines! After thirteen and a half years, just a couple of months ago, Pandora's body shut down on her. She couldn't eat, drink, or walk—she could only cry. Connie held her long that last morning, and then I took her to the vet, who left me alone with my faithful companion for around five minutes. I scratched her chin one last time and told her I loved her. Then the vet came back in, injected her with that ultimate sleep. Pandora's head became heavier and heavier on my hand, and it was over. I went outside and wept. So much a part of our lives was she that we have not yet been able to replace her. But, as long as this story lives, Pandora will live too.

❖   ❖   ❖

The story was first printed in 1997 in Review and Herald Publishing Association's trade paper Christmas in My Heart 6; *it was later included in the Focus on the Family/Tyndale House* Great Stories Remembered III *in 2000. My original story was much longer than this, with Arthur's having fled to New England after his wife had left him, seeking answers as he walked its beaches and hiked its mountains. But my three free-lance editors persuaded me to save that part of the story for another time—place it in escrow, so to speak. These three editor/writer friends—Sheree Parris Nudd of Gaithersburg, Maryland; Linda Steinke of Warburg, Alberta; and Corrie Whitney of Crescent City, California—became, with this particular story, the replacement for the students who earlier on hammered my stories into their final shape. Each of them has brought unique insights to the table, and catches things the others do not.*

In the rather short time it has been out, it has already become one of our most beloved stories.

His Last
CHRISTMAS

He was just an old man, an old man waiting to die. What possible difference could he make in the short time he had left? Furthermore, how in the world could he add anything to Christmas?

❖   ❖   ❖

"Who is he?"

"He? . . . Oh, you're new here, aren't you? He's been here for a month or so now. One of the good ones . . . *never* complains—makes up for those who do their best to make our lives a living hell."

"But who *is* he—doesn't he come with a name attached?"

Janet laughs, "Of course he does. Sorry. He's Mr. Abbey."

"Mister?"

"Oh, I know it is a bit unusual, calling him 'Mister' when we refer to most everyone else by first name, but, I can't really explain. In time, as you take care of him, talk with him, watch him, you'll know why we call him 'Mister.'"

"Now you really have me curious. . . . Is he kind of, you know, old-school formal?"

"Well, yes and no."

"Y-e-s?"

"Let's see, how can I put it? . . . I don't really know myself why it's so, because we have lots of other old men here, and we call 'em all by first name, old school or not. So it's not just his age—it's something more."

"Must be quite a bit more."

"Yes, you could say that. . . . I remember the morning he was admitted. He was wheeled in, and I helped to lift him onto the bed. He is very thin and doesn't weigh much; has almost no power left with which to move himself—oh, it's sad! . . . Yet he's not weak inside. Inside, he's probably the strongest person of us all."

"Now you *have* got me intrigued!"

"Is this a good time to talk?"

"Yes, I don't clock in until the afternoon shift. Take as much time as you can spare."

Janet leans back in her chair, a far-away look in her eyes. "Let's see, where was I—oh, that first morning! . . . No way I can ever forget it. He didn't say much—he doesn't say much. But his *eyes*—his eyes followed me as I moved around the bed and elsewhere in his room. His eyes were friendly—and there was just a smidgeon of a twinkle in them—but they also revealed a reserve I'm not used to in our patients here. They seemed to be weighing me, trying to size me up! That shocked me, because . . ."

" . . . most of the others think only of themselves and their problems?"

"You got it! And many of them are darn angry about being here, about being dropped off here by their families, about being defenseless—totally at our mercy—about knowing deep down that things will never get any better for them—*that they will die here.*"

There is a long pause, while Janet struggles to regain her equilibrium. "Yes, that's the worst of it. It's a lot like a dialysis wing I worked in a few years ago at Community General: we knew, and they knew, and they knew we knew, that things were unlikely to get better—not for long, that is. Almost all of them we'd see die. It broke my heart, so many of them were so young! I finally—finally had to leave. For some dumb reason, I thought it would be different here."

"Well, isn't it?"

"Yes, it is different, but not much. In dialysis, the body is shutting down on them. Occasionally, we'd see a miracle—a new drug, a new procedure, a new diet, healing from within by a higher power than medicine . . ."

"You believe in God?"

"Yes, I do—no small thanks to Mr. Abbey . . . but that's another story. In dialysis, miracles sometimes happen, and I guess all of us, deep down, hoped a miracle would occur with each of those patients we came to love the most. But, it's worse here; with age, there can be no miracle short of the Second Coming. Once the body begins to dismantle its white blood cell armies, once the inner organs begin to wear out, once the strength begins to ebb away—it's only a matter of time."

"You make it sound depressing. . . . I'm—I'm beginning to wonder if I should have come here."

"Oh no! Guess I haven't done a very good job of explaining myself. There *is* a difference here—or, rather I should say, there *can* be a difference. There can be a beauty, strange as it may seem, in one's last moments when one's inner spirit really shows through."

"I think you've lost me."

"All right, see if this helps. Several weeks ago, Charlie, a bone-cancer case, was screaming night and day. You literally could not get away from his voice. He was in pain, great pain (every breath hurt), and he made sure every one of his breaths hurt us too—*all* of us! Charlie was angry at life, angry at us, and angry at God. And none of this anger did he keep inside of him—that was not his nature. He was terribly self-centered. His room was next door to 202, Mr. Abbey's room."

"Oh, the poor man!"

"I haven't told you the half of it! Two doors down the hall on the other side of Mr. Abbey was another screamer—a woman. She wasn't dying, but oh how she wished she would! A fouler-mouthed patient we've never had here. Hour after hour she would rant and rave, screaming, raging, laughing maniacally—and every other word was a four-letter one."

"And in the middle of this was your Mr. Abbey. How did he take it?"

"Let me tell you. One night I subbed for a friend and took her graveyard shift. Normally, midnight to 8:00 A.M. is the quietest of the three shifts, but not *that* night. Both of those patients were virtually out of control. In the midst of it, my nerves on edge and wondering if I could possibly stand one more day of it, I walked in to Mr. Abbey's room to check on him and turn him (he doesn't have enough strength left to even turn over)."

"Oh, how sad!"

"Sad, indeed! Well, he was wide awake—how could he *not* be? Nobody slept that night. I walked to the head of his bed and he smiled. I was about to ask him how in the world he could endure it—then, I looked into his eyes, and they were filled with concern *for me!*

"No!"

"Yes, it staggered me. In his quiet and kind voice, he said, 'My heart goes out to you, and all the others you work with. You're probably wondering, *Is it worth it?—Could any amount of money possibly compensate for this?*'

"Well, I smiled a rather sickly smile and said (I had to speak rather loud in order to be heard), 'To tell the truth, Mr. Abbey, the thought *had* crossed my mind.'

"There was a long pause, as we both listened to that discordant duet. Then he said, 'I feel sorry for them both.'

"Disbelievingly, I sputtered out, 'for *them?*'

"'Yes,' he answered quietly, 'them. Mr. Zingfeldt has no faith in God to help carry him through. He can't possibly, . . . judging by what he says . . .'

"'*Screams*, you mean!' I retorted.

"He smiled. 'Yes, *screams* is correct . . . and the other—Mrs. Wilson, is it not?'

"'Yes.'

"'Mrs. Wilson must not believe in God either—or she would not continually take His name in vain.' A look of pain came over his face: 'That is what hurts me deep down inside: every curse against the God I love and serve, hurts. More than hurts. Not because I can't handle it, but because she is in such need of the Lord, of a friend. Were I able to move, I'd try to talk with her, offer to be that friend. Same with Mr. Zingfeldt . . .' Then his kind, loving eyes softened, and he said, 'But *you* could be that friend.'

"Almost horrified, I spat out, '*Me?* You've got to be kidding! I'm not even sure I still believe in God. And this nightmare we're both forced to endure isn't helping any, that's for sure.'

"There was a long silence, then he said, 'Miss Andrews, would you care to tell me more? This isn't—' and here his eyes twinkled impishly—'a very busy time for me. . . . I have time to listen if you'd care to tell me about it.'

"Well, I can't really explain it, but knowing Mr. Abbey had been a minister, I figured, *What the heck? This night is such a hell, maybe he can make some sense of it—perhaps even to my life itself.* So, there by his bedside I told him the story of my life—it has not been a happy one. Several times I broke down and wept. Tears trickled down his face too. My handkerchief did double duty that night. Mr. Abbey was not at all judgmental about the mess I'd made of my life; he just looked at me with his kind and loving eyes.

"It took a long time to tell—and why I'm telling *you* all this, I don't really know; but somehow I feel I can trust you with it."

"Without question. I *promise*. . . . So, what happened next? Do you mind telling me the rest of the story?"

"Not at all, might as well finish what I've begun. I spoke to him on and off throughout that awful, yet strangely wonderful, night. Each time I'd complete the rest of my rounds, I'd return and we'd talk some more. If ever a person walked side by side with his Lord, surely Mr. Abbey does. Before daylight ended that sleepless night, he brought me back to God—gave me a hope, a reason for living. . . . I've started going back to church."

"And, I'm . . . I'm a bit curious—did you become that friend?"

"Now you put *me* on the spot! Well, yes, I felt I could do no other. I *tried*."

"And failed?"

"Perhaps—yet perhaps not. Mr. Zingfeldt was Jewish and felt that if God would let one-third of his race be snuffed out during Hitler's holocaust, then either that God was not the God the Jewish people have worshiped for thousands of years, or worse yet, perhaps that perceived God didn't even exist. Believe me, our dialogue got beyond my depth often, and I'd have to get back to Mr. Abbey to seek counsel. It was a strange triad. Then, Mr. Zingfeldt entered into his final agony; we gave him powerful drugs because of the excruciating pain, his skin turned blackish, and, about a week ago, he died."

"Do you feel you got through?"

"I don't really know for sure. I like to think so. Don't have much to go on, though, for he was so drugged during those last days he lost all sense of reality. But, I was with him at the end. Just before he breathed his last rasping, gasping breath, awareness came back into his eyes, and he tried to say something—I never knew what. I reached for his hand, and I felt an answering squeeze (it must have taken his last tiny reserves of strength). He tried to smile . . . , and then he was gone."

"And . . . and the woman?"

"Mrs. Wilson? I had less success with her. She'd just scream at me, curse me—she seemed demon-possessed. Just last Thursday, we had her transferred. It was either her or us. So, guess I failed with her."

"Perhaps. Only time will tell."

❀   ❀   ❀

"Hi there, Janet. It's beginning to look like Christmas."

"It *does*, doesn't it! I was head of the decorating committee this year. First time for me; before, I never felt like it, not knowing for sure if I even believed in Christmas—or Christ. But now I feel differently. I'm filled with so much joy, I can hardly contain it."

"I can tell by your laugh. Every time I hear you, my day seems brighter—your laugh is so infectious."

Janet laughs, "You're kind; others describe it in less flattering terms. . . . But the place does look festive at that."

"And the Christmas carols—is that your idea too?"

"Yes, it seemed like the proverbial horse and carriage—didn't seem right to have one without the other. Oh, by the way, have you been down to Mr. Abbey's room lately?"

"You mean, have I seen the decorated wall everyone's been talking about? . . . Yes!"

"That's it! Isn't it something? I understand some of the family put it up. Wasn't easy, as they had to wear masks. So sad about Mr. Abbey's staph infection! He has more company than anyone else in the whole place, and it has made it so much harder for them to talk with him and tell him how much his life has meant to them. . . ."

"That's hard—'*has* meant.' It won't be long now, will it?"

"No, sorry to say."

"By the way, Janet, you haven't asked, but I felt that if Mr. Abbey could turn *your* life around, well . . . , maybe, just maybe, he might be able to salvage *mine*. I didn't see how anyone could possibly mess up more than I have: three divorces and two live-ins."

"*Did* he? . . . Not that I really need to ask. I can tell it by your face."

"You noticed?"

"Couldn't help it."

"Well, yes. Only I was a harder nut to crack than you; it took weeks before Mr. Abbey brought me . . . he brought me . . . to, to, uh . . ."

Janet reached for her hand. No words were necessary.

After a long pause, Janet changed the subject. "Back to that wall! As you know, the family posted on it most of the jobs and roles Mr. Abbey has had during his long life. I was so intrigued that I memorized them. Let's see if I can still remember all of them: salesman, tailor, lumberjack, farmer, teacher, minister, counselor, missionary, administrator (did you know he's even been a college president?), band director (evidently he is an accomplished musician himself, both as a vocalist and with various musical instruments), choir leader, painter, devoted husband and father—oh, the list could go on and on! *Everybody* has been down there to look at it!"

"Kinda sad, isn't it, Janet? Now that we know about his long and successful life, we respect him for it. But, don't you suppose that *every* patient in this place, if we only knew it, comes to us with a similar story? Oh, perhaps not as grand as Mr. Abbey's, but some might come close. In fact, I sometimes wonder . . ."

"Wonder what?"

"Oh, uh, well, I sometimes note how we treat most of our patients. We treat *children* nicer and with more respect than we do them! And I wonder whether or not we would act differently around them if we knew their life stories . . . the way we know Mr. Abbey's."

"Hmm. You may have a point there. . . . I'd never thought of it that way. To so many of us, they are not really people at all, but jobs, paychecks, rather unlovely (and often smelly) specimens of not-long-for-this-earth humanity. What a difference it would make if we went to the trouble to really *know* them!"

✣　✣　✣

"Happy New Year, Susan!"

"Happy New Year to you, Janet."

"Sad, huh?"

"You mean, about Mr. Abbey, of course—*Very!*"

"Did—did you get in to see him before Christmas?"

"Of course, but it wasn't easy, with so many others wanting to do the same thing."

"True indeed. I wasn't surprised by the many visitors who came — but I *was* surprised by how many of our coworkers found it necessary to visit that room, surgical mask or not!"

"And did you — did you hear him — uh . . ."

". . . hear him play his harmonica — for the last time? No, but I had heard him play before. But I heard it was *so sad* — everyone knew it was the last time. Stephanie told me Bob had to help hold up his harmonica. I'll — I'll never hear a harmonica again — without thinking of him."

"Did you look at him?"

"Did I *what?*"

"Did you ever *really* look at him?"

"Oh! I think I know what you're driving it. You mean, his face."

"Yes."

"I did indeed. It was . . . uh, in a way, beautiful. A rather strange word to use, isn't it, in connection with a man's — especially an *old man's* — face. But it's true, nevertheless. Strangely enough, several weeks ago the realization hit me that we aren't responsible for our faces when we're young, but we *are* when we get old! Look at — intently study — any given face in this entire complex, and you'll see truth, reality. . . . Whatever is inside has now seeped through into the face. It can't be hidden, not even by plastic surgery, for no plastic surgeon yet has been able to keep inner ugliness or evil from being reflected through one's eyes."

"I hadn't thought of it, but you're right."

"Yes, no matter how handsome or beautiful you were when young, you will be ugly — even repulsive — when old, *unless* you've been beautiful inside."

"True enough! And, on the other hand, even the plainest while young can be beautiful when old."

"Like Mr. Abbey."

"Like Mr. Abbey — not that he was necessarily plain when young."

"When did you see him for the last time?"

"Well, not at the very last, for his family was there until the very end. His wife was there a lot — she came to see him as regular as clockwork."

"An old-fashioned romance, they say—been married over *sixty years!*"

"Yeah, they don't make them to last like that anymore."

"More's the pity."

"No one knew when he would go; we only knew it would be soon. That last night, his daughter, responding to a sixth sense that told her time was running out, made a flying trip to see her father. She took one look at him and knew that this was it."

"We *all* knew. No matter which hall you were in, it was all the same; we didn't speak with mere words—it hurt too much—but if ever eyes mourned the truth, they did that last night."

"I had found an excuse to get down to his room Christmas Eve. The room was full of Christmas cards. The flowers people sent were shared up and down the hall, making it the most festive wing in the place! Several church groups came through the building, singing Christmas carols—I heard later that each one lingered longest just outside his door. During one of these, I happened to be in his room when he first heard their voices. How his eyes brightened—in fact, the most apt word I can use to describe it is 'radiance.' On his face was a look of radiance not of this earth. He turned to me, and said simply, 'I've always loved Christmas.'

"Curious, I asked, 'Why?' He didn't hesitate an instant—he *knew*. 'Because it celebrates the birth of my Jesus on this troubled earth.' It was indeed *his* Jesus; none of us could possibly doubt that Christ was his all in all. . . . But, how about *you*—when did you last see him?"

"Oh, it was about the ninteenth or twentieth, if I remember right. Anyway, as usual, I had to come back several times before I caught him alone. It's amazing how many of us sensed he was leaving and wanted a part of him while we still had him."

"Truer words were never spoken!"

"Well, when I came back in for the fourth time, there was in his eyes that look of loving, tender concern for me which always greeted me, only this time it was more intense than ever before, as if he sensed it was our last time together. He smiled and said, 'This . . . uh . . . is my last . . . Christmas.' His speech was very slow that night, as he had almost no physical reserves left. I won't replicate it, for it hurts too much.

"Well, I didn't know what to say, for I knew full well he knew that we knew it was indeed his last. He took me off the hook:

"'I have no regrets, Janet' (at my specific request, he'd finally graduated from 'Ms.' to my first name). 'The Lord has given me a full life, and I am ready to go. And He has given me such a warm and loving family—actually two of them: my biological children . . . and my children of the spirit, such as you. You are what I find hardest to leave. But it is time. My body'—and here he looked down ruefully to his strengthless arms—'is closing shop on me. Not too long from now, my faithful generator will flicker for the last time, and then go out.'

"I could not trust myself to speak.

"'And the next face I see will be that of Jesus!' What joy was in his face and voice! 'And,' he continued, 'in that world without pain, aging, and death, I want to see all my loved ones again. Will you promise to meet me there?'

"Too overcome to even speak, I could only nod mutely. Then George came in—and our last shared moment was over."

Breaking the long silence that followed, Susan said, with trembling lips, "The night he—he—he—left us, I was on duty. We all knew it was coming, coworkers and patients alike. There was an incredible hush. I don't remember a sound, except soft footsteps down the hall. I could almost hear the feathered sibilance of angels' wings.

"Then . . . Maria—remember how crusty and sarcastic she used to be?—well, Maria came around the corner, and one look at her face told me everything—he had gone.

"I took one look at her tear-stained cheeks, and took her into my arms, and I wept. We *all* wept."

❊   ❊   ❊

Today life goes on in those halls, but not life ever again as it had been before he came. He came with but one stub of a flickering candle—and left a glow warm enough to light the world.

❊   ❊   ❊

HOW THIS EIGHTH STORY CAME TO BE

Of all the stories I have ever written, this was the most painful to write. They say that one of the most wrenching experiences of our lives is when we reverse roles with our parents—when, due to the battering of the years, our parents lose their self-sufficiency and we children are forced to step in and become surrogate parents; when we are forced to make our parents' key decisions for them. That role reversal had already come to me.

Two strokes had laid my father low; now he was in a Roseburg, Oregon medical facility, having caught a terrible staph infection in an earlier hospitalization. Our entire family was there that Thanksgiving of 1996, each of us having to put on a mask before entering his room. Dad was now too weak to be able to turn himself in bed, too weak to even raise his hand without help. Yet his inner strength remained. We all knew he was dying, and so did he. We all knew that this would most likely be the last time we'd see him alive this side of the Kingdom. Each of us went in alone for our patriarchal blessing. We'd retain our composure until we left the room—then we'd run outside and weep. I told our family that, worst of all, as I looked at Dad's face on the pillow, there'd be a blur, and instead of his face I saw my own there—for after Dad died, I'd be the oldest male in the family. Our unmarried son retorted, "Dad, it was worse with me—I saw my face on the pillow, but there was no family to care!"

I realized then that Dad had been the rock I had built my life upon; his great love for my mother the impregnable bastion of my childhood and youth. Because that home was secure, he had freed me to become, to believe in myself. Now that rock was crumbling, cracking.

On April 9 of 1997 we received that dreaded call. Dad's spirit had returned to his Maker. Again the family returned to Oregon, only this time for—not a funeral, but a celebration of his life. It was there that the story of Dad's impact on those around him during those last days, weeks, and months began to be told. Dad preached thousands of sermons in his life, but perhaps his greatest one was told by the life he continued to live as his vitality drained out of his body.

So there I sat, eight months later, wondering how I could tell that story. For months the story had evaded me. Every time I tried to tackle it, a door would be slammed in my face. Perhaps it was because my father's passing was too real to me, and too close—I just could not gain perspective. The book deadline came and passed, and still I had no story. Finally, almost in despair, I turned the story over to the good Lord. I took the events, inspired as they were by my father's last few months (even the life story on the wall), and asked Him, if it be His will, to take over my pen. Incredibly, at that very moment of surrender, God loosened the logjam in my brain. What you have just read, I wrote nonstop in four hours—without so much as one pause. I could only say, "Thank You, Lord!"

❖   ❖   ❖

The story was co-published by Review and Herald Publishing Association and Tyndale House in 1998. It has served, already, as a great source of encouragement to older men and women who learned in those pages that each of us can make a real difference in the lives of others . . . up until our very last breath.

LEGACY

Just what is a legacy? Is it a masterpiece created by a great painter or sculptor? Is it a villa by the sea? Is it stocks and bonds worth millions?

Or might it be something entirely different?

❖   ❖   ❖

It was cold and foggy that bleak December day on the Oregon coast. But inside my aunt's farmhouse living room it was cheery, and a hot fire crackled in the big black iron stove. On the mantel was a stack of Christmas cards and letters and, in a corner, a small Christmas tree.

Suddenly, around the corner stalked Mr. Tiggelen, a proud old tomcat of venerable years and uncertain ancestry. But, lack of pedigree had never bothered Mr. Tiggelen; in fact, he reveled in his mongrel polyglot Americanism. *He* would establish the dynasty.

Called upon by my aunt to perform for me, Mr. Tiggelen leisurely responded in his own good time, letting me know he condescended to do so, not because I was in any respect worthy of it, but because he owed my aunt one of his royal favors. Old as he was, he hesitated before wheezing his way to the stool-top, licked his chops at the cheese my aunt held high above him, then stood up tall on his back legs to claim the prize, yet never for a moment losing his dignity.

After Mr. Tiggelen had paid his dues, he descended from the stool and swaggered out.

In the quiet moments that followed, I wondered: *Do I dare bring it up . . . again? Surely, if she had been receptive to my plea, she would have responded long ere this. And, for good measure, my uncle hadn't responded either—and now he lies in his grave up on that misty green hill overlooking the valley. Perhaps . . . I'd just better forget it for now.* So I said nothing and only leaned back into the softness of the couch, dozy because of the alder wood fire.

❖   ❖   ❖

I was a boy again . . . and my heart was leaping within me because I knew we were nearing the ranch. The first gate loomed ahead, and Dad's Ford slowed and stopped so I could get out. This had always been *my* job! The long wooden bar slid back, and the heavy gate lifted and opened at last; then I stood there holding it while the Ford chugged past me and stopped.

Ever so slowly, for I was ever so small, I struggled across the road, that balky gate fighting me all the way. After reinserting the bar, I ran up to the car for the best part of all: riding on the running board to the other side of Frazzi's vineyard. Some days we'd drive up to the Frazzi house and Mrs. Frazzi, large of girth, dark of complexion, poor with her English, and robust with her belly-laugh, would throw her plump arms around me, brag about how I had grown, and tow me over to the always overflowing cookie jar.

But not today. Down I leaped for the second gate, also of heavy wood. It, too, was a struggle, and resisted every inch, squawking all the way. Once again the Ford rolled past and stopped. Once again I got on the running board.

The next gate, of metal pipe and wire mesh, was easier. Overhead, I could hear the wind in the pines; occasionally, we'd see a deer bounding through the manzanita, madrone, and buckbrush bushes. Today the road was dusty; sometimes there would be snow on it instead.

On the running board again, and jolting our way ever higher up the mountain, my heart was beating so turbulently it threatened to leap out of me. At last, the big maple tree and the clearing. Thousands of apple trees to our left, and just ahead, at the top of the hill, was the walled home of the self-anointed "Old Man of the Mountain," Grandpa Rollo, and his jolly wife, Grandma Ruby, who was deaf.

All the way up that last hill, Dad laid on the horn; as he swerved around to the house, there they were waving, Grandma saying over and over to Grandpa, "Wh-y-y-y, Papa!" and to each of us in turn, "You d-e-e-a-a-r soul!" Background sound was provided by barking dogs.

Up there on top of the mountain, the seven hundred-acre ranch stretched away, to my childish eyes, to forever. I would explore it later. First of all, though, we'd go through the gate, through the evergreen tree windbreak behind the rock wall, to the little rock house in the middle. The door *always* squeaked. Inside, it was rather dark, but there on the lip of the rock fireplace were the purring cats. As often as not, one of them would be leaning against the great wicker basket of blocks.

The wind might howl and the rain would pelt, but inside that snug little cabin of a house—with so much love and laughter; with the fire in the fireplace; with the kerosene lamp's soft glow; with the fragrance of homemade bread, fresh applesauce, and cold milk just feet away; with one of the cats or kittens purring on my lap and the blocks already stacked into dream buildings—well, it was home; it was Shangri-la.

Then, we'd hear other horns, other slammed car doors, each punctuated by "Why Papa's!" and "You dear souls!" Then, more laughter as uncles and aunts and cousins poured into the walled enclosure.

Swirling mists blotted out the little cabin and the side house where we children stayed when we got older, with its swinging, banging doors with semi-clear plastic instead of windows, and not far beyond, the outhouse with its abridged Sears catalogue and pesky wasps.

Years passed, and we flew in silver DC3's to places thousands of miles away—places where bougainvillea bloomed in patios, royal palms bowed in torrential storms, freshly cut stalks of bananas hung on back porches, and exhausting heat drained one's vitality.

But, every once in a blessed while, the silver birds would bring us back home, home to the three gates, the "Why Papa's!", the "You dear souls!", the cats on the hearth, and the blocks.

Once, a new word entered my childish vocabulary. My grandfather was hauled into court by a neighboring rancher over water rights. The opposing attorney, attempting to diminish the value of Grandpa's ranch, asked the loaded question, "How much is your ranch worth?"

Grandpa's attorney, never missing a beat, stepped in and shot a question back: "Do you mean the value if it came on the real estate market? Or do you mean its *esoteric* value?" "Esoteric" was a big word for me, but after I looked it up in the dictionary and had Mom explain it, I thoroughly understood. The esoteric value was the greatest view in all the Napa Valley region, the multi-hued sunsets, the fog banks rolling in from the Pacific, the snow flocking the evergreens and apple trees, the little walled house on the mountaintop, the thoughts, the dreams . . . oh how—how could one possibly put a value on all that? Ah yes, it was easy for me to now grasp the attorney's question, for children value esoterically to begin with.

❀   ❀   ❀

A door slammed, and I was jerked out of the past and slammed into the present. I heard voices: my aunt was needed down at the barn. . . . Then there was silence again, and once again I slipped backwards into time.

❀   ❀   ❀

A number of years had passed and Grandpa and Grandma were growing old. The winters at the top of the mountain were hard and cold. The apple business was exhausting. . . . Then came the news— the big ranch was sold, and they were moving down the mountain to a smaller (eighty-acre) place.

The next time we went to see them, we came to their one gate only a mile or so off the paved road. There was a larger compound now, surrounded by a long mesh fence to keep the deer out. Initially, there was only a tiny cabin there, but over time Grandpa built a big, beautiful brick home, a veritable palace compared to the older one! Out the broad picture windows, one could look out across the valley to a small lake. There were rocks and boulders everywhere, but Grandma Ruby determined (now that the children were grown and gone, now that the apple ranch had been sold) to transform her little piece of earth into a flowering paradise.

It would prove a never-ending task, and Grandma would have to wrestle like Jacob for every blossom, for every lacy fern, for every rosebud. Now, when we honked and drove in, scattering cats and kittens in our wake, chances are we'd have to get out of the car, search out the business end of the hose, and tap her on the shoulder before we'd hear "Why, you dear soul!"—and looking over our shoulders, "Why, Papa!"

Then we'd haul our suitcases into the big new house. Inside, it was spotlessly clean—it was kept that way. And it was easy to do so because, to Grandma and Grandpa, the new house was too grand to live in. They compromised by installing an iron stove in the garage and moving in there. The main house was reserved for the family: all nine surviving children and their throngs of grandchildren. Grandpa now did most of the cooking (the applesauce and nut bread) in the tiny cabin, for Grandma had traded cooking for flowers. The beautiful kitchen in the main house was generally used only when company came.

When we'd come into the big house, there in the large family room was the great fireplace, and there on the hearth would be the wicker basket of blocks. There were never any other toys—just the blocks. As a child, I never really examined them or wondered how old they were—I just played with them. When my other cousins wandered in, they'd plunk themselves down on the floor and play with me.

As we got older, however, the siren call of horseshoes drew us outside to where those authority figures, the men, were challenging each other, trying to beat Grandpa. To us, a rite of passage was reached when we were deemed old enough to play. Every Thanksgiving, as the clan gathered from far and near, the clang of horseshoes could be heard all day long—except for during dinner when we all gathered around the long, groaning trestle table in the big house. Around it we saw a side of our parents we never saw anywhere else, for here they were still considered children by Grandpa and Grandma.

And how Grandpa loved to tell stories: stories like the one where my cousin Billy sidled up to him in the orchard and drawled, "G-r-a-n-d-p-a . . . I t-h-i-n-k I s-e-e a-a-a s-n-a-k-e." And, as Grandpa would tell it, he'd always counter, "Now, Billy, don't tell lies! You *know* there's no snake around today."

There'd be silence for a while, until Billy forgot about the admonition, and sidled up to Grandpa saying: "G-r-a-n-d-p-a, I t-h-i-n-k I s-e-e a-a-a s-n-a-k-e," and again Grandpa would warn him not to tell lies, and again Billy would subside into silence.

Then, Grandpa would grin as for the third time he'd hear, "G-r-a-n-d-p-a, I t-h-i-n-k I—I SEE A SNAKE!" And, no matter how many times we'd heard the story, we'd jump a foot off our chairs when Grandpa'd galvanize into frightened little boy action.

And there were other stories, such as the one about a man who used to take a shortcut home, from time to time, through a graveyard. Well, one dark and moonless night, he took that shortcut, unaware that earlier that day a new grave had been dug for a funeral the following day. Well, here he came: *"pad, pad, pad,"* and suddenly, there was no path; and *"whumpf,"* he plunged into the open grave. After he got up and gathered his wits, he realized where he was and tried to climb out, but it was too deep. So he called out for help, loud and long, but no one could hear him. Finally, exhausted, he gave up and sat down to wait for morning.

By this time in the story, tingles would be going up our spines as we waited for the next line. "Suddenly, he heard someone else coming: *"pad, pad, pad,"* and *"whumpf,"* another man fell in!" Pausing to make sure he still had his audience, Grandpa would then proceed to tell us that the newcomer, as was true with the other man, paced around and around the grave, trying to find a way out, but couldn't. In the pitch dark, the pacing man hadn't seen the other man crouched in a corner. Finally, the first man got up and approached the newcomer from behind, tapping him on the shoulder, and saying in a sepulchral voice, "You can't make it, buddy." Then Grandpa's voice would leap into the long-awaited punch-line:

"BUT HE DID!"

And we'd roar—even us kids, by now playing over by the fireplace with the blocks. And stories and jokes would continue to be told—and we never tired of hearing them.

When there was a break in the action, Grandma would give us haircuts. In those early days, there was no motor attached to the clippers as is true today. Rather, each time Grandma squeezed the handles together, a sheaf of hair would fall to the floor. But, those of us who were down the line a bit had to endure the heat generated by the clippers that got hotter with each haircut. Even worse, Grandma would occasionally yank hair out by its roots—and we would howl or scream, to no avail, because Grandma could not hear our wails. Being deaf, she could only read lips.

After supper, everyone would gather round the piano and sing. Grandma would gravitate over to the piano, put her hand on the soundboard, and seraphically smile as she *felt* the music! Later yet, games would be brought out, and Grandpa would challenge all comers to caroms—and he'd whop most of his sons. If they didn't let us kids play games with them, we'd play with the blocks.

Eventually, to the sounds of slammed car doors, good-byes, shooing away of cats, crunching gravel, and tears, the clan would drive away, one car at a time.

And so it went, season after season. Each time we came, before I opened the gate, I'd turn and gaze longingly up the hill towards the lost Shangri-la beyond the three gates. In all the years that followed, I could only bear to return once, but it was not the same: a multi-millionaire from San Francisco lived there now and had built something at the top of the hill I cried to see.

❊ ❊ ❊

Awareness came back to me gradually. The house was still silent, so my conscious mind picked up where it would rather not have. I remembered when it seemed—because of the battering of the years—best that Grandpa and Grandma should leave their Napa Valley garden spot and move north to Oregon so my only double relatives (my father's youngest brother, Warren, had married my mother's youngest sister, Jeannie) could be near enough to take care of them.

But now the rest of the family no longer came on holidays, and the Oregon coastal mist and rain kept Grandma inside a lot. I came to that house only twice, and each time I did so, it was not the same—not at all the same! They seemed a hundred years older than they had before. I did not see the blocks—I was too old to want to play with them anyhow. Gone was the vitality, the, what the Spanish call "chíspa," that made being with them such an adventure. Finally Grandpa just let go. And not too long afterward, Grandma, bereft of her lifeline into the speaking world, followed him.

By now, I had a wife and children of my own and was far too busy to dwell much in the past. But there came a time, some years later, when I began to remember. When I belatedly realized that, of all the things our family had ever possessed, I longed for only one thing: *those blocks!* I wondered if they had by now been thrown away. Who, after all, in this hectic life we live, would care much about an ancient basket of battered-looking blocks?

It took years, though—years of wondering about those blocks along the long corridors of the night—before I posed a question, in a letter, to my aunt and uncle, a question I wasn't sure I wanted to hear the answer to: "Those old blocks we used to play with—if they still exist, what do you say to giving a few to each grandchild who used to play with them?" The question was rhetorical: I didn't really expect an answer . . . and I didn't get one.

But in recent days, weeks, and months, I had found myself more and more often carried back to that time so many years before, to that time when those blocks were the most important thing in the world to me, the most prized, the most *loved*. Funny how it takes so many years in life before you realize value—if the house caught on fire, what you'd race for first.

I heard my aunt come in . . . and my heart began shuddering: *Did I really want to know?*

In the end, I knew that even if the blocks were gone forever, I just *had* to know!

So, struggling to keep my voice from shaking, I asked the fateful question: "Aunt Jeannie, do you remember . . . uh . . . uh . . . those . . . uh . . ."

"Ye—e—s," she answered.

"Well, uh . . . uh . . . it's about the . . . the . . . uh . . . *blocks* we used to play with, so many years ago. Uh . . . uh . . . I was just curious; . . . what ever happened to them?"

Matter-of-factly, my aunt ended the uncertainty of the years: "The old blocks? They're fine. They're here."

"They're *here*, in *this house?*" I sputtered inanely.

"Yes. They're here."

Pausing to regain my equilibrium, I finally managed to say, "Uh . . . do you mind if. . . . *Can I see them?*"

"Of course. Come with me."

In her bedroom, in the back of her closet, was a strangely familiar brown wicker basket filled with old blocks. She picked it up and took it into the living room, then handed it to me.

I was so stupefied I could not talk. Lord Carnarvon himself, on first stepping into King Tutankhamen's tomb in Egypt's Valley of the Kings, could not have been more overcome than I — I, who had long since given up the blocks as lost forever!

I just stared at them stupidly, unable to say anything that made sense. Finally, I sighed, "I'd almost kill for these."

My aunt smiled for the first time.

Time passed, and I continued to fondle them, unable to stop touching them. Finally, I asked her if she'd ever thought about my request years before. She said that she had, and that the answer was no. Then, seeing my woebegone face, a smile as big as Texas spread across her dear face: "But *you* can have them, if you wish."

"If I *wish?*" I gasped out.

"Yes, but there are conditions."

"What?" I demanded.

"That they always stay together, that they are never divided, that they remain in the family *always.* And that—" and here her smile grew even broader "—only when you find someone who loves them as much as you do . . . can you let them go."

❖   ❖   ❖

When I returned home with those precious blocks, I carried them with me into the passenger cabin, not daring to risk checking them on the plane.

A few days ago, for the first time in my life, I really analyzed the basket of blocks I had for so long taken for granted. The basket itself is most likely well over a century old. In it, there is an ivory-ish shoe horn, a very old darning sock egg, and an accumulation of seventy-three blocks, representing at least six generations: twenty-two uncolored alphabet blocks (one, perhaps the oldest, has burn holes in each of four sides, and dates back to the early 1800s); these are so old that the corners have been worn round by generations of children playing with them. One single "A" block, with color, dates to around the 1850s. Twelve multicolored picture blocks (forming a design on each side) dates back to the 1870s. Four very small blocks with raised figures date back to around 1890. Twenty-two alphabet blocks with raised colored lettering, date back to about 1910. And one modern nondescript colored block dates back to the 1940s — how it got into the box I haven't the slightest idea.

Apparently, each family for over a century added blocks to the basket. Undoubtedly, a number have been lost during the family's many peregrinations: from Massachusetts to New Hampshire to western New York to California (not long after the Civil War), then many moves crisscrossing California afterwards.

In the end, I concluded I was glad I didn't really know for sure how old they were. It was enough that my only surviving great aunt, memory razor-sharp in her mid-nineties, remembers playing with the blocks and thinking them "very old" even then. Are they perchance two hundred years old? I don't know. Were they played with by a distant cousin, Buffalo Bill Cody? I don't know. And the tree the oldest blocks came from? Was it standing during the Revolutionary War? Was it standing when the Pilgrims landed in 1620? I don't know . . . but it could have been.

In researching block history, I discovered that alphabet blocks date clear back to the 1600s, John Locke first advocating their use in his landmark educational book, *Some Thoughts Concerning Education*, 1693. Thereafter, alphabet blocks were known as "Locke's Blocks." They crossed the Atlantic and were played with by American children during Colonial times. By the mid-1800s thousands of middle- and upper-class American families owned such block sets as those earliest blocks in our family basket. Friedrich Froebel, one of the German founders of kindergarten education, urged the adoption of alphabet blocks in that curriculum, which really hit full stride in America late in the Nineteenth Century. (Andrew McClary's *Toys with Nine Lives: A Social History of American Toys*, North Haven, Connecticut: The Shoe String Press, 1997).

But, more to the point, why do these simple little blocks mean so much to people like me? Perhaps the best answer is found in Dan Foley's wondrous book, *Toys through the Ages* (Philadelphia: Chilton Brooks, 1962): "The magic land of childhood, which was filled with delight, vanished with the approach of adolescence, so, too, did the toys. Only a small fragment of the millions of toys made in times past, even during the last century, remain to bestir our nostalgia and to record the heritage of childhood." Foley then quotes Odell Shepard, who wrote in *The Joys of Forgetting* (Boston: Houghton Mifflin, 1929), "Our toys were almost idols. There was a glamour upon them which we do not find in the more splendid possessions of our late years, as though a special light fell on them through some window of our hearts that is now locked up forever. . . . We loved them with a devotion such as we shall never feel again for any of the things this various world contains, be they ever so splendid or costly."

❧   ❧   ❧

A few weeks ago, our Grey House high in the Colorado Rockies was about as Christmassy as a house can get: on a ledge was Dickens' Christmas Village; on the mantel, twelve stockings; in a far corner, a tall evergreen, ablaze with ornaments and lights. Outside on the deck, our multicolored lights could be seen from ten miles away. But, for me, there was something that meant more than all these things together:

Yes, there was Taylor, our first grandchild—only seven months old, but intent on toppling the tree so that he could suck on each branch. Short of that, if he'd had his way, the lower three feet of decorations would have been stripped bare. The only thing he showed comparable interest in were the blocks. He drooled on them, he sucked on them, and he took fiendish delight in swatting down the block towers we made for him. I can hear his joyful chortle yet! I would guess him to be one of the first children to have played with those blocks during the last third of a century (quite likely, our son Greg one of the last to have played with them during the late 1960s).

So it was that as I watched Taylor play, I felt a soothing sense of the continuity of life, of the past joining hands with the present, of a long procession of ancestors magically shedding their wrinkles and beards, gray hair and hoop skirts, and all plopping themselves down on the floor with the blocks, as children once again.

As for Taylor, I wondered if he'd love them as much as *I* did, as *they* did. Probably not, for our generation (even I was a Depression baby) had very few things to play with, compared to the king's ransom in toys we shower upon children today. Which makes me wonder: *Perhaps we were lucky, for we appreciated what little we had.*

So it is that never can I look at this basket of blocks without memories flooding in upon me: memories of Taylor, my son Greg, myself, my father, my grandfather, and a host of faded tintype photograph ancestors. Given that intergenerational bond, somehow it does not seem farfetched at all to me to imagine Grandma's greeting her homecoming family in the New Earth by saying, "You *dear* soul!" to each of us, then turning to Grandpa with "Why, Papa"—and Grandpa turning to me, and saying, "Joe . . . , did you, uh . . . uh . . . by any chance, bring the blocks?"

THE CASTLE-BUILDER

A gentle boy, with soft and silken locks,
A dreamy boy, with brown and tender eyes,
A castle-builder, with his wooden blocks,
And towers that touch imaginary skies.
A fearless rider on his father's knee,
An eager listener unto stories told
At the Round Table of the nursery,
Of heroes and adventures manifold.
There will be other towers for thee to build;
There will be other steeds for thee to ride;
There will be other legends, and all filled
With greater marvels and more glorified.
Build on, and make thy castles high and fair,
Rising and reaching upward to the skies;
Listen to voices in the upper air,
Nor lose thy simple faith in mysteries.

Henry Wadsworth Longfellow

❈　❈　❈

HOW THIS NINTH STORY
CAME TO BE

As I've gotten older, I've also become more retrospective. Undoubtedly the recent passing of my father and the earlier death of Connie's mother, have contributed to that mood. As we look at the accumulated clutter of the years and then imagine our children having to make sense out of it all, deciding which items to dispose of and which to keep, it is decidedly sobering. Since their homes are already overflowing with their own possessions, they'd have precious little room for much of ours.

Last summer's Hi Meadow Fire got to within three and a half miles of our house. When warned that we might have to evacuate, it really brought home to us the reality that, given fifteen minutes to pack, most of the things we own—or that own us—would have been left behind. In such situations, market value means little. We decided that such things as Connie's quilts, family photo albums, treasured letters, objects of sentimental value to us and our children—these we would have saved first. Even the treasure house of stories, illustrations, and books could not have been saved.

But we would have taken the basket of blocks.

So, as the time came to write my ninth story, and I asked God for a plot—I was impressed to write "Legacy." Perhaps the Lord felt the story would remind us that all too often we have misplaced priorities in life, that the things we give our very life-blood to gain we often, later on, ruefully discover weren't worth the price we paid for them.

All these thoughts came together in mid-January of 1999 as the story finally came together. But not just the story of these blocks of wood—but the story of my grandparents, their role in our lives, and the legacy these blocks represented to them.

❊   ❊   ❊

The story was first published by Review and Herald Publishing Association and by Tyndale House/Focus on the Family, in their respective Christmas in My Heart 8 *editions, in 1999. I read it to the staff of Focus on the Family at my annual Christmas reading there, but forgot to bring the basket of blocks with me. Two months ago, at my 2000 Christmas story reading, I placed the precious basket of blocks on the lip of the stage. Afterwards, one after another passed by, gazed intently at these artifacts from another time, and some even reverently touched them.*

And not until I find someone who loves them as much as I do—can I let them go.

City of
DREAMS

A train pulls out of Washington's Union Station. Among the hundreds of passengers were a man and a woman, but not together—not together in any way.

※　　※　　※

He was *not* in a good mood. For one thing, an accident on the Beltway backed traffic up for miles—he almost missed the train. For good measure, outside newly glorified and resurrected Union Station, the trees stood naked, shivering leafless in the biting December wind. The snow was grungy and mud-spattered; the sky was a stolid, unresponsive slate gray. And as if all that weren't enough, the acid icing on the cake was that terrible newspaper head-line screaming at him from the newsstands.

He dashed from the parking lot to the station, ran through the station, and at last reached the porter of the Chicago car just as he was preparing to board and close the door. He smoothed his dark, wind-tossed hair back into place and drew a hand across his rugged features, as if by so doing he could blot out the past few days. Oblivious to the glances that followed his tall, lean, and well-dressed figure, he strode down the aisle, looking for a seat. The train jolted into motion. With a sigh of relief he sank into a window seat, thankful he had no seat-mate.

Slowly at first, then with gradually increasing speed, the train *clackety-clacked* its way through back corridors of the nation's capital (unlovely too) as the December sun withdrew west of the Blue Ridge.

Night fell.

And the man at the window looked out at a vast sea of lights, but saw only a luminescent blur, heard nothing but the repetitive hum of steel wheels on steel rails and the mournful blasts of the air horn. When he'd collapsed into his seat shortly before, he'd been nothing more than a contorted bundle of shrieking nerves, so tightly wound that one little half-turn more would have shattered his mainspring. Never in his life had he been this close to that ultimate darkness. His heart pounded wildly, completely out of control.

Several hours passed before he came back to reality. The only image he could bring partly into focus in his foggy mind was that of the porter checking his ticket some time before, and even that was shrouded in mist. Suddenly he could hear people talking, could hear a boy and girl quarreling over a toy, could hear a baby cry. He was not alone after all.

Tension so filled him that he did not walk down to the dining car for something to eat. Instead he asked directions to the observation car. When he puffed to the top of the stairs, he felt as though he had dragged half of Washington behind him. Three seats from the front, he found an unclaimed window.

Of course it would have been quicker to fly, but he needed—desperately needed—time to think, to hide, before he faced those he knew again.

At long last, the accumulated tensions began to leave him, much like a slow leak in an automobile tire. Kaleidoscopic images and sounds came and went in seeming incoherence—low bridges and overpasses with their green, yellow, and red signals; Christmas lights in city streets; endless caravans of twin-eyed cars; trucks lit up like Coney Island; signals at crossings; sirens of ambulances and police cars; the now friendly *clackety-clack;* and the soothing echo of what reminded him of a foghorn. That horn-sound was the last sound he could remember as his body, battered almost beyond belief, shut down its engines and coasted through the night.

It was early morning before awareness slowly came back to him. Though the train had stopped a number of times during the night, he had been aware of none of them. Now, as the train gained speed on the westward slope of the Alleghenies, and dawn began to break through the mountain mists, he changed position, burrowed deeper into the warm Log Cabin quilt made for him by his mother seven Christmases ago, and went back to sleep.

An intercom call to breakfast woke him up at last. Brushing the cobwebs out of his eyes, he looked down at his wrist as his gold and platinum watch gradually came into focus. It was 8:47, and broad — almost glaringly bright — daylight. Suddenly, he was ravenously hungry.

After freshening up with a shave and a change of clothes, he stashed his belongings and found his way to the dining car. White tablecloths, gold-edged china, and iridescent goblets pleased his eyes. He was seated at a table with a retired couple from Edinburgh, Scotland, and a shoe salesman from Atlanta. Words were sparse because no one took the lead.

Halfway through his Spanish omelet, an attractive young woman in her early-to-mid-thirties followed a waiter to a table at the other end of the car. He caught only a glimpse of her face, but did take in the small feet, well-turned legs, and slim figure, inhaling the faintest of expensive French perfume, as she walked down the swaying aisle and was seated with her back to him.

Then it was back to the observation car. They had traded wooded west Pennsylvania for the snow-covered farmlands of Ohio. Here the snow, blinding white, made the world seem pristine, untouched by civilization's heavy hand. It was only now and here, as he and the small city of travelers floated ever westward, that he faced himself in the tribunal of his mind. Here on this train where no one knew him, he realized with a jolt just how small was his Inside-the-Beltway fame. The warm and loving family seated just behind him reminded him of how much he missed having children of his own; the ever-so-much-in-love couple three seats ahead brought home to him how unutterably lonely he was without a soul mate.

Inexorably, though he fought him every step of the way, the bailiff of his mind forced him back to those Washington headlines of yesterday — could it have been only yesterday? He had been his friend, the Senator had, as good a friend as he had known for a long time. No senator had been more revered than he — or more *loved*. Always the champion of the underdog, a rock of integrity in a sleazy age, he had become over the years almost a folk icon. Lately, there had been talk of his running for president; the nation seemingly yearned for another Lincoln.

And then came that snowy morning he wished with every fiber of his being that he could forget. When he got to the network building late that morning because of a massive backup on the Beltway, he found a note on his office chair from his chief; short and terrifying:

> *Charles,*
> *Come to my office just as soon as you get in.*
> *We need to talk.*
>
> J.R.

All the way down the hall, all the way up to the top floor, he wondered what it was that he had done wrong. Was he to get the axe Henry had last week? Completely out of the blue—just as was true of Susan two days before. The entire staff was near paranoid about the station's long slip in the ratings. Rumor had it that heads were going to roll, from top to bottom. Since the hostile takeover of the new owners, no one's job was safe; for there was no corporate memory at the top. And if he were next? *What would I do? I am over-extended on three credit cards; I shouldn't really have purchased that Lexus last July; nor should I have borrowed to take that last cruise. If I'm fired, where could I go? How could I face all those who tell me I'm next in line for the big time?*

He walked into the impressive reception area of the chief, which seemed expressly designed to awe subordinates into submission. He waited a long time—close to an hour. Meanwhile, he died inside. Finally he got the nod to enter. That walk to the other end of the room was one of the longest he could remember. The chief did not smile, but merely looked at him—silently—for what seemed forever with his cold, fishy eyes.

Then he told him—reminded him that the ratings were bad and getting worse, deep personnel cuts were imminent. Unless the rating decline was reversed, the station might not survive at all. What they needed was a miracle. Then he smiled for the first time, an *evil* smile. The miracle had been found: a story had surfaced— never mind from where—about a prominent senator, one of the uncrowned kings of the Hill. It had to do with something the Senator had done many years ago when he was young. Just between the two of them, the documentation was shaky, the source unreliable (had perjured himself more than once), but the bottom line was this: *We need the story. True or not!*

Yes, it concerned his friend the Senator, the one who had done him many good turns over the years, had been his mentor, in fact. Had welcomed him as a son into his family. And now here was his chief telling him that this was his one and only chance. If he refused to break the story under his own name and stand behind it, he could clean out his desk; a severance check would be mailed to him later. Given no time to deliberate and pressed for an immediate answer, he caved in.

Next day the story hit Washington and the nation like an 8.5 earthquake, and he was treated as a celebrity. The chief praised him and raised his salary $2,000 a month. Without bothering to ascertain whether or not the story was true, the harpies of the media went into a feeding frenzy, the speculation and innuendo going far beyond the original accusation. Declaring the Senator through was the nicest thing they said about him.

And yesterday morning the Senator had been felled by a massive stroke—instantly fatal.

❊   ❊   ❊

Now, the morning after, Charles stood face to face with his conscience. He was reminded of the Huey Long prototype in Robert Penn Warren's *All the King's Men,* who maintained that, if one only searched long enough and hard enough, sooner or later in the strata of the years, no matter how good the person, *something* could be found with which he could be destroyed. So it had come to pass, with this one not-so-small qualifier: Charles strongly doubted that the story was true.

Now burning thoughts rushed at him, searing his heart and soul with sizzling tears: *It is said that there is no such thing as a true friend in Rome on the Potomac; not one of those supposed friends wouldn't stab you in the back if the stakes were high enough. Same for the media. With five hundred cable channels needing to be fed, their collective maw is insatiable and not very picky about whether a story be true or not, so long as it is sensational and can help ratings. . . . And here I am, one of the worst! A Judas to my best friend in Washington!*

Is this the life I wish to live? A life devoid of friendship, kindness, respect, integrity, empathy—or even simple goodness? Is this what I want my life to represent when I am gone: that I never passed up an opportunity to tear down rather than build up?

❀ ❀ ❀

His self-recriminations skidded to a halt as the woman of the dining car walked past him to the front seat. As she turned to sit down, for the first time he had the opportunity to study her face. To begin with, it was not one a red-blooded male was likely to forget. Furthermore, it bore undeniable signs of trouble: her lovely brows were wrinkled with inner concerns, and her eyes met no one's. Like him, she was traveling in a self-contained world.

Beautiful women were nothing new to him. Through the years, a number of them had come into his life; and all of them had gone on. Some of them might have stayed had he but asked them to, but he hadn't, for he had long ago developed a horror of commitment. Like Oscar Wilde's Dorian Grey, he lived only for today—and for his ego. But now he felt his body clock ticking: this Christmas Eve he would be forty. FORTY. *FORTY!* Life was passing him by.

A white country church with its sky-seeking steeple outside his window reminded him of a subject he rarely thought much about anymore: God. When he spoke about spiritual things, invariably it was in jest, in ridicule. But that church reminded him of his childhood; to just such a church had his parents brought him every Sabbath. He had once believed; God had once been central in his life.

But all that was before . . . before. . . . Even after all the long years he could not face thinking about it without a catch in the throat, without tears. All that was before his father had left his mother, brother, and him, for another woman. From that day to this he had refused to set foot inside a church (other than for an occasional concert, or funeral). But now, with yesterday's headlines still torching within, he was no longer so sure about his way of life. In fact, he felt bankrupt of all the positive qualities the Senator had embodied prior to the day he helped destroy him. The Senator had often invited him to attend church with him. He had always declined.

And the Senator's wife had been like a mother to him. His own mother had died just two years ago—had skidded through a guardrail on Highway 1 during a spring storm. Her passing left a great empty space in his soul—great guilt, too, for she had prayed for him every day, prayed that he would invite God back into his life. He never had. At the remembering service they had for her, he had kept his composure until the last—until someone had sung Mother's favorite song, "Tenderly He Watches over You." Then he broke down and cried until there were no more tears to cry.

Indiana swept by, but he didn't see it. Then came Illinois. The towns became larger and larger, and finally, when ahead could be seen the skyscrapers of Chicago, all the passengers were called back to their seats. The train shuddered to a stop, and the city within a city disembarked.

During the six-hour wait, Charles walked the streets near the train station. He walked because he didn't want to face the headlines—the same subject regardless of the newspaper. One headline really jolted him: The column, written by a respected journalist, questioned the veracity of his now famous "scoop." It seemed as though, thread by thread, the fabric of his life was unraveling, and he did not know where there might be a stopping place.

On one of these streets, the front door of a century-old cathedral stood open. For some inexplicable reason, Charles felt impelled to go in. An organist (renowned it turned out) was interpreting Bach. The very floor shook. Charles found a seat in a dark corner and let the music bombard his soul. Wave after wave thundered in and engulfed him. During "Jesu, Joy of Man's Desiring," he chanced to look up at a stained-glass window depicting Christ with the one lost sheep. Without knowing how he got there, Charles found himself on his knees, shedding the first tears since his mother's death. What all this meant, he did not know. All he knew was that, in some inexplicable way, he had turned a corner. His last words before he stood to his feet were, "Lord, guide me, please—bring someone to show me the way."

❖   ❖   ❖

Almost, he missed this train too! He had lost all track of time in the cathedral, having it out with his soul. The train was already moving, in fact, but the porter in the last car, seeing him sprinting along the track, helped him swing aboard. Just in time he had remembered his suitcases in two terminal lockers. Relieved not to be left behind, he moved up through the cars of the "City of Dreams" until he came to the two set aside for through-passengers to Portland. As he entered his car, halfway down on the right, the sun chose that moment to shine through between buildings on a now familiar figure, a woman by the window, a woman with rich brown hair burnished with copper. She turned to smile at a three-year-old child across the aisle, and her smile was both tender and yearning. It stopped him in his tracks. As quickly as it had come, it was gone, and she had turned back to the window. She was alone, and she wasn't a woman one expected to find alone. He found his heart pounding as he neared her seat, and to his chagrin, his broadcast quality voice shook a little when he asked her if the aisle seat was taken. She said "no" graciously, and picked up a book on that seat so he could sit down. Then she resumed her viewing out the window. But she had to look his way when the porter came to check their tickets: both were checked through to western Oregon, so now he realized, to his inner delight, that they'd be traveling together for almost three days. Much could happen in that length of time.

Charles was amazed at himself, for he was known in the D.C. area as one of the most effective and persistent television interviewers around. He had worked his way up the ladder, each rung solid below his feet before he moved to the next. In recent months and years, more and more important assignments had come his way. More than a mere photogenic talking head, his encyclopedic knowledge of people, history, geography, and the political process, gave him a distinct edge; a razor-edged wit and a disarming ability to laugh at himself did the rest. He'd been told the anchorman job was as good as his sometime the next spring. He had enjoyed being important, being on a first-name basis with the nation's power brokers. There was no one he dared not tackle one on one in a hard-hitting interview. Yet here he sat next to about 120 pounds of feminine beauty, and found himself unable to get a conversation going. Where was his vaunted glibness now?

She opened her book and began reading. Kibitzing a bit, he discovered that it bore the title of *Quo Vadis*. He had heard about the book years before, but knew virtually nothing about it. Suddenly he found himself discomfited; he didn't even know what to do with his hands. He got up, and from his suitcase in the overhead rack he pulled out the latest issue of *Newsweek*. Mindlessly, he leafed through it, back to front, not knowing at all what was on any given page. Suddenly, at the front of the magazine, he discovered that the lead article had to do with his "friend," the Senator, and his perceived chances for the presidency. He froze there, the magazine open, and the kindly face of the Senator staring at him, the well-known chuckle lines in his face and the impish twinkle Charles had come to love.

The woman at the window chanced to look at the image and broke the silence, "Oh! Did you see the papers today? Wasn't that terrible news about the Senator! Almost tears my heart out, for he was one of the good guys, one of the only political figures in Washington I really respected. . . . What a president he would have made! — and now, just like that, he's gone!" And, with a catch in her throat, she turned back to the window.

Charles found his face turning crimson, unable to say a word. He wondered if she knew who had broken the story. Oh, how he hoped not!

The "City of Dreams" finally shook itself free of Chicago and its multitudinous suburbs, and with ever-increasing speed turned west. The woman at the window read on, engrossed in her book. He still didn't know her name. Ostensibly, he was reading the latest Grisham novel he'd retrieved from his suitcase, but in reality not a word was registering in his mind; for he saw but her, drank in but her, and inhaled but the ever-so-faint fragrance of her.

Once she looked up, and he dared to say, "Must be quite a book!" And she smiled as she looked down again, saying simply, *"That,* it is!" and resumed reading. Stymied there, he tried to resume *his* reading, but couldn't, for the print continued to blur and the words made no sense at all. He thought of going to the observation car but was riveted to his chair, not wanting to lose a millisecond of the vision at the window. It wasn't just her looks or her perfect form that took his breath away; it was something far deeper. In her hazel eyes were mirrored sorrow, pain, heartbreak — but also strength, courage, and joy. He only sensed these things, for he had looked straight into her eyes only a couple of times; but as an interviewer he had learned years ago that the eyes are indeed the window to the soul. They alone cannot lie. What he *did* know was this: one could look into those eyes for a lifetime and never plumb their depths. Never before had he been at close quarters with eyes like these.

In December, evening comes early, so soon the curtains of night descended on the prairies. There was no sunset because a snowstorm was sweeping down out of Alberta—a "Canadian Clipper" the engineer called it. At first the flakes floated lazily down, but that changed quickly as the full force of the storm was felt. Not much could be seen, except the lights of small towns they passed through, but the wind could certainly be felt and heard.

Around eight o'clock Charles asked his seat-mate if she was hungry; she was, so they found their way down the swaying train to the dining car. They were seated across from a young couple—honeymooning, it turned out—from Bavaria. Their destination was Monument Valley and the Grand Canyon, two places they had long dreamed of seeing. In the process of introducing themselves, Charles finally learned the name of the woman at the window—it was Michelle. The German couple, Hans and Hildie, had been waiting all day for the opportunity to ask somebody questions about the West, so both Charles and Michelle lost their shyness quickly as they assumed the thrust-upon-them roles of host and hostess. How Michelle sparkled and dimpled as she helped to answer the many questions. And of course she and Charles had questions too, especially about the Bavarian Alps and the fairytale castles of Mad King Ludwig. Since it was Hildie's birthday, a waiter brought them a candle-lit cake—which naturally led to questions as to *their* birth dates.

By the time they walked back to their seats, they were friends. Now he was eager to learn more about her. He learned that she was the daughter of a small-town minister; had been educated at a Midwest Bible college, double majoring in speech and journalism, subsequently completing the coursework for the masters in philosophy and a Ph.D. in theology at Vanderbilt. She was just now completing her dissertation—subject: the early Christians during the time of Emperor Nero. That's why she was so fascinated with Sienkiewicz's *Quo Vadis*. She currently worked as an assistant editor for a newspaper on Maryland's Eastern Shore, and was heading home to Astoria, adjacent to Oregon's northwestern-most cape.

How about him? Well, he was a child of divorce, educated at St. Johns in Annapolis, masters in history at University of Maryland in College Park, and Ph.D. in history of ideas at Georgetown. Worked now for a Beltway television station, and was planning on spending Christmas with his only brother and family, who lived near

Timberline Lodge on Mt. Hood. He did not then tell her that he hadn't seen his brother in twenty-one years, and that his brother was dying from a rare disease for which there was no known cure. It was clear that her family was warm, loving, close, and Christian—and his was all that hers was not.

About an hour or so later, he asked her about *Quo Vadis*. Would she mind telling him what it was about? She was silent a moment or two, then, choosing her words carefully, said, "Well, it's about a princess from ancient Poland named Lygia and a Roman tribune named Vinitius. She is secretly a member of the early Christian Church, and he does not believe in religion at all—I don't want to give away the plot, but the story has to do with Nero, the burning of Rome, and the terrible persecution of the early Christians."

"And Lygia and Vin—Vin—uh . . ."

"Vinitius."

"Oh yes, Vinitius. . . . What happens to them?"

Even in the darkness he could sense her smile: "For *that*, you'll just have to read the book yourself."

Not long afterward, Michelle wrapped a light train blanket around her shoulders, positioned a small pillow against the window, and dropped off to sleep. But for Charles, sleep did not come that easily. Thoughts swirled around in his head like a Tornado Alley twister. There was so much to think about that he felt incapable of sorting it out. Every minute that passed, the "City of Dreams" carried him farther away from the nightmare he had left behind in Washington. In some respects, he felt himself to be in a different world, a different time warp—a world he was increasingly reluctant to ever leave.

Which brought him to that slender form leaning against the window, sleeping naturally and easily as only those with a clear conscience can. He knew very little about her, for she was adept at erecting barriers between small talk and personal talk. Obviously she had had a lot of practice dealing with men like him down through the years. Well he knew that many, if not most, of the human moths that flutter around the flame of beauty, are there for no good. For her own self-preservation, a beauty must develop a thick veneer. Even so, most beauties have disastrous marriages. Almost invariably, they are sought out and courted for all the wrong reasons. Certainly his track record in this respect had been no better. He sighed.

The midnight hours passed and the sleeping form remained only a touch away—but he found himself responding to her unspoken trust in him. Gradually there was stealing over him something totally new in his adult lifetime—tenderness. So new, in fact, that at first he did not even recognize what it was.

About 2 A.M., the train stopped in a small prairie town. Christmas lights could be seen inside house windows and outside on eaves and trees. Now he could see, by the light from street-lamps, just how thick and fast the snow was coming down. Half an hour passed, an hour . . . and the car gradually became colder. When Michelle had twice shivered in her dreams, he quietly stood up, retrieved the warm Log Cabin quilt, leaned over, and, ever so gently, wrapped it around her. A deep sigh told him that her subconscious had gratefully acknowledged the difference. People around them began to awaken and question each other. Finally a steward came through the car, explaining the situation in whispers to those who stopped him: the problem had to do with a connecting train slowed by near blizzard conditions to the north. So many passengers were transferring to this train that it was felt they just *had* to wait.

A little over two hours after the train stopped, the other train loomed ghost-like out of the darkness and falling snow. Soon the sounds of doors opening, footsteps, people bumping into things, directions from stewards, questioning whines from sleepy children, and fretful babies, added to blasts of frigid air from the open doors below, woke up most of those still sleeping. Finally, even Michelle. Initially, she seemed disoriented, not knowing at all where she was. Gradually, awareness came back to her, and last of all, she began to question how that blessedly warm quilt had come to her.

She turned to him, smiled a sleepy smile, and said, "Out with it; how did I acquire this quilt? And furthermore, what in the world's happening? It's *cold* in here!"

So he told her all that had transpired. She looked at him with softened eyes. "You wrapped me with your mother's quilt so I wouldn't get cold, yet there you sit shivering! Come, Charles, this is a big quilt—got to be at least a queen! Here, take this end of it and get warm!" Implicit in her words was this: *What a man this is! Not only did he not make passes in the dark, but covered me so I'd be warm, remaining icy cold himself. Now I know he can be trusted.*

Suddenly there was a jolt, then another, and the now full train was on its way again. Everyone—*especially* those on the late train, who had been worrying they'd be left in a cold train station for another day—quickly dropped off to sleep; Michelle almost instantly, Charles about an hour later. A couple of times during the night he heard the muted sound of the air horn far in front; but it was a good sound, a comforting sound, and he smiled listening to it.

Morning came at last, and the "City of Dreams" hurtled through time and space, trying to make up for lost time. Stiffly, yet quietly, Charles stood up so as to not awaken the sleeping woman at the window, then went downstairs for his shave, ablutions, and change of clothes. As he climbed the stairs, the train began slowing down, for the Queen City of the Plains, Denver, was just ahead. The snow continued to fall, but more lightly now. When he got back to his seat, Michelle had just awakened and sat gazing at him through adorably sleepy eyes. He could hardly control his runaway heart.

She excused herself and returned twenty minutes later, her cheeks a freshly scrubbed pink, her shiny hair pulled into a loose knot. A short, polar fleeced shirt floated over the soft cotton mock turtle neck tucked into stone-washed jeans. She seemed as comfortable in this Rocky Mountain naturalist look as she had in the tailored silk blouse, wool jacket, skirt, and dress boots she'd worn onto the train the first day.

At Denver, they disembarked, ordered breakfast in a nearby café, and re-boarded, and the Amtrak "City of Dreams" began the long, long climb to Moffat Tunnel. As they climbed, the volume of snow increased as well. Once through the tunnel, they found seats in the observation car, knowing that the scenery from there on was about as beautiful and spectacular as can be seen from a train track in America. Frozen rivers, ice-edged waterfalls, snow-flocked trees; Winter Park, Fraser, Gore Canyon, Glenwood Canyon, and still the snow continued to fall, but intermittently now. Here and there they saw elk, deer, bald eagles, and once a snow-encrusted fox that watched them go by with quizzical eyes.

Then came night once again, and they moved back to their car. Both found themselves strangely shy and quiet during dinner. Once, their hands touched, reaching for bread, and an electric shock passed through his arm. They didn't talk much afterwards; both were tired, but especially *him*, for the stress of the last few days had begun to wear him down. This time it was he who fell asleep first, and this time it was she who watched him, watched and wondered.

When they woke up, outside their window was the Salt Lake City train station. Here they would leave behind the southward-bound cars. The snow had stopped during the night, and the morning was golden. Oh, it was a heart-stoppingly beautiful day! They disembarked and walked joyously through the newly fallen snow, so dazzling and white. This morning, there was a different look in her eyes when she looked at him, yet almost nothing personal had been discussed in their conversations together. Then the "All Aboard" signal was given, and the long silver snake headed north to Idaho.

Both seemed aware that, unless a miracle occurred, this would be the last full day they would ever spend together, but nothing was said about it—not until they had come back from the dining car in early afternoon. Deep within him, Charles knew with absolute certainty that he loved her already as he had never loved another in his almost forty years of selfish life. She awakened in him a yearning for real friendship-based companionship. Oh, the fires of desire had burned within him at sight of her, but they were now tempered by tenderness, concern for her comfort and wellbeing, and a fierce but gentle protectiveness. Should he lose her, he felt confident that he would never find another who could compare to her; so in truth it was now or never.

But he also knew that he was at the turning point of his life in other respects. Career-wise, for starters; relationship with friends and family; and, more importantly, his new post-cathedral experience with God. In those respects, Michelle could not have entered his life at a worse time. Yet, had he not been at these crossroads, would he even be thinking this way about her? He couldn't help but notice that she bowed her head and prayed before each meal, so clearly that relationship had priority over all others in her life.

Suddenly a little boy stood beside him, the just-turned five-year-old perpetual motion machine who belonged to the family six rows behind him. Children had full run of the train—to them it was one long playground. The child, Tony, was *always* asking questions. Earlier that morning Charles had heard the boy's mother plaintively saying to a woman across the aisle, "Yes, Tony is the youngest of four—had he been the oldest, he'd have been an only child."

Big Tony, Tony's father, had quite a story to tell. He and his twin brother had been adopted out to separate parents shortly after birth. Neither had ever known what had happened to the other. In recent years, Tony had instituted a search for that brother who represented such a large missing piece of his selfhood. Now, thirty-six years later, that brother had been found—and Big Tony and his family were to spend Christmas with them. Thanks to Little Tony, everyone in their car now knew the story.

Well, here was Little Tony staring at him and Michelle, engrossed again in *Quo Vadis*. In his high piping voice, which the entire car could hear perfectly, he asked a question that had been troubling him: "Are you two in love?"

Charles just sat there in a state of shock; by the window a lovely brunette was blushing seven shades of scarlet. All Charles could think of to say was, "Why do you ask?"

From the vicinity of the boy's father came an embarrassed, "Tony! What a rude question to ask!"

But little Tony didn't consider it rude. So he continued, "Sometimes you act like you're in love—the way you sort of look at each other when the other isn't looking. If you're not, it sorta seems like you'd like to be."

Then he was gone, forcibly retrieved by the strong arms of his father. But the little rascal got in the last word after all. As Big Tony propelled his unquenchable heir back to the bosom of his what-next-can-he-possibly-say-or-do family, the familiar voice piped up once more, loud and clear, "But Daddy, questions help me know things!"

Waves of laughter rolled through the car. Michelle found something unusually interesting to look at outside her window.

When his heartbeat had returned to normal, Charles thought again about Big Tony and the missing piece of his life waiting for him in eastern Oregon. Just as *his* brother, a missing piece, too, was waiting for *him*. A portion of his family who might not be around much longer. How foolish to have wasted all these years! Why hadn't he bridged the abyss between them sooner?

Which reminded him that time was fast running out on another front—and that realization decided him. Turning to the woman at the window, in a voice that shook in spite of his determination to keep it steady, he said, "Michelle, when you come to a good stopping point, I'd like very much to share something with you."

With a smile, she slid her marker in and closed the book, then said, "No better time than now—what is it?"

"It'll take a while, Michelle, but I have a very special reason for wanting to tell you a story," he said.

"Y-e-e-s?" she answered, somewhat uncertainly.

So, greatly condensed, he told her the story of his life, told it truthfully even though doing so flooded his heart with wave after wave of pain. The Washington years were the hardest of all. When he got to the events of the last week, his pace slowed. He came to a complete halt several times, and had to wipe his eyes with his handkerchief. In the telling, he spared not himself, did nothing to minimize the monstrous thing he had done. But he didn't stop there. He told of his first night's torment in the observation car, of seeing her and noting the pain lines in her face; of the cathedral, organ, and stained-glass window in Chicago.

Then he finished his story with these words: "If you were just any woman, I wouldn't be telling you this. But you aren't. You have come into my life at a moment when I am all at sea, with many more questions than I have answers, and I am strongly questioning all the values by which I have lived. I wish I could come to you strong, with solutions rather than questions. I did find the biggest solution of all in the cathedral, though. First and foremost, I now know that a life without God just isn't worth living; the same is true of values based on biblical principles. I didn't even know whether God would accept me back, but I prayed in Chicago that He would forgive the prodigal son that was I—and He did. I asked Him to send me someone to guide my stumbling steps; I know so little about how to get right with God.

"Second, I feel the time has come for a major career change—I can no longer work for a boss I cannot respect—whom I even loathe—but I haven't the slightest idea where I'll go from there. I only know I cannot work there another day.

"Third, even though it will be the hardest thing I have done in my lifetime, I shall never live at peace with myself until I ask the Senator's wife for forgiveness for the despicable thing I did to her husband.

"Fourth, I plan to make family central in my life: to love and cherish my brother, and show it; and should I lose him, to serve as a surrogate brother to his family.

"Fifth—and I know full well what a risk I am taking in even saying this, but it is a greater risk not to. Some people don't believe in love at first sight—I know I never did. But I do now. From the moment I first saw you, my heart yearned toward you, and I loved you without even knowing you. During the last couple of days I have only come to love you more, even without hearing your story. Believe me, I know how sudden this must seem to you, but I'm not asking for a response. Even if you should say, 'Charles, you have more gall than I have ever known, and I want nothing more to do with you—ever!' Even if that be true, I plead for but one favor: do me the kindness of telling me your own story."

She did not meet his eyes but stared out the window, absolutely silent, for what seemed like forever to him. He could only wait by her side, leaving his fate in her hands. Finally, she turned from the window, stared straight ahead for a few pensive moments, then began to speak, but refusing to meet his eyes:

"I was born to a man and a woman who deeply loved each other—they still do." Then she went on to tell him *her* unvarnished story: the brief period of rebellion against her parents; the times when she had questioned God; the career problems she had faced, and was still facing—and the story of Richard.

They had fallen in love at the Midwest Bible College; he had asked her to marry him; and she had accepted with joy. But, the weekend before the wedding, she had found out that he was not the kind of man she could respect, and she most certainly refused to marry a man she could not look up to and admire. So she had called it off—the hardest thing she had ever done. In retrospect, though, it proved to be the right thing, for he had broken the heart and shattered the life of the girl he'd ended up marrying several years later.

Yes, there had been other opportunities to marry, but in every case, love and respect never coalesced in any one man. "Guess I've been too picky, but I've determined that not until I find a man who loves me as much as my father loves my mother, who I can respect as much as I respect my father, and who I can love as much as my mother loves my father—only then shall I marry.

"Lately everything seems empty. Men seem to see no deeper than my outward appearance. I want them to see my caring heart. And I've always known that marriage between a believer and a non-believer would not work, bringing with it a lifetime of sorrow and misunderstandings. As for the children caught between, almost invariably they'd be lost to the Lord, unless a miracle occurred.

"My deepest crisis hit when I held the newborn child of a dear friend. I've always yearned for God's greatest gift—children—but the dull ache increased to life-shattering pain when I held that baby! My biological clock didn't just tick, it exploded! All the suppressed longing for a home, a soul mate, for children, burst open inside me just the day before I boarded this train. The pain you saw in my eyes reflected my anguished pleading with God to end my long years of loneliness—if that be His will."

Then she was silent again, looking out the window for a long time. Idly, she picked up *Quo Vadis*, but kept losing her place, a far-off look in her eyes. But at no time did she establish eye contact with him.

Night came, and they were as they had been at the beginning: casual strangers churning out small talk. It was as though each had raised the shade to enable the other to see the naked soul, then after doing so, lowered it again, and then gone on as though the shades had never been raised. It was almost surreal.

Dinner was quiet, and Michelle was absent-minded; Charles was just plain miserable. Had he been stupid to be that candid with her? But how could he *not* have been?

Afterwards, remembering what he had said to her about praying for a guide, she spoke to him about God, assured him that of course God had accepted him; that it was never too late to come back, as long as life pulsed in his veins. They talked far into the night, about things that since childhood had held no interest for him: God, the plan of salvation, and how God seeks wandering children and brings them home again. He asked many questions, and she answered them all. Shortly after midnight, he gave his heart to the Lord, and she took his hand as she prayed a prayer of dedication. He followed with a prayer of commitment.

He was long in going to sleep, filled as he was with both a feeling of great joy and great loss. He could see that he had gained the Lord. But gaining her was not to be. Finally, he fell into a restless sleep.

❀   ❀   ❀

They were making a corkscrew descent of the Blue Mountains when the first rays of Christmas Eve Day came through the window. Michelle woke first. She looked across at Charles, his face drawn and etched with pain, yet at the same time illuminated by a joy and peace that had not been there before. She stepped over his legs without awakening him and found her way into the observation car—to think and to pray.

Some time later she returned to her car just as the train was slowing for its first stop in the Columbia River gorge. An air of excitement filled the car. This was it: the thirty-six-year moment of truth. She stopped in the vestibule as Big Tony and family, carrying gaily colored packages and suitcases, got off the train into the cold, foggy morning. But there, to greet them, it seemed, must have been the entire town, complete with banners, band, and balloons—and the other brother. She watched as the two brothers dropped everything, like two gunless gunmen in *High Noon*, then ran to each other. That entire side of the train cheered!

Then she glanced at Charles, expecting to see on his face a reflection of Tony's joy. Instead, she found him leaning against the window, his shoulders shaking with gut-wrenching sobs. *It's his brother*, she thought. *No wonder he had a hard time finally telling me about him!* At that moment, a dam deep within her broke, sweeping with it the wreckage and anguish of the long, lonely years. She knew full well he was a deeply flawed man, yet who but God could be perfect? His Christian walk was a new one rather than one strengthened by time. There, she would have to lead, at least at first. Should she accept him, there would be a tough road ahead, job-wise and financially, for both of them. She too had tired of the artificiality of her life, the six million people she could never get away from in the Washington-Baltimore corridor, and the simple life and faith she missed.

And the ever-changing mighty breakers of the Pacific she longed for with every atom of her being. Her uncle owned a newspaper in Astoria, and it needed both a publisher and editor. His last letter had urged her to take one of those positions and find someone for the other, as he was old, ill, and tired. Perhaps that would be the answer—Charles, too, had told her how he was tired of urban life and wanted to live near the sea. Astoria would be a good place to raise children—neither of them were too old for parenthood *yet*.

Again her eyes took in the Christmas celebration outside her window—the coming home of two lost boy/men, the engulfing, the smiling through tears. In her heart, Tony was Charles, also going home to a brother after the long years. Suddenly, the last inner barrier was swept away—can one ever really know another? She hadn't really known Richard—and they had dated for four years. Even after a lifetime together, a man and woman still wear masks before each other. No, time is not always the answer. In a sudden flash of clarity she realized that it isn't length of association that roots love, but the sharing of ideals, hopes, dreams—God. Two can grow together.

The only questions remaining were these: Did she respect that man by the window as much as she did her father? No . . . , not yet. That was a mighty tall order. But quite likely she would in time. Could she grow to love that man by the window as her mother loved her father? Could she? Of *course* she could! To get off the "City of Dreams" without him would be—would be . . . she couldn't even visualize it, it would hurt too much. Now she knew that true love rarely makes sense: It is either there or it isn't. It's a realization that life without each other is not even an option. Even when heaven and hell come together within it—even should it last but a day, an hour—that moment shared would be worth it all. All at once she realized that, unbeknownst to her, the Lord had answered her prayer—had brought to her a man, a man who would give her love and tenderness, friendship and understanding, wrapped up in protectiveness and tied with strength. Oh, what greater Christmas gift could a woman ever ask for than *this!*

The "City of Dreams" jolted into motion once more, a blizzard of hands waving from both sides of the windows. The "City of Dreams" was, after all, just that. Every last man, woman, and child had first boarded the train with dreams, dreams that they hoped would be fulfilled when they reached the other end. So, it was not mere advertising hype to call it "City of Dreams."

Beyond the city limits and heading down the great river to Portland, Charles turned to find her in his old seat, glory in her eyes. At first, he could not even fathom the change in her—the new tenderness in her eyes, the new so-much-more in her eyes, the new *everything!*

His eyes widened.

Then her made-to-be-kissed lips curved adorably, lips he had yet to touch.

She shattered his composure first with what day it was:

"Happy Birthday, Charlie,"

then completed the demolition with

"Merry Christmas, Darling."

❋ ❋ ❋

HOW THIS TENTH STORY CAME TO BE

It was mid-November of 1999, and I had not yet decided on either the title or the subject matter of the tenth Christmas story. Finally, I made it a matter of intense prayer, and God gave me the subject and the protagonists. But long ago I discovered that while God may provide the bare bones plot of a given story, He expects the author to write from known experience, conceptualize characters and plot through the prism of his or her life perspective. And so it was with this story.

Unbeknownst to me, I had been preparing to write this story for thirteen years. During the ten years we lived in the Washington, D.C. area, I read The Washington Post *every day. Gradually, as the years passed, I began to gain a rather clear picture of Inside-the-Beltway thinking and behavior. I learned how cut-throat it tends to be. Ambition, power, control, influence, selfishness—all are operative words one reads continually about.*

Then, in the years after we moved, we kept up on the Washington news, which, if anything, only grew worse—especially the obsession with power, the willingness to prevaricate or twist the truth in order to gain one's ends. Even in the White House, truth suffered horribly. Perhaps one question posed by President Clinton best capsulized that miasmic atmosphere: Once, when questioned under oath, he countered with, "What do you mean by 'is'?" The media, too, has continued to blur the line of distinction between truth and falsehood, good and evil. And in law, truth increasingly has given way to technicality. No longer is it a question of guilt or innocence, but of who can afford the slickest attorney (or, case in point, the O. J. Simpson trial: a battery of attorneys). Result: the increasing cynicism of Americans, young and old, and the decline of moral absolutes—the secularizing and watering down of spiritual faith.

Next, having always loved trains, I decided to create a train romance. Having taken a number of transcontinental trips originating in Union Station, it was easy to create the atmosphere. In fact, almost everything (including dialogue) in the story—except for the romance itself—we actually experienced, observed, or overheard during these rail trips. Sadly, however, the Salt Lake City to Portland run has been discontinued.

At the beginning, I had no idea how the story would end. Each morning, before I wrote a word, I asked God to direct that day's story-flow. In fact, I surprised even myself with the ending, for never before had I written a romance with this short of a fuse. I thought my three readers might balk at it, but none of them wanted to wreck that last line—so it stood.

It turned out to be a story of new beginnings, even though that had not been my original intention.

❖   ❖   ❖

This story was printed in trade paper by Review and Herald Publishing Association and in hardback by Tyndale House/Focus on the Family in Christmas in My Heart 9. *The response has been heartening, but limited, as its journey just began in the fall of 2000.*

White WINGS

Below, through rifts in the clouds, she could see snowy mountains, glaciers, and serpentine rivers. Alaska! Then the great silvery-white bird began its long descent to Fairbanks.

FAIRBANKS

Fairbanks was nothing she had imagined it to be, and everything she had not. She had imagined it to be frozen in ice and snow, complete with furred Eskimos, prospectors with icy beards, and dog-sleds. Instead, it was as if she'd been dropped into a medium-sized country town most anywhere in America. It was a warm summer day with no snow in sight. Flowers—flowers in pots, window boxes, and gardens— were everywhere. Fairbanks glowed with their vibrant colors. Just out of town, a paddlewheel steamboat plied the river. The buildings— hotels included—were plain. An unpretentious sort of town.

Night came, but someone forgot to tell the sun. It was late before a brief period of twilight gave lip-service to night. It was the time of the midnight sun, preceding the time of the midday moon. The Arctic is an Alice-in-Wonderland world, with everything the reverse of what you expect. Only when she pulled shut the thick drapes in her hotel room and shut out the light could she finally drop into an exhausted sleep. Her dreams were troubled ones, but the recurring theme had to do with a prisoner vainly trying to escape from a bleak, maximum security prison. The soundtrack consisted of mocking laughter echoing down endless halls of iron-barred cells. She woke up exhausted still.

ON THE RAILS

R-r-r-r-i-n-g! went the alarm. "Morning already!" she complained, but dutifully got up. Had to, or she'd miss the train. An hour later found her at the depot, taking in the *McKinley Explorer*, long and glittering in blue and silver, with freshly washed Vista Dome glass—her home for the next two days. There was something about a train that had always called to her, wooed the long-caged, restless spirit within her. Trains—wings on rails to carry her far away from duties and responsibilities, from realities of a leaden hue.

Then the "All Aboard" sounded, and she climbed on and up the narrow stairway into the Vista Dome of her assigned car. Her outfit of fine cashmere whispered wealth in spite of her modest demeanor. Finding a window seat about a quarter of the way down, she stowed her necessaries overhead and sat down, watching the action outside as well as sizing up the passengers still boarding. She wondered how many others were in Alaska for the first time. Most passengers boarded in groups or in couples. Rare was the single, for most lone passengers had already clustered. She began to feel left out, a third thumb.

Next to the last to board was a man about 5'10", well-built, casually dressed, and topped off with a tan Tilley hat. As he approached the empty seat next to her, he paused indecisively, then moved on six rows to another empty seat. Surprisingly, she felt an unexplainable sense of loss.

There was a jolt, and the train was in motion. The crew was jolly, busy at their mission of transforming passengers into friends. First of all, they took a roll call: Where was each passenger from? From everywhere, it seemed—a big batch from "New Yawk" and "Joisey," others from various states in New England, and yet another from California; quite a few from Texas and Florida, four from Germany, three from Japan, two from South Africa, and one from France.

Breakfast was announced, and a porter came by to make up the tables. Three Jewish travel agents asked her if she'd like to be their fourth. It was a good beginning, for at breakfast downstairs she quickly shed her loneliness. The thawing process was evident at other tables as well. Breakfast tasted delicious, the upstairs crew doubling as their cooks and waiters.

Back under the Vista Dome, she found herself unable to read—the Alaskan wilderness was just too fascinating. The first moose (half immersed in mid-river) almost tilted the train off the rails as everyone rushed, cameras in hand, to that side of the tracks. But what impressed her most was the sheer immensity of the land contrasted with the scarcity of people. According to the crew, Alaska was both wonderful and lonely—especially lonely if you were one of those who lived in a house away from all roads, such as several homesteads they pointed out along the way. The crew seemed to know all the inhabitants by name, even where they had come from and how long they had lived there by the tracks (the railroad their only lifeline).

In the seat just in front of her was a thirty-something couple with their two children, a boy nine and a girl six. They hailed from Phoenix and planned to rough it for the summer in an isolated cabin. If they managed to stand it that long, they'd then decide whether or not to stay for the winter.

"Jack is tired of civilization," admitted Mary, his wife, "and he persuaded me to spend the fall up here—but I'm wondering if we haven't bitten off more than we can chew. There'll be no electricity, no indoor plumbing—it'll be life stripped of all but its bare essentials. Now the children," and here she looked at them fondly, "just consider it to be one big lark. . . . They don't realize that our diet'll be mostly fish." She sighed softly, but not loud enough for Jack to hear.

A little over three hours out of Fairbanks, the passengers were told to watch for their first sight of Mt. McKinley—or "Denali," the "Great One," as the Eskimos call it. Usually it was socked in by clouds, but who knew? They might get lucky this time.

But they didn't get lucky—Denali remained shrouded in her cloudy garments. So huge is America's highest mountain that it creates its own weather. The Himalayas are higher, but they don't begin at only 1000 feet in elevation, then soar over 19,000 more feet to 20,300 like Mt. McKinley does.

The train stopped at Denali Station, and everyone boarded buses for their hotel complex. That afternoon, at 3:30, Juliet climbed into a light plane with three other passengers. Destination—Denali.

Almost she still didn't get to see it, for the clouds were so high and dense. Then, at 17,000 feet the plane broke out of the mist—and there, directly in front of them, was the most awe-inspiring sight she had ever seen. It literally took her breath away. For perhaps fifteen or twenty seconds, the sun came out and transformed cold gray into blinding white, topped by the bluest of blue skies. Then the vision disappeared, as the fog and rain closed in. But that ever-so-brief moment of beauty would be part of her always. Even the pilot, who'd been chattering virtually nonstop, became mute at the sudden apparition. They flew back to Denali Station in silence.

It rained all night.

It was still raining when they boarded the *McKinley Express* next morning. Only this time, Tilley Hat (for so she had come to call him) stopped in the aisle next to her and politely asked if he could join her.

She smiled and nodded.

And so it began.

❈   ❈   ❈

After small talk came introductions. His name was Robert MacDonald, and he was a small town newspaper editor from Granbury, Texas. Her name, he discovered, was Juliet Romano, and she owned and operated a shop in Aspen, Colorado. "Christmas in the Rockies," it was called.

The ice broken, she laughed, and said, "I've a confession to make."

"What's that?"

"I've been calling you 'Tilley Hat' in my mind."

"You *have?* . . . Most people don't even know this hat *has* a name."

"Well, I do, because my brother Richard has one. He maintains there's a kinship involved in its ownership—that no Tilley-hat wearers can be other than friends."

"True indeed. Just yesterday, in the Seattle airport, a fellow wearing a dark green one came up and introduced himself. Said he was visiting from South Africa, and had bought the hat at the factory in Canada. . . . And, I must confess—I had a name for you too."

"Oh?"

"You'll probably think it strange, though."

"Why is that?"

"Well, I called you 'Madonna of Sorrows.'"

"Why?"

"Oh, I don't know. Perhaps because you have the soft auburn-haired loveliness of a Raphael Madonna, and perhaps because you appeared to be so sad."

"Hmm. I didn't know it, uh, showed."

"Maybe it's because, being an editor, I'm used to studying people . . . their many moods, their personalities, what makes one different from another. Can tell what mood an employee is in before a word's been said."

Juliet didn't rise to the bait, but merely admitted, "You may be right."

And he left it at that.

Right then the train began to slow, seemingly a hundred miles from nowhere. Questions were on everyone's face. *Why here?* Then the family from Phoenix got up, Mary's face a blanched white: *This was it. Like it or not, she no longer had a choice.* The train stopped, then quickly started again . . . and there by the tracks, they stood waving. By their side were their belongings—their food, sleeping bags, tools, and necessaries. All they'd have to survive on for the next three months.

The day passed in a blur of mountains, trees, streams, birds, animals, isolated cabins, and hamlets. Of special note: one bald eagle, one fox, and two bears. Late in the afternoon, the train pulled into the depot of Anchorage (containing in this one city almost half the population of Alaska).

Next day, it seemed only natural that Juliet and Robert sit side by side in the bus to Seward, arriving at that seacoast village late in the afternoon. The town of Seward was named after William Henry Seward, Lincoln's secretary of state (retained by President Johnson), who purchased Alaska from the Russians in 1867 for $7,200,000, making him the laughing-stock of America. "Seward's Folly" and "Seward's Icebox" were two of the kinder contemporary designations of that vast land, with 20 percent as much land as the entire continental United States. Why, it stretched almost 11 percent of the way around the world—2,600 miles. And all that for two cents an acre. "Seward's Folly," indeed!

In the harbor, looming out of the crystalline water like a great white swan, floated their ship.

THE JUBILEE

This was to be their home for the next week. Fourteen years old, this Carnival Line ship was 733 feet long, weighed 47,262 tons, carried almost 1,500 passengers, and was staffed by a crew of 670.

After checking in, and before going to their respective staterooms, Robert haltingly asked a question: "Juliet. . ., this ship is so large that we're not likely to see each other unless we plan now to do so. We're both traveling alone . . . and uh . . . , speaking just for myself, the trip would be so much more enjoyable if I could share it with a friend. Do you think . . . uh . . . ."

"Of course," she responded, "I'd like that too."

Thus they stood together on the top deck at 9:00 that evening, when *The Jubilee*, after several long blasts of its horn, majestically moved out of the harbor and into Blying Sound. They watched until the lights of Seward disappeared from sight.

Late that night, she cuddled up in the well of her window, looked out at the moonlit water, and listened to the waves slapping against the ship's hull. Too tired to think, she let her mind drift at will. About midnight, she dropped off into a dreamless sleep.

Very early the next morning she awoke to the same sounds—the low hum of the engine, the waves slapping the hull—and experienced the same slight roll of the ship. She smiled, sighed, and dropped back to sleep.

Nine A.M. found her at the breakfast bar. Robert was already there at a table by the window, a large mug cupped in his hands. Her arms shook a little as she set her tray down. *Why this sudden and uncharacteristic surge of joy?* She couldn't remember the last time she'd faced a day with this much happiness.

How quickly the day passed!

College Fjord, as well as the fjords of Valdez, then a small boat tour of the Valdez/Prince William Sound area, with wildlife every-where—seals, otters, eagles, hawks, gulls. Both Juliet and Robert being amateur photographers and naturalists, their sense of a kinship of the spirit couldn't help but be increasingly evident as the hours passed.

Inside *The Jubilee*, meals and snacks were available around the clock, and activities such as nature lectures, variety revues, quiz shows, musicals, films, games of chance, deckside sports, and shopping, all added up to a ship that never slept.

That night a storm hit, and having left the sheltered bays for the open sea, *The Jubilee* was pounded by towering waves. But Juliet, there by the rain and wave-slashed window, reveled in the tempest. So long had she been assailed by inner storms that the external one she now experienced brought her nothing but a kind of primitive, savage joy.

In the morning, after breakfast, the sun out and storm gone, off to their left the vast snow-capped peaks of the Wrangell-St. Elias National Park (three times the size of Yellowstone) moved slowly past their ship—or so it seemed. Only in Alaska would an 18,000-foot peak, Mt. St. Elias (2,000 feet higher than the highest peak in the lower 48), be virtually ignored. As a matter of fact, seventeen of America's twenty highest peaks grace this land. Just across the Canadian border from Mt. St. Elias is Canada's highest mountain, Mt. Logan, at 19,850 feet, only 450 feet shorter than Mt. McKinley —but no American ever hears of Mt. Logan!

As she and Robert scanned the magnificent mountain range with their binoculars, into their line of vision flashed two sets of snow-white wings—seagulls. For almost two hours the two gulls put on a performance neither Robert nor Juliet would ever forget—now skimming the waves (only inches above the water), now circling the ship, now soaring so high above they were only blurs, yet always in synch, wings never touching, as choreographed as a ballet. "Together, yet alone," mused Juliet. . . . Then they were gone—they never saw them again.

Then came quieter waters and the famous Hubbard Glacier. The great ship drew as near as the captain dared, then stopped in the midst of a field of small icebergs. Mesmerized, the passengers watched the "calving": office-building-size sections of ice breaking off and crashing into the sound. Both Robert and Juliet had seen this phenomenon in film a number of times, but to actually experience it firsthand was something else entirely! Each time, there was a crack of thunder followed by the slow-motion fall of a new iceberg and a great splash of milky water. Juliet pulled her scarf tightly around her neck, for the wind coming off the glacier chilled her to the bone.

Historic Skagway was next, jumping off point for the Klondike Gold Rush of 1898. Juliet and Robert took the train to the top of Chilkoot Pass. It was here that almost thirty thousand prospectors were forced by the Canadian government to haul up two thousand pounds of provisions before they were permitted to go on to the Yukon. Translated, that meant that each prospector had to find a horse with stamina enough to make it to the top with a hundred pounds of supplies a minimum of twenty times! Not surprisingly, more than three thousand horses died here, not being equal to the strain and bitterly cold weather. And those unfortunate prospectors who couldn't afford to acquire horses were forced to carry two thousand pounds of provisions to the top on their own shoulders!

TWO STORIES

Lovely Juneau, accessible only by sea, was next. Of all the towns and cities they saw, they loved Juneau most. As was true up and down the Alaskan coast, they marveled at the pristine water, the almost complete absence of pollution and urban sprawl—America as it once was.

So many float planes had they seen taking off from the waterways that they finally chartered one. What an experience! The view of mountains, lakes, glaciers, rivers, and fjords was breathtaking. During the afternoon, they landed on several glaciers and one remote lake. On the shores of this crystalline lake they saw two grizzly cubs, a wolf pack, and half a dozen bald eagles. It was a Shangri-la most difficult to leave. They made it back to *The Jubilee* with only twenty minutes to spare. As the white float plane took off again in the late afternoon sun, Juliet thought, *White wings. If only I had white wings to take me away from everything!*

That evening, after dinner, they found a quiet place just inside the top deck. Both were quiet and contemplative, and each was increasingly aware of the other—and that they were skating on mighty thin ice. It was high time to level with each other. All around them shipboard romances were taking place, for there is something about a ship that induces them. Perhaps because shipboard life seems so out of time, the rest of the world is forgotten. The only reality is the "now," with both the past and the future treated as if they never were and never could be. In such an island in time, no relationship appears impossible, no matter what obstacles might lie in ambush upon leaving the ship. But now, on this wondrous night, both felt their stories could no longer wait to be told. Robert's was first:

"I'm afraid you won't find my story to be a happy one, Juliet. I'm Texas-born and grew up in south Fort Worth. My father was a minister and my mother a stay-at-home mom. My childhood was, by and large, happy, and my parents' marriage a solid one. I've always loved books and writing, thus I majored in journalism and history at Texas Christian University. Along the way, I fell in love with a lovely blonde from Dad's church. A prom queen, she was the campus dream girl. Somehow, I don't know how or why, she chose me over the others."

I can tell you why, thought Juliet.

"Seven years went by. Gloria was happy in her nursing job but yearned to have a child, . . . but no child ever came to us. It about broke my heart, too, for I also felt incomplete without children in the house.

We both attempted to compensate for the child void by being workaholics. Gloria took extra shifts at the hospital, and I stayed late at the newspaper. A friend of Dad's had owned the Granbury Tribune, and he brought me aboard as assistant editor after I graduated from Texas Christian. Eventually Gloria and I saved enough money for a down payment on the paper, paying the rest on time. Well, the Tribune became the child we couldn't have. Immersing myself into the community, I joined Rotary and Kiwanis, as well as being a director of the Chamber of Commerce. The paper grew, as most anything does if you give it your all.

"Needless to say, none of this strengthened our marriage. We began to drift apart. We had a long talk and decided to attend a marriage encounter weekend sponsored by our church. There — that weekend — we realized how close to divorce we had drifted. We renewed our vows. Then we packed our things and headed home."

There was a long pause while he struggled for control. . . . Finally, he picked up the thread of the story again:

"It was night on the road south of Fort Worth. We'd just passed Cresson, when around the corner came a pickup out of control, going way too fast to hold his curve trajectory. I hope you never experience that utterly helpless feeling of seeing two headlights in the opposing lane cross the yellow line heading dead-center for you. Because of the speed, there was no chance in the world of getting out of the way, and to jerk the wheel would be to flip our SUV. Nor was there time for the proverbial replay of one's life story you hear about in such situations—only time for Gloria's 'Bob, Bob! He's going to'—and then the deafening crash.

"The pickup horn stuck on. With that terrific impact, I felt certain the next face I saw would be the good Lord's. But no, I was still alive and aware. Checked my left foot—it moved. Same for the right. Same for each hand. I was in tremendous pain, gasping for breath, and crying. But hearing nothing from Gloria, I turned—and wished I hadn't."

"Oh!"

"Yes, she'd taken more of the hit than I. True, her airbag deployed, but the impact was so great that she was pushed halfway into the back seat. I could hear her whimpering, making gasping noises."

Again he paused for control, then continued.

"A doctor just behind us saved her life. Called an ambulance on his cell phone, and we were rushed to a Fort Worth trauma center. Gloria was wheeled into the operating room. Had the best surgeon in the city. But nothing he could do was enough."

"She *died?*"

"No, but I wish she had. What happened to her was worse. So many vertebrae were crushed that she was paralyzed from the neck down. And since her trachea received such a direct hit, she lost the use of her voice as well."

"*Oh no!*"

"Yes, she, my once lovely Gloria, only twenty-nine years of age, became little more than a vegetable. Brain still functions—and eyes. But nothing else does—or ever can."

"Oh! Oh!" was all that Juliet could say.

"So there she lies in her hospital bed in what used to be our bedroom, or in the front room by the window that overlooks Lake Granbury—that's where I wheel her when I go to work. A nurse watches over her while I'm at the Tribune. I come home twice a day to check up on her. She gets her food through tubes."

"And absolutely no hope?"

"None whatsoever."

"And you've had no communication whatsoever with her for—for . . . how long?"

"Six and a half years. The *only* communication is through her pain-wracked eyes and, occasionally, a slight hand response to a question. Just imagine what it would be like to be locked in a body that refuses to obey the brain! That's the worst of it; she *knows* what has happened to her, and she *knows* what has happened to me. I'm certain she wishes herself dead . . . but she's strong, strong in spite of her broken body."

"And the driver of the pickup?"

"That's the part of the story I've had the hardest time with—he got out of it with hardly a scratch. And he'd been going close to a hundred miles an hour, according to the police report."

"And her expenses?"

"Had to take the driver and his insurance company to court. A settlement finally, just last year, paid her medical bills—$850,000 at last count, paid her lawyer, and left me enough to get by, but only if I keep her there at home."

"So here you are . . . still young. . . . Trapped in . . . uh . . . uh—"

"Trapped in a marriage that's no marriage? With absolutely no hope of anything else? True, on both counts. But I go on, one day at a time."

"I admire you. Not many men would have stayed by her."

"Well, I made vows to stay by her, in sickness and in health, in good times and in bad, till death do us part. Repeated those vows to both God and man—*twice*. And death has not parted us."

"But *how* have you coped with it? Haven't you become angry and embittered, or lost faith in God?"

"Oh, I'll admit to some dark days, and even darker nights, there in that house, as silent as a tomb. And I've cried till I have no more tears to weep. Begged God to call her home to Him. I know she's ready to go. Asked God about me too: Would I ever again have a companion, a wife? Was I doomed to celibacy for life, in my mid-thirties? It's been hard, Juliet, awfully hard, for there have been a number of attractive women, some of them at the office, more than willing to take her place . . . even without the marriage license."

"So how did you get *here?*"

He smiled for the first time. "Well, since I still felt bound to the Gloria that once was and was thus unwilling to take what was . . . uh . . . available, gradually it began to get to me. My health began to suffer. I became more irritable at the office. After having been generally cheerful all my life, I sank deeper and deeper into despondency. In fact, it got to the point where Mom and Dad began to fear for my life. They came over to the office one afternoon and handed me a long envelope. When I opened it, there was a ticket for this Alaskan cruise."

"What wonderful parents you must have!"

"Yes, I'm blessed. . . . They furthermore said not to worry; they'd watch over Gloria while I was gone."

"Oh my!"

"And what does 'Oh my!' mean?"

"Oh, I wish I'd known all this earlier."

"What good would *that* have done?"

"Guess it wouldn't have."

"And if you had, you might have been nice to me just because you felt sorry for me. I wanted you to like me for myself alone."

"I *do* like you for yourself alone. . . . I just wish there was more I could do to assuage your pain and bring you the happiness you'll never have at home."

The look in his eyes told her she'd been unwise in adding that second sentence. Quickly, she struggled for control before going on, then she said, pulse racing and her breath ragged, "I think, Bob, I may have inadvertently offered more than I can give. I . . . I think it's time I tell *my* story."

"I'm listening."

"Well, let's see. . . . Earlier on I felt extremely sorry for myself, but . . . after hearing *your* story, I count myself lucky in comparison."

"Let me be the judge of that. I strongly suspect you've experienced more than your fair share of pain as well. Go ahead."

"Alright. . . . I was born in Monterey, California. My father owned a beachfront hotel there, and my mother helped him run it. I'm one of three children. I grew up happy. Well, I *was* happy until the day Dad told Mom he'd met someone he loved more than her.

It happened the day after I graduated from high school. It shattered Mom. She was never the same happy mother after that. She took Dad to court; it was a long and angry trial, and she saw to it that all Dad's dirty linen was hung out to dry on the Monterey clothesline. In the end, she got half—Dad had to sell the hotel. Mom bought a mansion on Carmel's Seventeen Mile Drive, and there she exists today. I can't really call it living—still angry and bitter after all these years. I can't be in her house for more than twenty-four hours without going bonkers. I've never had a home to go back to since, for Dad dropped out of my life completely."

"How sad!"

"I packed my things two days after graduation, cleaned out my savings account, and moved north to Santa Cruz, where I got a job waiting tables at a restaurant. Later on, I enrolled at the university. Majored in psychology. Perhaps because I was so mixed up myself. Got my B.A. Half-way through my masters, I met Max. He was drop-dead handsome, smooth, worldly, well-to-do, and was considered the catch of the campus."

"And you decided to remove him from circulation?"

"Oh, I wasn't quite *that* calculating." She laughed that warm, throaty laugh that sent tingles up his spine, and continued: "The truth of the matter is that I was terribly lonely and was tired of being poor and waiting on tables. So when he told me how beautiful he thought I was and offered to take me 'away from all this,' I accepted, with stars in my eyes and hope in my heart. We married that very night. Justice of the peace. And honeymooned in Spain."

"Didn't want a church wedding?"

A shadow passed over her face. After a pause, she continued, in a very low voice: "*I* did, but he didn't. I had attended church up until my parents' divorce, but I was so angry at God for letting Dad walk out on us that I'm afraid I gave God up at the same time. But I missed that dimension in my life and hoped I'd marry a Christian, and thus have an excuse to attend church again.

"But, as you see, I married Max instead. And he's never felt any need for God. Only money. And he's made lots of it: bought and sold hotel after hotel, making money each time, until he finally bought the Five Star hotel he owns in Aspen now."

"*He* owns?"

"Yes, *he* . . . had me sign a prenuptial agreement to that effect. I was too naive then to fully realize what I was signing. It was years before I finally woke up to the realization that everything but the house was all his."

"Did . . . you have children?"

"Yes, thank the good Lord. Three: a boy and two girls—nine, six, and four, respectively. They are my comfort."

"Oh?"

"Yes, I'm sure you're aware by now that I'm *still* a lonely woman. Max gives me plenty of money; bought the Christmas store for me. Laughingly said, 'Go and play with your toy—it'll get you out of the house.' But he doesn't give me much else. I try to be a good wife to him, entertain his clients, never reject his conjugal demands if I can possibly avoid it. If I do, he gets angry and gives me the silent treatment for weeks at a time. . . . And, uh, in spite of all this, he—he—has not been faithful to me."

"And yet you stay?"

"Of course! True, I didn't promise to stay with him for life, in front of God. But in my heart, I promised God I would. Since our marriage, I've attended church whenever I possibly could, for I've needed God so. I take the children with me. Max deeply resents our going and usually has something cold and biting to say about it, but we go anyway. But it's hard, because Aspen is so New Age—has hardly any churches. Grocery stores either. The reality is that Aspen is nothing more than palatial homes empty for all but a few weeks of the year, with the average home cost now exceeding three and a half million. It's *not* a family town, and thus few marriages last long there. So I have to go clear to Glenwood Springs to find a church. And I have almost no real friends in Aspen—other than my employees at the Christmas shop."

"I had no idea Aspen was like that."

"Oh, I haven't told you the half of it! It's not just the transient super-rich who float in and out with their chauffeurs, butlers, maids, nannies, and servants. It's also the people who stay in those top-flight hotels—where the nightly rates are stratospheric. Even at that, many stay weeks at a time, in suites. Max tells me that a good share of them are miserable in spite of all their wealth. So are their spoiled kids. Why, just two weeks ago, a woman screamed out to the front desk manager—could be heard throughout the entire floor—'Just because I'm the second richest woman in America, you've no business overcharging me!' Yes, she made *quite* a scene."

"They're not *all* like that, are they?"

"No, of course not, but they are disproportionately so—unhappy and hard to satisfy. Even the trust kids, who 'toil not, neither do they spin'—they don't have to work for a living because of their inherited wealth, so they flit from here to there, into substance abuse, sex, gambling, and thrills wherever they can be found. No, money—if one may judge by Aspen—certainly doesn't bring much happiness with it. Without work, life has no purpose."

"So how do *you* find happiness?"

"Through my children, my work at the store, and God."

"Not through Max?"

"No. Oh, let me qualify that. I think he loves me in his own way. He's a child of divorce too. His parents gave him all the money he wanted and none of the love. That's why I don't know if he's even capable of true love. Since he wasn't given it at home, apparently he's incapable of passing it on."

"And the children?"

"Oh, he's proud of them and pets them if they're well-behaved and don't get on his nerves. Heaven help the one who does!"

"As for me, I don't think he's likely to divorce me—not as long as I keep my looks, that is. He considers divorce to be . . . uh . . . 'messy,' is his word for it. As it is, he has the best of all possible worlds: a wife who loves him far more than he deserves, children who both admire and fear him, employees who tremble at his every word, and women who fawn over him. He travels all over the world. . . ."

"But doesn't take you?"

"But *never* takes me—says my place is with the kids."

"So, how did *you* get here?" he grinned.

"Funny you'd ask. It's this way. Guess I was looking kind of down. One night, when he'd been in Tahiti for most of a month—at least I *assumed* he was in Tahiti, as he rarely calls me—everything sort of caved in on me at once: the realization that our marital love was so one-sided, that I was 'safe' only as long as I accepted his infidelities and coldness, and as long as I kept my youth and looks. So there in our fifteen million-dollar mansion, envied by most everyone who doesn't know me well, coveting the love some of my 'poorer' married friends take for granted, I cried out to God. 'Oh, Lord, it's all so hopeless! There's no light at the end of my tunnel—only dark and more dark. I don't know how I can take it any longer. I'm not asking out of my marriage—I walked into it with my eyes wide open. And I don't want my children to experience the desolation and rejection I did when Dad walked out of our home. No, all I ask, Lord, is *hope*—hope that my life will not always be dark. And a friend, a true friend who'll accept me just the way I am. Unconditionally. A friend who'll cherish me and tell me I'm worthy of friendship. A friend who'll walk into my life—and stay. Give me a sign, Lord, that You haven't forsaken me!' I cried myself to sleep that night."

"You poor dear!"

"Two days after that prayer, I received a cablegram from Max. And here it is." She reached into her purse and unfolded a yellow piece of paper that had obviously been read and reread a number of times. This is what it said:

Dear Juliet,

Still in Tahiti. Bored stiff. Home Tuesday. Today's your birthday, and I forgot to give you anything. You're such a good wife, better perhaps than I deserve. Take ten thousand or so and go on a cruise to somewhere. You've never gone anywhere. I'll take care of the children this time. Go!

Love, Max

"Unbelievable!" muttered Robert.

"Isn't it! So, as I always wanted to go to Alaska, I was able to get the ticket for this cruise."

"And Max, do you think he's changed?"

"Well, I thought perhaps he had, but on his return, he was the same old Max, a bit disgruntled in fact at what he'd let himself in for. If you want the real truth, I think he'd been afraid my unhappiness would end up aging me." She laughed, "It most likely *was*, so it'll probably turn out to be an astute business investment for him after all."

"So God answered your prayer?"

"Yes, bless Him! . . . And brought me that friend. A friend who understands that friendship . . . and no more—deep, heartfelt and, hopefully, for life—friendship is all that I can offer, for both of us have made vows before God. . . . I hope I have the assurance of yours in return."

"Without a question! And my admiration with it." Then he turned from her and stared into the night, not trusting himself to say anything more.

WHITE WINGS

The next day, it was on to Ketchikan, aglow in the ultramarine. They shopped and went out on a small boat looking for birds—and found them. Saw the salmon flailing their way up the river in which they were hatched, their God-given instinct driving them up the river to spawn and die.

"How do they *know?*" Juliet wonderingly asked him.

"According to a fisheries executive I spoke with in Juneau," Robert answered, "it's some quality, some unique chemical element in the river itself that calls to them thousands of miles out in the Pacific; calls and summons them home—to the mouth of the river, up the river, no matter what obstacles stand in the way, to the very spot in which they hatched. Only then do they spawn. Only then can they relax, give up the long fight, and die."

"What a God we have!"

※　　※　　※

Then the great white swan spread her wings, and they were off to the Inside Passage. Every hour now, every minute, every second, tasted bittersweet, for up ahead in the clouds they could sense the southern terminus of their island in time.

The next day—their last day together—as they stood watching whales cavort and blow on both sides of the ship, Robert pensively asked her if he might leave a very special gift with her.

"Of course!"

"Well, Juliet, it's really a gift from God—and it alone has given me the courage to face each day."

"Whatever it is, I need it too. . . . Go ahead."

"Are you familiar with David's Psalm 139?"

"I don't think so. Please share it."

"Very well. I've memorized the parts that mean the most to me:
   O Lord, you have examined my heart
   And know everything about me.
   You know when I sit down or stand up.
   You know my every thought when
      far away.

You chart the path ahead of me
And tell me where to stop and rest.
Every moment you know where I am.
You know what I am going to say
Even before I say it, Lord.
You place your hand of blessing
  on my head. . . .
You watched me as I was being
Formed in utter seclusion,
As I was woven together in the dark
Of the womb.
You saw me before I was born.
Every day of my life was recorded in
Your book.
Every moment was laid out
  before a single day had passed.

Psalm 139:1-5, 15-16 (New Living Bible)

"I'd never heard that before. Would you mind repeating it once more for me?"

He did. Then there was a long silence, broken finally by her: "Reminds me of a passage in C. S. Lewis's *Mere Christianity.* In it, he maintains that since God is not in time as we are, He sees us as a vast tree, with the past connecting the present to the future—each of us interacting with each other according to His divine master plan."

"In other words, God is a sort of grand chess master or master choreographer?"

"Precisely."

"That nothing takes place, even casual conversations, by mere chance?"

"True."

There was a long pause; then Robert thoughtfully observed, "If all this is true, then God put me on that train and on this ship, and put you on board as well, just because He loves us both—dearly. . . and wants to comfort us, give us the courage to carry on back home, to bring us happiness to offset the pain. It's sort of divine damage control for choices He permits us to make."

"True on all counts."

It was the last night of their island of time, and the full moon silvered the waters of the Inside Passage. Here and there, off to either side, twinkled lights—lights from homes—graphic evidence that the Last Frontier lay behind them and civilization ahead of them. Some sixty passengers shared the moment with them. Mesmerized, they watched silently as the great shadowy prow of *The Jubilee* sliced through the dark waters below, phosphorescent billows sweeping away and away on either side, and only the sounds of night birds breaking the serenity of the night.

Looking intently into his eyes, she spoke these words, "Bob, I'm so very grateful God brought you into my life. Your friendship, listening ear, and love have given me the courage and the heart to return to a house that is cold, to a man who loves me little, and to children who love me much. . . . You've made me believe in myself again, Bob— believe that God not only cares but has a plan for the rest of my life. I can now take up my responsibilities with a song in my heart."

After a long silence in which he struggled for the right words, he said, "I am ever so grateful for your faith in me, respect, empathy, friendship, and love. I now realize that above all the unspoken anguish in my wife's eyes—and the answering torment of my own— that above all this, God knows and understands, and has a plan for all the days of the rest of my life. . . . I, too, can go home with a sense of joy."

Then he took her hand in his and prayed the Lord's blessings on them as they went their separate ways only hours from then.

Next morning, after promising to stay in touch, they bade goodbye to each other, not at all sure they'd ever see each other again.

❊   ❊   ❊

That December, Robert received a long letter, written on seagull stationery. It began with these words:

Christmas in the Rockies

Dear Robert,

It's almost Christmas, and the children and I have decorated our house, emphasizing Christ rather than Santa. I read Christmas stories to them every night—how they look forward to it! Max neither understands nor approves, but we make our own happiness.

How often I have relived our island of time, our city of refuge. How often have I seen again the white-winged plane from which I caught that one glorious glimpse of Denali; that white-winged seaplane that carried us to that remote lake, where I wanted to *stay;* that white-winged swan named *The Jubilee,* and the two white-winged gulls off the Wrangell-St. Elias coast. How I envied them their freedom, and how I yearned to follow them. But you helped to teach me a great lesson: life is not that simple. We are *never* free to live a life dedicated to self. Like it or not, each of us is connected—connected to parents, brothers, sisters, aunts, uncles, grandparents; connected to husband, wife, children, friends, and community. Like that phosphorescent wake we watched that last night on *The Jubilee,* each word we say, each act, each decision of our lives leaves its wake—and that wake rolls on and on into eternity itself. So, though we may fly like the gulls, we're never free. No freer than God Himself, who created us—and then is stuck with us for all time.

So, should we disregard all this, and turn our backs on the impact of our acts and words on those who love, depend on, respect, and admire us, then the consequences would likely be far greater than any brief high we might have felt during the breakaway. The cost would be far too high.

But how precious are these wings, wings that bring us friendship and love that will never die.

A few days from now, you'll receive a package. I first saw it in a shop in Juneau. For this limited edition, a master carver created two soaring snow-white gulls, wings spread in flight. Their wings do not touch, can never touch, as they are frozen this way for all time. One sculptured piece stays with me always; the twin goes to you. May God grant you and yours a Christ-filled Christmas."

❀   ❀   ❀

It was two days before Christmas when his package reached her. In it was a two-page letter:

Granbury, Texas

Dear Juliet,

Received your wonderful present. Nothing could possibly have brought me more joy! Have placed it on our fireplace mantel, where we can both see it every day. While nothing has changed in this house, I've taken it upon myself to change the atmosphere. I, too, have decorated the house for Christmas in a lavish way, even with the crèche I used to put up at Christmas. When I positioned it on a small table where Gloria could see it, the closest thing to a smile I've seen on her face in seven years appeared, and the dull stare temporarily left her eyes. I even play Christmas CDs for her. And—you'll laugh. . . . No, on second thought, you won't. I even read Christmas stories to her. Nothing is wrong with her hearing. In—in the Kingdom, I'll ask her what she thought of them. *Your* soul-mateship gave me the courage and joy to change the atmosphere in the house: to show Gloria that I love and respect her still, even if she can no longer articulate that she yet loves me too.

And I have a present I hope you'll like. I'm no poet, but I wrote this poem for you, then copied it onto parchment paper. My copy will remain on my office wall. Just as is true with your copy, two snow-white seagulls have been painted against the Alaskan sky and *The Jubilee*.

White Wings
Far far north in the land of the midnight sun,
*   We saw two seagulls with snow-white wings.*
Together, yet alone; never saw them touch
*   As they serenely floated down the air rivers of the sky.*
How my heart yearned to be a gull like they:
*   Free to soar into Alaska's azure sky,*
Free to roam far out to sea,
*   Free to stand on Mt Elias's crest.*
Could I but be freed from the trials of my life,
*   The coldness, the never ceasing anguish;*
Freed from the squirrel cage of spiraling darkness,
*   Spinning, ever spinning, but never a ray of light.*
The Lord answered my heartfelt plea
*   By sending me a white-winged gull*
Who floated with me down the air rivers of the sky,
*   Who sang with me the joy of life.*
Now that I have returned to my squirrel cage,
*   Now that I have shouldered once again my cross,*

All is changed, for there on my mantel
Are two snow-white gulls:
Together — yet alone.

❄   ❄   ❄

HOW THIS ELEVENTH STORY
CAME TO BE

Like everyone else, a writer goes through periods. My most recent one resulted from a mix of stories I've been putting together for WaterBrook/ Random House on the subject of tough times. Louis Venden points out that eleven of the twelve Apostles died violent deaths, and that God does not normally reward our "good works" with happily-ever-afters. In fact, joy and pain go hand in hand in life, with pain predominating. Also, in recent months and years, more and more true stories (some involving people I know personally) have come to my attention — men, women, and children who bravely make the best of it, even out of pain and heartbreak. Thus, the conviction came upon me that at least some of my stories ought to reflect this ever present reality.

Early in October 2000, I sat down on the upper deck of our Colorado home, birds, chipmunks, and squirrels flitting or scampering all around me. And there I sat with a blank piece of paper in front of me. Then, as I always do before I write, I prayed this prayer: "Lord, on this so beautiful day that You've granted to us, I ask You for a gift. If it be Your will, give me a story that You feel needs to be told, one that will be both a blessing and a source of courage to those who read it. Happy, sad, or both, I'll accept whatever plot You give me."

Then I leaned back and waited. Within ten minutes, the Lord had given me the protagonists and the beginning of this story. Not until three days had passed would I know how the story might end.

The catalyst was our first ever (but, hopefully, not last) cruise to Alaska, last fall for our wedding anniversary. This story would not have happened without that cruise. The wreck scene was taken from our February twenty- fifth head-on collision, when a speeding driver smashed into us. But we were luckier than were Robert and Gloria in this story because we have healed almost completely. Granbury I knew well for fourteen years.

As for Aspen, two autumns ago, Connie and I stayed one night, at off- season rates, in one of that resort town's grandest hotels. I overheard the "second richest woman in America's" tirade myself. I had a long discussion with the maitre de about it and what it was like to serve America's super-rich.

The prototype for Robert is my father-in-law, Derwood Palmer, who —

when his wife of over half a century, Vera, experienced a massive stroke and was no longer able to communicate except by a squeeze of the hand, move any part of her body, or control her bodily functions—tenderly and lovingly took care of her in their home for almost five years. When we asked him how he stood it, he said, "It's not hard—when it's your girl." When Mom died, Dad didn't have any tears left—he'd cried all he had already.

As for the role of friends and soul mates in our lives, I've been mulling that over ever since I put together Heart to Heart Stories of Friendship (Focus on the Family/Tyndale House, 1999). I could not even imagine a life devoid of the cherished friendships that so enrich, encourage, and bless my life! We live in such a perverted society today that deep friendships between men and women, men and men, and women and women, all are twisted into evil by those who have ceased searching for innocence and goodness in others. But one of God's greatest gifts is just such a friendship. As for the poem, "White Wings," God withheld that from me until the morning after the story came to its close.

❖ ❖ ❖

This story will also be included in the trade paper Christmas in My Heart 10 (published by Review and Herald Publishing Association) and in the hardback edition (published by Tyndale House/Focus on the Family), fall of 2001.

EVENSONG

PRELUDE

Constance gazed at her seven-year-old daughter through pain-wracked eyes. The miniature edition of herself stood there staring out the window, lost in thought. Her resemblance to Constance was striking—even to the pain etched on the child's face.

"Mommy, do you think Father really loves me?"

"How could he help it, dear?"

"Mommy! You're not answering my question!" Serious eyes peered out, framed by long, golden hair.

"Well, I *think* he does—in his own way."

Beth sighed, "'In his own way' somehow doesn't make me feel very loved."

"Doesn't *my* love count?"

Leaping up from the armchair and giving her a strangling hug, Beth exclaimed, "Of course! You know it does! It's . . . it's . . . just that I want my . . . uh . . . father to love me too. Well, not Father—what I *really* want is a daddy. Someone who will laugh with me, joke with me; I can muss his hair, sit on his lap, listen to him read stories to me. And somebody who won't go away, but will stay with us *always*.

"Oh, Mommy, I didn't mean to make you sad. Don't cry!"

"It's all right, precious; it's just that I too wish things were . . . uh . . . different."

"When do I see Father?"

"In two weeks. He's gone to Switzerland."

"But he *knew* I'd be here today. He sent our tickets. He got us this room in this hotel that I love," she said as she clambered onto the chair by the window, "where I can see that beautiful bridge."

"I know, dear. Yes, he knew. I suppose something came up."

"With Father, something's *always* coming up."

"Well, dear, at least you and I can have fun together."

"But what are we going to *do?*"

And that was the quandary. She'd been afraid this would happen—again. Ah, what forces she had set in motion twelve years before—back when she had thought beauty meant happiness. Every beauty pageant she'd ever entered, she'd won—even the one at Northern Arizona University in snowy Flagstaff.

And how excited she'd been when *he* had noticed her. He was the buzz of campus—a real live earl and said to be filthy rich. Good-looking too! Came out here to see the "Old West!" Even wore cowboy boots and a Stetson.

And then when it had gotten serious, she'd been too star-struck to delve beneath the surface. Just think. As a countess, she'd be addressed as "Right Honorable" and "My Lady." Her eldest son would be called a viscount while his father lived; her other sons would be lords and her daughters, ladies. Oh, it was just too exciting!

But when Robert flew her to England to meet his widowed mother, she experienced her first reservations. Lavish apartments in London, a visit to the Castle in Scotland, parties, balls, and formal dinners. Robert's mother was rather cold to her, and Constance once overheard her saying to her son, "A pretty little thing, but not much in the way of family connections. If she had money, that would be some comfort at least, but she doesn't even have *that!*"

Constance fled to her room in tears. Robert followed, assuring her that nothing else mattered but the two of them. Surely if they loved each other, "Mum" would come around.

So they married; she became a countess and was soon almost giddy with the whirlwind of parties and socializing. Robert seemed proud of her; and her beauty, coupled with her title, opened all doors to her.

Then a child was born to them—a girl, much to Robert's disgust. In fact, he didn't seem to even want the baby around him. When Constance refused to turn her baby girl over to a nanny, that was the last straw. Robert stormed out of their bedchamber and, for all practical purposes, out of her life. "Mum" did not come around either. More and more Robert stayed at the club, or in his London bachelor's flat. She rarely knew where he was. It might be Monte Carlo (his crowd loved to gamble); he might be away on business; he might be at a polo match, horseracing, or chasing foxes. He might be anywhere in the world but home with her. *Home?* What a laugh! She had no home. Neither did little Beth. All that was bad enough, but then came the tabloid photos of Robert with one woman after another—but never with her.

Finally, when she could handle no more of his public mockery of their marriage, she applied for divorce. Instead of its bringing him to his senses, he encouraged it. Once final, he gave her a generous settlement and suggested she move back to America with "Elizabeth" (he never called her "Beth"). Within six months, he was married again, this time to an old-time family friend, one who reveled in high society and was, not coincidentally, the daughter of a lord. Within five years, two sons came to them. As for his daughter, he condescended to see her only once a year. And his new wife made it clear that the little girl was to come and go quickly. Her sons would inherit most of the estate and assets. Getting the message, her stepbrothers were cool to Beth as well.

Only after the fact did Constance realize another thing she'd lost—her relationship with God. There had been no place for God in the whirlwind of pleasure eddying around her and Robert. And without God to anchor in, the marriage so full of promise at the start, instead self-destructed.

So, deeply wounded, she took Beth and moved back to America, to old Santa Fe, where she finished college and did internships in rare books, art, and antiques prior to establishing her own business. And she and Beth sought out God.

Still lovely, Constance was besieged by suitors, but she didn't dare get close to any of them. She no longer trusted her judgment where men were concerned. Besides, there was little Beth—she must not put her at risk again.

Suddenly she became aware that night had fallen; the lights on Tower Bridge had come on; Beth had fallen asleep; and she was alone with her thoughts. *Alone.* More and more in recent months she had felt that aloneness—a sense that half of her was missing. At night, the bed was big and there was no one to cuddle up to, to put his arms around her, to talk with her, to laugh with her, to love her. And Beth needed more than just a father. As she'd just made abundantly clear: she needed—*desperately* needed—a daddy. She was such an adorable, precocious seven-year-old. She read on the fifth-grade level (and read omnivorously). Worldly wise beyond her years, this child was yet innocent, idealistic, and intensely loving.

O God, she prayed, *You see what a mess I've made of my life. But You also know how sorry I am! I know I don't deserve Your help, but I'm so lonely, Lord. Is there somewhere my soul's other half? Is there someone out there who'd be my soul mate, and who loves You as much as I do? Who would unconditionally love Beth too? I know You've got far more important things to do than bail out a foolish woman, but, O Lord,* please *find him for me.*

For some time she just sat there in silence, her brain in neutral. Softly she rose and walked toward the window. Inadvertently she bumped the dresser, and something fell behind it. *Oh no, not my passport!* But it was. Very carefully, so as not to wake Beth, she slowly pulled the dresser away from the wall, reached behind, and found—not just her passport, but something else—a leather case!

That woke Beth. "Mommy, what are you doing?" she asked sleepily.

Constance turned on several lamps and sat down on the bed. "Come over here, dear, and let's find out what's in this thing."

It was indeed a case—slim and of high-grade leather. Some other occupant of Room 507 must have bumped this same dresser, with the same results. Only that person left without noticing that the case was missing. Then, later, upon discovering its loss, would not have known where he'd left it. At least she assumed the owner was a he: The case looked masculine.

"Open it up, Mommy!" demanded Beth.

She did, and inside was—"Well, what do you know!" she exclaimed. "A journal!"

"What's *that?*" asked Beth.

"Oh, it's a diary . . . just like yours and just like mine."

"Oh goody! Let's read it!"

"Do you really think we ought to?" she responded doubtfully.

"Of *course!* How else will we find out who it belongs to?" the little girl answered. "Besides, you *know* you're going to snoop—you always do. And you know *I'm* going to snoop—I always do. So we might as well snoop together!"

So, chuckling at their inability to resist snooping, they fluffed up their pillows and settled down to read.

"Read it out loud!" ordered Beth. So she did.

JOURNAL OF WILLIAM HARRISON

"It's a man. I knew it would be," interrupted Beth.

DAY ONE

On Board British Airways, Denver to London

"Oh goody! He's from Denver. We've been there."

"Perhaps, dear. He may be from somewhere else."

I don't really know what it is that I'm fleeing from or what I'm expecting to find in Old England. I only know that a Higher Power willed it.

Nights have been long in recent days, weeks, and months. I've had such a hard time getting to sleep. It has been almost six years since that terrible July night when a truck driver veered across the median and smashed into our Lexus, killing my lovely Julia almost instantly. Oh he was contrite, that truck driver was, and admitted to the police that he'd skipped several mandatory rest stops . . . and had fallen asleep at the wheel. But his being sorry couldn't bring my beloved Julia back.

"How sad! The poor man!" said Beth, sighing.

Constance continued reading.

At first, the pain of losing her was so intense, it blotted out time and reality. It was like a nightmarish movie that never got to its screen credits at the end—because there was no end. Because this was real, not mere fiction. Time after time, I'd reach for her in the night, only to find

*once more that she was not there, would never be there again. That I was
alone in the midst of my life journey. Alone at 33.*

"Thirty-three what, Mommy?"

"Thirty-three years old, dear."

"Oh."

*Toward the end of the second year, the anguish began to diminish. If
it hadn't, it would have killed me. Early that October, as Bob (what
would I have done without close friends like him?) and I were hiking in
the Grand Tetons, it came to me that my mind and body were finally
un-numbing, coming back to an awareness of life, of its beauty. The
singing and cascading creek, joyfully leapfrogging its way down to the
Snake River.*

"Is the Snake River in Colorado?"

"No, dear. He was hiking in Wyoming. Maybe we'll find out if he
lives there."

*The always curious, hyper, and scolding squirrels, never silent or still
if they could help it. The ubiquitous magpies that would follow us all the
way, demanding handouts. . . ."*

"Stop, Mommy. What's . . . uh, u-biqui—"

"'Ubiquitous,' darling, means that they're *everywhere.* You
remember those big black and white birds, don't you?"

"Oh, yes—they're such pests! One even ate out of my hand. Felt
funny!" she giggled.

The wind . . . soughing in the pines . . . brought me my first peace.

"What's soughing?"

"You know, dear; don't you remember how you love to hear the
pines whispering in the wind?"

"Oh, yes! Sometimes it sounds like a waterfall—a *long* ways off!"

"Well put, my dear. You may grow up to be a writer someday."

"Mommy, I like the way he writes. Wonder if *he* writes books?"

"Could be, dear."

*I turned to my hiking companion and said, "Bob, I've just had an
epiphany."*

Stolid, unimaginative Bob muttered, "Had a what?"

"An epiphany."

"What's that?"

Beth chortled: "Oh, that's funny! He's old, and he doesn't know what big words mean either!"

Her mother smiled and continued reading.

"Oh, sorry. It's . . . uh . . . a sudden realization of a great truth, an unexpected insight into life."

"Oh?"

"Yes. . . . I just realized that my life is not over. That it will go on . . . and that there's still beauty all around me. And joy. And that I've wasted far too much time already. It's time to begin writing again too."

"I *knew* it!

"I suspected it, too, dear."

"'Bout time," agreed Bob, always stingy with words.

Beth's laugh sounded like tinkling chimes in a soft wind.

It was indeed 'bout time, but Scripture reminds us that there's a time for everything.

But in life, the price of skipping a stage is a delayed time-bomb later on, so I had to work through grief in order to be able to re-enter life, to become productive again.

It would have helped had we been blessed with children. Julia had longed for a boy, I for a girl. But it was not to be. Just a week before that wreck, for the first time we had discussed the possibility of adoption. Oh, the seraphic look on her dear face when I agreed to initiate the long process of adopting a child. We hadn't yet decided whether the first would be a boy or a girl—but we did want both eventually.

But we had no child as yet, so I endured my grief alone—and longer than was good for me. But now, at long last, I came out into the blinding light at the end of the serpentine tunnel. Out to life.

"Mommy, stop! . . . I want to think before you go on. He says so much in a few words that my mind gets too full."

"I know what you mean, dear."

"Let me think, and don't rush me. . . . Oh, now I know what I want to say. He *loved* her, didn't he?"

"Yes, dear."

"And he would have loved a little girl (if he'd adopted her) almost . . . as much."

"Just as much, darling."

"More than Father loves me?"

"Oh, honey!" Constance took Beth into her arms—she just couldn't bear to admit the cruel answer out loud. Instead, she returned to the journal.

"Let's see, where was I? Oh yes, there's extra space here—it means time has passed, and it's now later than it was."

In time, much healing has come. And happiness. I've found both in hard work, in getting my mind off of self, and in focusing on others instead. God has been good—has respected my space. Has picked up His end of the phone when I've called. For a long time I called Him only once in a while; then it was oftener and oftener. Now, we never hang up at all.

"What does he mean, Mommy?"

"He means, dear, that God is always in his heart, his thoughts, so he talks to Him all the time now."

"Like we do with each other?"

"Yes, like that."

"Oh."

Lately, I've been asking God if it's His will that I remain alone the rest of my life. I'm still young, could still be a husband again—a dad. But it scares me to think about going through the relationship meatgrinder again.

"Huh? Is he trying to be funny?"

Constance laughed, as she hadn't in months. Finally, wiping her eyes, she chuckled, "He means, dear, that courtship is tough work, and it's easy to get sort of chopped up by the other person."

"Like Father chopped *you* up?" . . . Then, taking a look at her mother's blanched, pain-ridden face, she rose on her knees and hugged her, murmuring, "I didn't mean to hurt you, Mommy! Forgive me?"

"Of course, dear . . . but it hurts because you're right. There have indeed been times when I, too, felt more than a little chopped up. Now, let me read on."

I look around me, and almost no relationship seems to last very long anymore. In fact, most people my age don't value the institution of marriage.

Constance, realizing that this section was too deep for her child, and that Beth was already drifting off to sleep again, tenderly tucked the spread under her chin, kissed her on the forehead, and returned to the journal, determined to get beyond this section before she read anymore aloud.

. . . it's all downhill from there, nothing more to look forward to. It's only, "I wonder how long we'll be able to stand each other?"

And the ones who do marry don't take it very seriously. First bump, and they're "outa here." Oh, of course there are many who miraculously make it through somehow. But, if they do, it's no thanks to cinema, TV, or the print media. Where are our children to find traditional role models? Where are they going to see portrayed decent men and women who really believe promises such as "Until death do us part"? Rarely do such people appear on either the big or the small screen anymore. When they do, they are mocked, they are ridiculed. That really scares me. How does one dare to bring up a child in such a dissolute age?

This was the end of that day's entry. Constance closed the journal, put on her nightgown, slipped into the bed closest to the window, and looked out at the Tower Bridge, ablaze with lights, her thoughts tumbling like clothes in a dryer.

❊ ❊ ❊

Two hours later, and she was still wide awake. Jet lag—and this unknown voice in the journal—precluded sleep. Finally she gave up, turned on her small bedside reading light, and reached for the journal.

DAY TWO

Still on Board Brit. Air to London

Left Jackson Hole early yesterday morning, drove all day, and boarded this great plane early last evening in Denver. And is it ever full! Furthermore, there are more babies and kids per capita than I've ever seen on a plane. What a night it has been! Rarely did silence last more than minutes. Almost continually, babies whimpered, sobbed, cried, or screamed.

Just across the aisle from me are two young British families. Two brothers. They've been skiing in Colorado. One of them has a toddler (year and a half to two years old) who has been out of control for hours at a time. Screams so loudly he periodically turns scarlet and gags. The parents strap him into a car seat attached to a pull-down platform, and then just sit there, blithely ignoring the continual screaming. They don't touch him, take him into their arms, speak to him, or address whatever the problem is.

Finally, absolutely exhausted, landed at Gatwick International Airport. Took a while to get through customs and pick up my luggage. Then boarded the express shuttle to London.

THISTLE TOWER HOTEL

Wasn't able to write in the shuttle, but now I'm all checked in at this beautiful hotel on the river Thames. Outside my window is the majestic Tower Bridge. A few hundred feet from the hotel is a piece of history I've heard about and read about all my life—the ancient Tower of London. It all seems like a dream: I keep thinking, this can't be real!

I still don't know why God sent me on this trip, but I'm convinced it was for a reason. My part, as I see it, is to follow my itinerary and chronicle my reactions. I've read that unless one immediately writes down one's travel-related observations, they are lost.

So, before they become hazy, I'll write down my first impressions of this, America's mother country. First, I can't get over driving on the wrong side of the road. Gives me the heebie-jeebies! All these thousands of vehicles constricting these narrow lanes crowd each other in a continual game of chicken. Yet no one seems angry or succumbs to road rage like we see in America. Time and time again, I saw drivers brake to a quick stop and wave another driver into the traffic flow. And motorcyclists jauntily speed along between the opposing streams of traffic!

It is cold and drizzly, and the land looks green and damp—everything looks mossy. Instead of fences, hedgerows on property lines. Lots of birds. Here and there Beatrix Potter-type houses, and large country estates. Lots of busses, small trucks, and cars; very few SUVs, probably because petrol costs about five dollars a gallon! Stoplights the reverse of ours: red, yellow, then green. Houses and businesses are smaller than I'm used to, with precious little space separating them. Taxis everywhere, but small and charcoal-colored rather than yellow. Signs point to places sounding strangely familiar: Heathrow Airport, Wimbledon, Arundel.

As congestion increased I sensed we were moving into London proper, the heart of the British Commonwealth. Again, I was impressed with the quietness—no blaring of horns, and rarely did I hear sirens. Then came the Houses of Parliament and that most familiar of sights, Big Ben. Oh, *and that upstart: the London Eye, a Ferris wheel towering over four hundred feet into the skyline, on the banks of the Thames. They say it takes forty minutes to make one rotation. A wildly popular tourist attraction with the best view in London.*

Sense impressions came at me from all directions, and faster than I could assimilate them. The old and the new, the past and the present, coexist side by side. The streets are narrow and crooked, which is only to be expected as most were constructed hundreds and hundreds of years ago.

And at last the Thistle Hotel, 650 rooms overlooking the Thames and St. Catherine's Marina. Checked in, then up to room 507. Outside, dead center out my window, is the Tower Bridge, new by London terms (built late in the 1800s). Upriver just a little is moored a great British warship, vintage World War II. And outside is the unceasing flow of the London anthill.

Sleep deprivation catches up with me at last, so I crawl in.

Sleep deprivation was getting to Constance too. She scanned the next few pages, put down the journal, turned off the light, and drifted off into dreams.

❊　　❊　　❊

Constance was awakened by soft arms around her neck, kisses, and importuning: "Wake up, Mommy, wake up!"

Stretching languorously, her mother sleepily retorted, "What on earth for?"

"The journal! I want to see what comes next. You didn't . . . you didn't? You *did*, read on after I went to sleep! Shame, shame, shame on you!"

"Yes, dear, but just a little—the philosophical part. I stopped when I came to the part I knew you'd like. Apparently Mr. Harrison went to see an interesting place in London each day he was here. What do you say that each morning we read about his experiences there, and then go follow him and see if we agree with what he wrote. Wouldn't that be fun?"

"Yes! Let's."

"All right. As soon as we get back from breakfast, we'll begin."

DAY THREE
The Tube and the Double-Decker

"I know! Let's pretend we're tourists too—never been in London before."

"And see if we can learn something new?" added her mother.

"Right!"

Slept late as rain still falling. Breakfast at hotel's second-floor Tower Restaurant. Around the circular walls are pictures of famous and infamous historical residents of the Tower of London.

"What are . . . in–famous people?" asked Beth, wrinkling her forehead.

"They are famous people that were bad.

"Oh."

But most are admired people who didn't deserve to die by the axe. People such as the ill-fated wives of Henry VIII, Sir Walter Raleigh, etc. I look forward to seeing the Tower later on during my visit.

But I dedicated today to learning how to get around this vast city. Walked several hours before I finally found out how to get a week's ticket on the Tube. Then descended deep into the bowels of the earth . . .

"He's funny," giggled Beth.

. . . and boarded the subway, the system of travel that keeps London alive. Stops are close together, so there's no need to take surface transportation. Inside the cars, people are polite to each other. They read, they speak in low tones; some sit, some stand. Quite a polyglot mixture of nationalities.

"Polyglot?"

"It means *many* nationalities, dear."

Lots of women in London's workforce, and lots of tourists, even in off-season. Brits call this process "tubing."

After surfacing, couldn't help noticing the sheer size of the crowds flooding the city like so many rushing ants. And they're all in such a hurry to get somewhere! Even though I walk at a rather fast pace (faster than the average in the U.S.), they pass me half again as fast. Brits hurry everywhere! Not surprisingly, according to a London newspaper I read this morning, 80 percent of Brits suffer from extreme stress. Many physical breakdowns because of it.

Of what value is a life, I wonder, that is torqued up to such a frantic pace that there's no time to think or dream; no time to nurture, to make deep friendships, to grow in love, to draw ever closer to God?

No time.

"What's nurture? I kind of think I know what it means, but I'm not sure."

"Well, it means to nourish or take care of something or someone. It also means to help raise a child, like I'm trying to do with you, dear."

Boarded "Big Bus" after I learned how to use the Tube. Being it was bitterly cold, stayed on the lower level. Got a kick out of the guides. Each thinks he's (or she's) a stand-up comedian. The first one really knew his stuff. There wasn't a thing we went by that he couldn't identify. Had a wicked sense of humor—and his favorite targets were the Royal Family and the Prime Minister. Right now the Prime Minister is really getting it for his reversal on family values and his waffling on fox hunting. He came into office trumpeting the need for strong marriages and families, but so many of his associates now have failed marriages that they've all caved in on the issue. And the gentry are really furious at him for telling them they shouldn't run poor foxes to death with their horses, dogs, and guns.

It's an interesting system: their most powerful leader is not even chosen by the people, but by party leaders. So when the people get fed up enough, they throw everyone out of office at once!

And I'm intrigued by their terms: "bonnet" for car hood, "bloke" for "man," "to let" for "to rent," "lift" for "elevator," and (my favorite) "spend-a-penny" for the "street-side john."

Beth covered her mouth in her failure to keep from laughing.

And now it's night again, and I sit by my window staring out at that dream-like bridge. It's getting to me. It's magical.

❀　　❀　　❀

"Well, honey, did he get it right?"

"Oooh! I'm tired. But he was right. People *are* polite to each other, politer than at home. And they do hurry. Remember when I tried to keep up with one woman? I had to *run!*"

"Yes, I agree. And he was right about the bus guides too. It was so funny to see our guide swing out of the bus like Tarzan on a vine on the way to 'spend-a-penny.'"

DAY FOUR

Kensington Palace

It was a new day in London, and the skies were cloudy. After breakfast, Constance opened the journal and began reading.

Breakfast in the Tower Restaurant. Really full today as several bus loads of tourists came in last night. Food good, as always.

Took the Tube to Kensington Palace. In summer they say Kensington Gardens are one of the beauty spots of the city, but you wouldn't know it this time of year. Wind cut like a knife.

William and Mary lived in this palace. But as I walked through the vast rooms, it was hard for me to conceive of anyone actually living here (so large, so formal, so ornate, and then so full of staff, courtiers, and visitors). When could rulers who lived here have been themselves? When (and where) could they have spent time with their mates, their children?

Beth mused, almost as if talking to herself, "I feel the same way about Father's castle. Even where he lives in London. It's not comfy, but . . . uh . . . sort of like being in a museum."

Saw the Princess Di clothing collection. Beautiful dresses! After her breakup with Prince Charles, Di and her two sons lived on the other side of Kensington Palace. I felt sorry for her, for it was quipped that Charles was the only man in the world not in love with her. The idol of the world, but not of her own husband!

Can never forget getting up in the wee hours of the morning to see the wedding spectacular on television. The whole world watched that fairy tale unfold. But even then, Charles had to be prompted to show her any affection.

I wonder if he's really capable of love. Never will I forget the story of the little Charles who ran towards his mother, after she and his father had been on a round-the-world cruise on the royal ship, "Britannia" — been gone half a year. Half a year to a child is forever! So he ran into her arms. Well, not quite. She stopped his rush by sticking out her right hand for a handshake! How could a child who was treated so coldly by his own mother be capable of real love with wife and children?

"That's the way Father is with me," mused Beth. "Sort of cold. It hurts. He doesn't even smile at me most of the time. Makes me afraid of him. Doesn't act like he loves me at all."

Constance remained mute.

And many Brits send their boys off to all-male boarding schools in order to "toughen them up." Thus they grow up without the softening influence of their mothers.

Several months ago I saw a group of British tourists in Jackson Hole. I was curious enough to strike up a conversation with them.

*Apparently they had all left their wives and children back in England,
preferring to share their holidays with old schoolmates instead.*

Something's not quite right here.

Constance stopped reading and put the journal down, a pensive
look on her face. "He's right, Beth. When a man's wife and children
take second place to the schoolmates of his youth, something is most
definitely wrong!"

*I find myself fascinated by British newspapers. They reflect a
worldview that is decidedly continental. America's not mentioned much,
and rarely in a complimentary fashion. Not that I blame them—we
export so much of the seamy side of life.*

❖   ❖   ❖

*It's one o'clock in the morning, and I can't sleep. So I look out the
window at that glorious Tower Bridge, all lit up like a Christmas tree.
I see the deep purple streaked with silver and gold of the river, the people
still walking under umbrellas on the banks and on the bridge, the
ghostly headlights of cars, trucks, and busses. Where are they all going?*

*I'm lonely. Oh, how I wish I had someone to share all this beauty with.
Someone to talk with, commune with, to be my other half, to love.*

❖   ❖   ❖

Upon their return from Kensington Palace, again there was only
silence, each sitting there by the window, each harboring thoughts
that were too heavy to ride the flimsy rails of speech.

DAY FIVE

St. Paul's Cathedral

Uncharacteristically somber after a restless night, mother and
daughter wondered what the writer would have to say on this day.

*I've picked up quite a collection of books and pamphlets about places
I plan to see. By reading them ahead of time, I'll be able to fill in gaps
history-wise or correct misperceptions ahead of time.*

*St. Paul's. All my life I've wanted to see it, experience it. Once, in a
history class, a teacher showed us some World War II newsreels. Never
will I forget the voice of Edward R. Murrow, the sounds of anti-aircraft
guns, the wailing sirens, the bombs exploding—and searchlights
spearing the night. And, invariably, somewhere in the newsreel, there
would be the dome of St. Paul's. And to contemporaries who watched*

those newsreels, as long as St. Paul's was still there, England was still there—and not yet did Hitler rule the world.

"Who's Hitler, Mommy?"

"A very bad man, dear, who was responsible for the death of millions of innocent people."

"Oh."

Outside St. Paul's—and the pigeons were still there! It's funny, what did I think of as I looked up at that imposing façade and long flight of steps? A freckle-faced little boy and a pixyish little girl, pigeons, and "Let's go fly a kite."

"Mary Poppins! He's talking about Mary Poppins, Mommy!"

Mary Poppins comes back to me, a film I've seen over and over.

Inside St. Paul's, its immensity staggers. The only comparable cathedral dome in the world is St. Peter's in Rome.

Constance read on as Harrison told the long, tumultuous history of the cathedral, with antecedents all the way back to 604 A.D. Again and again it had been destroyed or ravaged—by fires, by Vikings, by the soldiers of Oliver Cromwell's Commonwealth, and by the Great Fire of London in 1666. Today's St. Paul's was designed by the legendary architect Sir Christopher Wren immediately after that fire.

These walls have seen the funerals of Admiral Horatio Nelson, the Duke of Wellington, and Winston Churchill; the marriage of Charles and Diana and the celebrations of Queen Victoria's Diamond Jubilee and Queen Elizabeth II's Silver Jubilee. Handel and Mendelssohn played on this great organ.

When I finally walked out of the cathedral it was with a feeling that one of the missing pieces of my life had been found.

Later that evening, Beth pensively observed, "I wish . . ."

"I wish *what,* dear?" tenderly prompted her mother.

"I wish—we could have seen Mr. Harrison when he stood there looking at the pigeons . . . but thinking of Mary Poppins."

DAY SIX

The British Museum

Beth grimaced when her mother read the heading. Not another museum! But perhaps he would somehow make it sound interesting. After quite a bit of history, which Beth found beyond her, came these words:

Couldn't help noticing all the children. Led by their teachers, boys and girls lay on the floor and on benches, leaned against tombs, gazed into glass cases, made relief drawings, took copious notes, listened to lectures. To them the great museum was one vast schoolroom — it was history come alive. How I wish I had a child of my own. How wonderful it would be to bring her here and share these treasures with her!

Unnoticed by her reading mother, a tear trickled down Beth's cheek.

What was most significant of all to me? Undoubtedly that it reaffirmed one's faith in the Bible. For centuries skeptics discounted the Bible, maintaining that much of it was but myth, that many of the nations appearing in its pages never existed at all. The Hittites for instance — no record of such a people! Yet here in this museum is archeological proof of the Hittite Empire.

As for Assyria, dominating its section of the museum are massive human-headed winged bulls (heavy enough to sink a ship). It suddenly hit me, as I stared at them, that Jonah must have seen, and perhaps even touched, these (or ones like them) as he walked up and down the broad streets of Nineveh, declaring, "In only forty days, this great city will be destroyed!"

"The Jonah that was swallowed by a whale?" asked Beth, wide-eyed.

"The very same, dear."

"Wow!"

But the Museum's Holy Grail is the Rosetta Stone.

"What's the Holy Grail?"

"It's a very sacred object associated with our Lord that Knights of the Round Table (according to tradition) longed to find. Would give their very lives to find."

Few in this throng knew enough history to seek it out — even some of the guards didn't seem to know about it. Finally, I found it, calmly blending in with the rest of antiquity in a simple glass case. Hard to believe that this small stone with three kinds of writing on it could be one of the most valuable things on this planet. That up to its discovery in 1799, no one had a clue as to understanding the two languages of ancient Egypt (hieroglyphics and demotic). But here on this stone was one text, in hieroglyphics, demotic, and ancient Greek. With Greek as a key, repeated in this stone, scholars have now unlocked the entire history and culture of ancient times.

Beth asked plaintively, "When we get there, you'll show it to me and explain?"

"Yes, dear."

But the artifact I searched for the longest you had to know by name and ask over and over where it could be found. Suddenly, there it was — the two-thousand-year-old Portland Vase, only 9 1/2 inches tall, but one of the world's most precious works of art, the inspiration for Josiah Wedgwood's great line of Greek-inspired china, pottery, and crockery. The single most famous cameo-glass vessel to have survived from ancient times.

"You have a cameo pin, don't you, Mommy?"

"Yes, I do. And we both love it."

The base is deep cobalt blue, and the cameo glass applied to it depicts mythological love and marriage. The artistic detail is so exquisite it takes your breath away. Perhaps the Apostle Paul may have seen this vase in his travels.

The vase has been on display since 1810, and thousands have thronged to see it from all over the world. One of those who drank in its beauty and miraculous preservation was the English poet John Keats, who in his famous "Ode on a Grecian Urn," concluded with these words:

> When old age shall this generation waste,
> Thou shalt remain, in midst of other woe
> Than ours, a friend to man, to whom thou sayest,
> 'Beauty is truth, truth beauty'—that is all
> Ye know on earth, and all ye need to know.

Only months later the short, tragic story of Keats' life was over.

I have seen so much this day, my mind is a blur. Felt like a time-traveler swept thousands of years into the past. Each of these artifacts was touched, molded, caressed, admired by men, women, and children in other times—as alive once as I am today. Today telescoped Time in my mind.

I shall come back to this place.

This time it was the mother who spoke first. "He knows a lot, doesn't he? History, literature, architecture, art . . ."

"A *lot?* He seems to know everything! . . . How lucky she'll be."

"Who, dear?"

"His little girl—when he gets her."

❊   ❊   ❊

"Well, it was quite a day, wasn't it?"

"Yes, Mommy . . . but my feet hurt!"

"Mine too."

"But, you know what? I think I learned a lot today . . . a lot more than I'd have learned . . . uh . . ."

"If we hadn't had the journal?"

"Yes."

DAY SEVEN
The Tower of London

"Where do we go today, Mommy?"

"Right next door—the Tower of London."

"Good. 'Cuz my feet are worn out."

A stunningly beautiful blue-sky day it has been! Perfect for taking in the ancient Tower of London. Even though it isn't tourist season, it was crowded. Hard to imagine that those walls date clear back to William the Conqueror in 1066. It has been everything: royal palace, fortress, prison, place of execution, arsenal, royal mint, menagerie, and repository of the Crown Jewels.

The Yeoman Warders (Beefeaters) who herd visitors through the castle are extremely good at what they do—which is to bring history alive. Had always assumed that the Tower (called the "White Tower") was complete in itself, not that it was the center portion of the strongest castle in England.

Like most visitors, what I most wanted to see was the Crown Jewels. But couldn't help thinking as I gazed at all those diamonds, emeralds, rubies, pearls, and gold that even those do not guarantee happiness, but rather the reverse. According to an old aphorism, "Uneasy is the head that wears a crown."

"What's that?"

"An aphorism? Oh, it's a quotation, a folk saying."

Saw room after room chock full of history, but what moved me most were the people who lived and died within those walls. So many famous people died here, had their heads chopped off in the courtyard. A number of queens: Anne Boleyn, Catherine Howard, Lady Jane Grey. Martyrs such as Sir Thomas More and Bishop John Fisher. Royal favorites such as Robert Devereux and Sir Walter Raleigh. Spent quite a bit of time in the two rooms in the Bloody Tower where Raleigh spent so many years of his life (13 years just during his longest incarceration there).

As I looked out into the courtyard at the same view Raleigh saw every time he looked out the window, again there came to me a sense of the past elastically tied to the present. All my life I've been reading biography, history, and historical fiction in which the Tower of London plays a key role . . . "and he was taken off to the Tower" was a common way of saying he would soon be dead. But only after seeing the actual castle (virtually impregnable) does fact validate fiction in my mind.

I feel very subdued and melancholy this night as I stare out at the bridge named after the Tower of London. It has not been a particularly happy day, yet in another respect, it has been one of the most informative and insightful days of my life.

❆   ❆   ❆

"Well, what do you think?"

"My feet are just as tired as yesterday."

"Is that all?"

"You mean, did I like it? Yes. . . . And did he tell the story true? Yes. He made me think."

"How, dear?"

"Well, that crowns don't make you happy. And all the crowns in the world couldn't make up for being locked up so many years—like poor Raleigh was."

DAY EIGHT

Westminster Abbey

"So, where to today, Mommy?"

"Let's see . . . Westminster Abbey."

There's so much more I want to see in London, but time precludes that. However, I've saved one day—and all of it is going to be devoted to the single most important historic building in Great Britain—Westminster Abbey.

It was here that then Princess Elizabeth married Prince Philip (in 1947); it was here that she was crowned Elizabeth II; and it was here that the whole world watched and sobbed as the beautiful Diana, Princess of Wales, finally found peace.

"I remember, Mommy. It was *so* sad! Remember, we both cried.

"I'll *always* remember, dear."

Westminster Abbey dates back over a thousand years to 950-960. A hundred years later, King Edward the Confessor decided to make Westminster the focal center of the kingdom. When William, Duke of Normandy, defeated Harold at the Battle of Hastings in 1066, the English monarchy became French. William was crowned in Westminster Abbey.

As an historian of ideas, I'm fascinated by periods. Future historians, looking back at our time, will no doubt classify the twentieth century as the Age of Skyscrapers (or computers, of course). But the first millennium spawned the Great Age of Faith during which Europe's soaring Gothic cathedrals were built. They started in France, spread across the channel to England, then to Spain and all across Europe, reaching their peak during the years 1100-1400. I'm amazed at how it all seemed to happen at once. What made those great perpendicular Gothic cathedrals possible was a simple wall-supporting device called the "flying buttress." Thanks to it, cathedrals could leap 100-150 feet into the sky, and walls could be mostly glass.

God was preeminent in the lives of Europeans then; the Crusades certainly proved that. Life expectancy was low; disease wiped out most of those who became ill; chances were that most women would die of childbirth complications; and wars were frequent. In such a world of uncertainty, God was the only constant, thus the yearnings of the people were reflected in their Gothic cathedrals, each a community effort. Westminster, Salisbury, Coventry, Rheims, Chartres, Notre Dame, Cologne, Toledo, Barcelona, and so many more, all were born during this brief period of spiritual rebirth. To my way of thinking, mankind has never created a more beautiful type of structure. And look—almost a thousand years later, most are still standing! Before I die, I'd like to worship in each one.

Westminster is a queen among them. What must it have been in its glory days, before the depredations of Henry II and Oliver Cromwell's marauding troops? John Field, in his Kingdom, Power, and Glory *(London: James & James, 1996/1999, 147), observes that:*

> *"So here it stands, this close-packed chaos of beautiful things and worthless vulgar things, after more than a thousand years of tumultuous history. It has somehow resisted the despoiling of two religious revolutions, fire, neglect, vandalism, riots, air*

raids, Westminster schoolboys, eighteenth century funerals, tomb-rifling, tourists, sea-coal, industrial pollution, traffic. Simply contemplating its miraculous survival nurtures faith."

Though today it is ecumenically all things to all people, yet the great Abbey's purpose—Christian witness—remains. The stabilizing and reassuring rhythms of a thousand years remain with us still. Matins at 7:30, Eucharist at 8:00, Evensong at 5:30. Unchanging.

"Like a great ocean liner built on Thorney Island but never launched, in each age it gathers souls and harbours them, and bears them silently on, not through space, but through time" (*Field, 154*).

❈   ❈   ❈

All my life I'd heard of "Evensong," and now I was going to experience it. Outside the great Abbey the cacophony . . ."

"What's that, Mommy?"

"'Cacophony?' Oh, it means so many sounds at once you can't think. And they are often sounds that grate on your ear and nerves."

Laughing, Beth agreed: "I think that's a good word."

. . . the cacophony created by seven million people forever on the move; inside, the serenity of a church built for the ages. Only those wishing to worship were permitted inside the gates during the services.

Once inside the Northwest Tower, I just stood there transfixed as I looked up, up, and up at the great Gothic columns and through the iridescent stained-glass windows. The deep-toned bells were ringing, summoning the faithful, the restless, the weary, the despondent, the heartsick, to drop whatever they were doing and seek quietude.

I softly walked down the main aisle, found a chair between the quire and the sacrarium, then looked up and out through the rainbowish north and south transept windows and listened to the bells.

Then we heard it, the Choir of Westminster, solemnly led by beautifully attired vergers holding aloft the symbolic verges; the choir (composed of both boys and men) was singing all the while, accompanied by the great Westminster organ. I shivered. So it must have been in Solomon's Temple—how could one not be reverent in such a setting?

Our program began with these words:

"Welcome to this service. You are sharing in a tradition of worship that has been offered since 1065 when the Abbey was

founded by St. Edward the Confessor. You are joining people from all over the world. Whatever your faith and belief, especially if you have little or none, we warmly invite you to take part as you can.

"Much of the service is sung by the Choir alone. You worship chiefly by listening, meditating, praying, and letting the music and words take your minds and souls into God's presence. Please join in the hymns and in those parts of the service printed in bold type."

The service proceeded, with lessons from Genesis and Romans, followed by Timothy Dudley-Smith's nativity hymn that deeply moved me, perhaps due to the fact that so many young voices were singing words such as these:

"Child of the stable's secret birth,
the Lord by right of the lords of earth,
let angels sing of a king new-born
the world's weaving a crown of thorn:
a crown of thorn for that infant head
cradled soft in the manger bed.
Eyes that shine in the lantern's ray;
a face so small in its nest of hay,
face of a child who is born to scan
the world of men through the eyes of man;
and from that face in the final day,
earth and heaven shall flee away. . . .
Infant hands in a mother's hand
for none but Mary can understand
whose are the hands and the fingers curled
but his who fashioned and made our world:
and through these hands in the hour of death
nails shall strike to the wood beneath. . . ."

After the vergers had led the choir and clergy out, the organist let out his stops, and the organ shook the very foundation of the Abbey. When he finished, echoes reverberated against wall after wall, and on into infinity.

❀   ❀   ❀

Then I got up and studied the rest of the cathedral. Canon N. T. Wright was kind enough to lead me to Poet's Corner where the likes of Chaucer, Shakespeare, Dickens, Herrick, and Houseman are immortalized.

Much later I made my way out into the sunset, so overloaded with sensory impressions and undealt-with thoughts that I almost felt I was in a trance.

❅   ❅   ❅

"Well, honey?"

"Oh Mommy, this was the best day yet! He was right in all he said about the Abbey. I—I just wish I had the right words to say what's in my heart. It's so *full!*"

"I know, dear. So is mine."

"But, of everything I've ever seen in my life, I think I like Evensong best. . . . Can't tell you why. It's just that it was so-o-o beautiful!"

DAYS NINE-ELEVEN

Canterbury

"Mommy, I'm sad."

"Why, dear?"

"We're coming to the end of these fun trips. He said yesterday was his last day in London."

"Why don't we see what he has for today? Let's see. Oh my!"

"Oh my, what?"

"He went to Canterbury!"

"Read it!"

After a week in London, it was time to move on—move on to legendary Canterbury, site of pilgrimages ever since Archbishop Thomas Becket was murdered in the cathedral by minions of Henry II on December 29, 1170. And certainly Chaucer's Canterbury Tales, *Tennyson's* Becket, *and T. S. Eliot's* Murder in the Cathedral *have helped to keep Canterbury alive in hearts and minds down through the centuries.*

I took the train so as to really see the countryside. It's only about an hour and a half journey. Immediately upon disembarking, you feel you are in a medieval town. In fact, it dates all the way back to the Romans. In 597, Saint Augustine and his fellow missionaries brought Christianity to Britain. Here is where they settled down and built their first church.

A taxi took me to County Hotel, the cellars of which have been there ever since the twelfth century. Doubtless Chaucer was familiar with it himself.

Outside my window, instead of the luminous Tower Bridge, were medieval buildings and streets, townspeople, students from all over the world, and tourists. The bells of the cathedral remind the visitors that it continues to rule the town.

The poor cathedral has certainly not had an easy time of it. The sanctuary built by St. Augustine was sacked and set on fire by the invading Danes in 1011. In 1066 it was wrecked beyond repair by a disastrous fire and had to be rebuilt from the ground up. In 1174 it was ravaged by fire again. In 1377 the old Romanesque nave was demolished in order to construct the great Gothic one. In 1540 Henry VIII's henchmen carried off cartloads of its greatest treasures. But worst of all were the Puritans who, during the 1640s and 1650s toppled the altar and monuments, ripped down the hangings, and badly damaged the organ. Timbers were removed and both ceiling vaulting and roof were stripped. The archives and libraries were plundered. Stained-glass windows were smashed; but fortunately most survived, for they represent one of the greatest treasures of today's England. two million visitors a year still come here (compared to St. Paul's two and a half million and Westminster's three million).

Since Evensong has got into my blood, when the bells began to ring late in the afternoon, I wended my way towards the cathedral. Inside, the worshippers being rather few that day, they motioned me to sit in the majestic quire (choir) itself. After the bells, the Canterbury Choir came in, led by the vergers and speakers. Again I was overcome by the synthesis of the visual and the aural:

"What's 'aural'?"

"What you hear, darling."

"Oh."

. . . the radiance of the windows of the Corona, the intricacy of the vaulting, the great columns soaring heavenward, the ancient hand-carved quire, the boys' and men's voices rising and falling, the speakers' voices, the organ's full-throated vox, and those like me who participated in order to experience the presence of God once again.

❖   ❖   ❖

I've been to Evensong again, and I've explored the cathedral top to bottom. Of all the cathedrals in England, this one is unique. What with its ties to St. Augustine, its being the cradle of English Christianity, its *being the mother church of the worldwide Anglican Communion, and having its own murder drama, well, it's got it all.*

But I love it for yet another reason. It is quieter here, more serene. The town is relatively small and still medieval, so it's easier here to get lost in a time warp.

Tomorrow I return to London for my last Evensong.

"Mommy, let's go!"

"Go where, dear?"

"Canterbury! He said it's only an hour and a half away."

"Oh, I don't know. . . ."

"What *else* do we have to do?"

"Guess you're right, dear. Let's get there in time for Evensong.

❈ ❈ ❈

"We *did* it, Mommy!"

"Yes, dear, we did it—even getting reservations in the County Hotel. I like this town, this cathedral, very much. It is more peaceful than London, and I especially need that peace right now."

"Me, too, Mommy. Especially when Father doesn't want me."

DAY TWELVE

Evensong

"We got our same room again, Mommy?"

"Yes. They promised to hold room 507 for us. So there's our bridge. It hasn't gone away. . . . It was special in Canterbury, wasn't it? And we saw so much that second day."

"Yep. Loved the whole town."

"Are you ready for the last day's journal entry?"

"No! I don't want it to ever end!"

"I'm afraid it has to. Let's see how he ends it."

Am back in my old room at the Tower Thistle. And the bridge is still there. This afternoon, one last time, I attended Evensong in Westminster Abbey. It was raining, but inside I felt protected, warmed, and nearer my Creator than I did on sunny days. The Abbey felt more like a refuge.

As always, I scanned the faces of those who were sharing Evensong with me . . . searching for her. Who she will be, I don't really know. I only know that I've been praying for her ever since my first Evensong.

Asked God to bring her into my life so that I won't be so lonely anymore. And perhaps she's just as lonely as I.

You *are*, Mommy, you are!" interjected Beth.

Constance blushed ten shades of red, and reached across to tickle Beth. "You silly girl! Why, I don't even know the man!"

Beth wriggled in delight that she had her mother on the defensive. "Do too. Did you know Father as well when you married him?"

"Well . . . evidently not, dear. . . . But you're acting a little crazy today."

Beth only looked searchingly at her mother.

But back to Evensong. My heart is so full this last night in London that I'm just going to let this journal ramble to a close. The very name, "Evensong," whispers peace and tranquility. My mind is still seething, still churning, with no closure on this trip. I've been more deeply moved by the Evensongs I've attended than by any other service I can remember. Not just by the service itself, but by the commitment made by the Church of England: that day in, day out, one of the verities of British life is that one can depend on meeting God every morning at Matins and Holy Communion and every evening at Evensong. In most American churches, one worships God on Sabbaths (but in truth, many only attend on high days such as Christmas or Easter).

Modern life appears to be, more and more, akin to a blitzkrieg, to fire and storm, to an irresistible invading force. All around me every day the world seeks to batter me into its own mold. Everywhere I turn, everywhere I go, even in my own home, the world clutches at me. Computers, the Internet, faxes, e-mails, telephones, pagers, radio, videos, television, cinema, music, newspapers, magazines, books, billboards (Studies reveal that the average twenty-year-old has already been exposed to more than a million commercials!)—taken all together, it's almost impossible to hold out against it.

But just think, what if we all had the opportunity to escape the world twice a day—or at least at Evensong—and for a few blessed moments seek out God, asking for strength and divine peace? Might we not be a different civilization? What if, not just Episcopal churches, but churches of all faiths, kept their doors open all week long? What if all churches had bells, and they rang them morning and evening, calling anyone who sought strength for the day, and the Lord's peace, to come in? Might not even Britain's 80 percent who are stressed to the breaking point somehow find peace? Maybe we can't all afford to build great Gothic cathedrals, but surely we could recognize the role that beauty and esthetics play in our sanctuaries. Look at God's blueprints for the glorious Tabernacle and Temple in the Old Testament. And too often we blunt the soul with the cheap, the pre-fab, the just plain ugly, instead of searching for beauty, for the sublime.

So much for my soapbox. Nobody's listening to me anyhow.

Beth's laugh tinkled adorably, "He doesn't even know he's being listened to, does he?"

"No indeed!" laughed her mother.

Just what am I looking for, in this world of hedonism, secularism, and obsession with pleasure and self-gratification?. . .

"Big words again, Mommy."

"Yes, dear. 'Hedonism' means to live only for pleasure—not others; 'secularism' means a life without God; and the other words mean the same things."

"Oh."

I'm looking for a woman who will wear well. . . .

"Wear *what* well?"

"Oh, you darling little ducky," laughed her mother, "he means a woman he wouldn't get tired of, even when she gets old."

"No one could ever get tired of *you,* Mommy."

"You and your one-track mind," said her mother, smiling, "but I thank you for the compliment just the same."

Of course externals are important, but what's inside is even more so. Is she kind, loving, unselfish, empathetic, sweet, giving, honest, altruistic, industrious?. . .

"Stop, Mommy."

"I knew you'd stop me—you always want to understand every word, bless your heart. 'Empathetic' means you try really hard to see life through other people's eyes, so you can understand them, comfort them, and encourage them. 'Altruistic' means you do nice things for people 'just because' instead of expecting them to do nice things back."

Beth wore a thoughtful look, then sighed, "Those are hard to do."

Does she love beauty wherever it might be found? Does she love children?

"He must like children a lot!"

"Apparently, dear."

Will she revel in walks along the beach, hikes in the mountains, getting lost in old bookstores? Will she love both the familiar and the far-away places? Will she cry at sad movies, sad music, sad books?

"He's talking about *you*, Mommy."

"Hush! You romantic child!"

Will she consider each day to be an adventure, a gift from God, an opportunity to make a difference in the lives of others? Will she be intelligent and enjoy the deep things of life? Will she have a good sense of humor (she'd have to, to survive me).

"He makes me laugh!" broke in Beth.

Will she stay with me for life (not just until she finds someone she likes better than me)? Most of all, will she have a deep and abiding faith in God? If she should not, not all these other wonderful qualities could possibly compensate.

Tomorrow, I board the great silver bird for home. I really wonder, though, why I've literally poured my heart out onto these pages, making myself so vulnerable (should anyone else perchance see them). But that's so unlikely that I certainly can rule that out!

"Wrong again, huh Mommy?"

Her mother only smiled enigmatically and read on.

But you, Tower Bridge out there in the falling rain, do you see me? You know, Bridge, I feel I know you well enough to confide in you. Tell you what. I'd like to come back to this very city this Christmas season. Come back to London to see Dickens' Christmas Carol performed, to see St. Nicholas ride in on his white horse, to see all the Christmas decorations.

Most of all—is this dream truly impossible?—I'd like to have her with me. I'd like to hold her hand during Evensong, and make her blush by whispering to her how lovely I think she is and how much I love her.

And . . . sooner or later, I want a little girl that looks just like her.

Please, dear God?

There was a long silence, broken finally by Beth's "I'm *so* glad he didn't forget me."

"You darling, darling child!" responded her mother, hugging her.

❊   ❊   ❊

"Mommy, you've got to send it back to Mr. Harrison.

All right, let's look in every crevice of this thing. . . . Not here. Not here. Not he—Oh! There's something in this pocket. A business card with his Jackson Hole address."

"In Wyoming?"

"Yes."

"Oh goody! I *love* Wyoming!"

"You, my dear, are impossible. But, for *your* sake, we'll copy the card and mail the journal back to him."

"With a letter from me in it—and a letter from you—explaining things?"

"W-e-l-l . . . I guess that would be polite of us."

"Mommy, sometimes *you* are the one who's impossible."

POSTLUDE

As Constance and Beth strolled the aisles of Harrod's department store, Beth suddenly exclaimed, "Look, Mommy! Here's his newest book!"

Who, my dear?"

"You know very well what who! The only who we've been talking and thinking about! Sometimes I don't know about you, Mommy. . . . Look, here's his picture! Just like I thought he'd look!"

"Oh?"

"Yes. Tall, handsome (but not too much), smile thingies in his cheeks and eyes—and he's looking at me and telling me to just be patient. Don't *you* like him?"

"Why, uh, yes. He looks like a nice man."

Beth did not respond in mere words, but her eyes could have killed.

❖ ❖ ❖

It was snowing in the Tetons. Harrison walked over to the window of his great log cabin home, flanked by flocked evergreens, and stared across the valley at a sight he never grew tired of: Mt. Moran and the saw-bladed Teton peaks, leaping into the sky nearly eight thousand feet from the valley floor. Without question, one of the grandest sights on this planet. So high was his ranch on the east mountainside that he could see both the falling snow and the sunlight glowing on Grand Teton Peak, framed for the moment against an azure sky—then that vista narrowed as the storm engulfed even the high country.

He returned to his seat by the crackling fire in the towering three-story-high rock fireplace. His thoughts, with a determined will of their own, carried him back to London. Just what had he accomplished there? Was it all a fool's journey? He mused, *I'm still convinced God sent me there—but for what purpose? As far as I know, she was not there. And all that work I put in on my journal—lost!* His last hope had been dashed by a telephone call from the general manager of the Tower Thistle Hotel: "Sorry, sir, but I had security check your room. No journal anywhere."

Idly, he turned to the large stack of unread mail. It made him tired just to look at it—the work it represented, especially the book-related fan mail, for it was virtually impossible to keep up with it. But one package was thicker than the rest, and it was hand-addressed. The smoothly flowing calligraphy was something out of the past, not the computerized present. The stamps, too, were chosen for their beauty. No blah metered postmark here. He opened it.

Unbelievably, here was his lost journal! He couldn't believe it! But how—? Perhaps the letters would tell the story. He opened the most interesting looking one first. Never could resist letters from children with their large scrawled or hand-blocked letters on the envelope. So undeveloped spatially that almost invariably they'd run out of space and have to cramp the rest of the letters into a huddle at the end. But this one made it. A girl, he guessed, seven to nine years of age. Inside was some crayoned artwork—the Tower Bridge!—remarkably good for a child. Already she had developed a sense of symmetry.

He turned to her letter and smiled as he read it.

Dear Mr. Harrison,

Thank you for writing your journal. Mommy found it behind the dresser. Please don't be mad at me because I made Mommy snoop. I just couldn't have lived without seeing what was in it!

We, at least I, love it. I don't know about Mommy. She hides how she feels more than I do. We read every word. Weren't we naughty?

I like you very much. Would you write to me? Or are you too busy to write to a girl who is only seven years old?

I have a lot more to say, but Mommy is rushing me. Next time I'll say more. If there is a next time. Oh I DO hope so!

Love,
Beth

The other letter was written in that same beautiful script. In it, the girl's mother told him the story of their finding his journal, their decision to read it, their following in his footsteps each day, and their finding his card.

Let me tell you a little about my precocious little Beth. She's such an intense little darling. She'd been terribly disappointed (upon our arrival in London) when the object of our visit failed to show up. So there we were with lots of time on our hands and nothing to do. Your journal gave us an excuse to play tourist and see England from the perspective of an American visitor.

More significantly, during the reading of it, Beth became more and more fascinated with you. I've never before seen her take to a person as she has you. In fact, had it not been for her, this packet would have included no letters, just an explanatory note. She's absolutely set her heart on hearing back from you. It would mean so much to her if you would—even if it were but a short note.

There was more, but it was guarded and rather reserved. He read between the lines and wondered whether or not she was still married.

Of course he answered Beth's letter. Both letters. He couldn't help thinking as he did so whether God was at the bottom of all this. In closing, he asked both of them if they'd be interested in continuing the correspondence.

They were, so letters began flowing between Santa Fe and Jackson Hole.

❈   ❈   ❈

"Got my third letter today," bragged Beth.

"I got one too," admitted her mother.

"He got my picture and likes it! Says he'd like even more the original to it some day," chortled Beth. "Did you send him one of you?"

"No, dear."

"How come?"

"Because . . . oh, how can I explain? . . . Well, it's because I've already been burned when a certain man didn't look beyond my face and figure. I want—*someday*—to be, uh, appreciated because of what I am inside."

"But how would he know that you're beautiful?"

"Well, I guess that's a chance he'd have to take, dear."

"Have I told you lately that sometimes you're impossible, Mommy?"

"Yes," laughed her mother.

❖ ❖ ❖

"Got another letter. Picture too."

"Good. What did he have to say?"

"Why? Didn't he write you too?"

"Yes," blushed her mother. "Never mind."

❖ ❖ ❖

The question that had been gnawing on him most was answered by Beth. Volunteered, as he hadn't known how to ask it:

Let me tell you about Mommy and my father. He didn't love her very much, so they divorced. He doesn't love me very much either. I can understand why he wouldn't love me, but I can't understand why he wouldn't love her! Cuz she's the most wonderful woman in all the world! When I tell her how pretty she is, she just smiles and says, Darling. She calls me that a lot! The only beauty that counts comes from inside you.

In his sixth letter, he asked Constance for her phone number. Thereafter, the friendships took on a new voice-enriched dimension. He would smile to himself when Beth would say, "It's Mommy's turn to talk now." The telephone topics ranged from news of the day to the Eternal. Constance plied him with questions relating to his faith journey. He listened intently as she updated him on Beth. It almost seemed he'd always been her friend, as she shared with him her likes, her hopes, her dreams. Gradually, Constance found herself opening up more and more. Having the letters focused on God and Beth first, then their shared love of books and the arts, helped that. She didn't spare herself. After a time, when her confidence in him had increased, she openly confessed her wandering from God and the mistakes of her past. Increasingly she realized that she shared things with William—now Bill—that she'd never told anyone before. One day the conviction came to her that she could talk so openly with Bill because—she *trusted* him. That she should ever again completely trust a man so jolted her that she dropped into a nearby chair to savor the idea. A smile tickled the corners of her mouth, and she gave fervent thanks that Beth—back in school—didn't see her at that moment. Beth would have seen her very soul shining from her face . . . and would have known the reason.

For Beth harbored none of her mother's compunctions and reservations. Her correspondence with Harrison remained as it had been from the first: open, confident, wistful, yearning. As though she had searched for him all her life.

E-mails came next, and he'd call them from various cities where he was doing book-signings. His voice on the phone did things to Constance that Robert's voice never had. Yet, she resisted his efforts to get together with her and Beth in person. Why, she really wasn't sure, but she sensed that what they had was such a rare meeting of the inner spirits that to inject the physical dimension prematurely might very well jeopardize . . . *everything.* Knowing how deeply she had been hurt, he—rather grudgingly, it must be admitted—acceded to her wish.

But in doing so, he became party to something rare in contemporary society. In their letters, each fell in love with the very soul of the other. The real-life chemistry, a wild card that could be dealt with later. Should that crucial dimension not be there when they finally met, well, they'd remain soul mates anyhow. Meanwhile, Constance's and Beth's love for God increased and deepened.

He sent her a music box that played only one song—"To Love Again." Beth was fascinated by it and was always winding it up just to hear it again.

One day, as he was looking through his mail, he found a large envelope with the now familiar childish handwriting on it. Smiling, he opened it to see what Beth had to say. Down the page a little were these words:

Mr. Harrison. Feels funny to still call you that. You mean so much more than that to me. And to Mommy. You make her so happy her eyes dance. She sings all the time. Yet we never really see you. We only imagine you. That's kinda sad. Had my eighth birthday yesterday, and you weren't there. I missed you. I'm growing up without you. Do you want me to grow up without you? Do you really love me as much as I love you? Do you really love Mommy? If you do, *do* something! I cried yesterday when you didn't even call to wish me Happy Birthday. Then Mommy reminded me I'd never told you when my birthday was. But you should have asked! Now Christmas is coming, and if you don't come for that, I shall die.

Nothing in Harrison's life had ever moved him more than this letter—this letter from a girl who was already bridging into adolescence. Did he want her to complete that bridge without him? Did he want her and Constance—she now let him call her Connie—to celebrate Christmas without him?

Not on his life! . . . He reached for the phone, called his travel agent, and ordered three tickets to London.

❖   ❖   ❖

It was Christmas in London. The great city had bestirred itself to prepare for the season of the Christ Child and was as festive as one ever sees it.

The great bells of Westminster Abbey were ringing out the news that Christmas Evensong was only minutes away. A beautiful woman stood next to the gate with an almost carbon-copy child beside her. Both wore an air of extreme expectancy, awaiting the arrival of a man they had never seen.

Then, around the corner he came at a brisk pace. Seeing them, he slowed, recognizing the little girl by the photo she'd sent him. Ostensibly, he saw only the shy child standing on one foot, the other nervously digging into the pavement, but, in truth, he never missed a nuance of the vision standing by her side.

As he reached them, he knelt down in front of the child and said, "Merry Christmas, Princess."

She said not a word but solemnly searched his eyes. Meanwhile her mother missed nothing of the tableau.

Then the little girl bypassed everything that didn't really matter—such as small talk—and rushed to resolution. Her voice shaking because she cared so much about the man's answer, she asked the question she'd been living with night and day for so many long months:

"Are you going to be my daddy?"

Just as solemnly, he answered, "Would you like me to?"

"Yes. More than anything in all the world!"

As he asked his next question (apparently so lightly, almost in fact banteringly), he *knew* that the reality of Connie was greater — *far* greater — than all his dreams. Now that he had finally seen her in person, he knew he could never leave London without her. Not another day of her life did he want to miss!

"What about *her?*" He looked up and held the gaze of the woman named Constance. "Does *she* come with the package?"

"I — I don't know," slowly answered the little girl, struggling against tears. "Sometimes I just don't know what to do with her."

A roguish look came into the woman's eyes, and the wisp of a smile. She looked down at the still-kneeling man and asked a question of her own (a slight tremor in her voice): "Are you sure you want me in the package too?"

Before answering, he again looked at Beth, and was engulfed by a tidal wave of love for this child who was almost single-handedly responsible for this moment of decision. Neither could he even consider leaving London without *her!* Here was the daughter of his dreams — only he'd already missed over seven years of her life. He'd not miss another day! Gathering the still, trembling little girl in his arms, he tenderly kissed the tears in her eyes, and stood up. Then he turned to the woman and said, "Beth and I have a question." Even without knowing for sure what he would say, Beth kissed his cheek softly and ran her starved fingers through his hair. "Our question is this," he continued. "Will you marry us, to have and to hold, from this day forth, in sickness and in health, as long as we live, so help you God?"

Now it was the woman's turn to puddle up, smiling at them both through brimming eyes — with so much love and trust in her eyes that the man knew the answer had already been given, regardless of what mere words might say.

"I'll give you my answer after Evensong," was her answer in words.

Beth broke in, "You're silly, Mommy. And a terrible tease."

Turning to the man who held her in his arms, she said, "Daddy," and her voice shook as for the first time in her life she called a man that precious word, "will you hold me all during Evensong, and hug me and whisper that you love me? . . . Oh Daddy!" Words failing her, she could only convulsively cling to him and weep in relief that the long journey of two was over and the journey of three was about to begin.

Speech failing him, he could only answer by tightening his arms around her. The mother drank in every drop of the moving scene. Whatever remaining reservations she might have had were swept aside by her daughter's yearning question, the man's response, and the sight of her daughter in Bill's arms. How her heart sang that he had gone to Beth first!

But to keep up appearances, she tried (unsuccessfully, it's true) to be severe by asking him, "And what do you have left for *me?*"

The newly minted daddy mistily smiled at her, but his voice yet teased: "Well, Beth has taken possession of everything but my right arm. If it promises to hold you close to me, will that do?"

"For the moment," she answered demurely. But her twinkling eyes held both promise and a great love the man recognized for what it was: the answer to his heartfelt prayers.

And so a little girl called Beth, a woman Beth called "Mommy," and a man Beth called "Daddy" (a sacred circle of three) walked into Christmas Evensong.

❊   ❊   ❊

HOW THIS TWELFTH STORY CAME TO BE

I worked on ideas for this story half a year before the subject finally jelled. In fact my first story plot sputtered to a complete halt, as dead as Marley's proverbial doornail. The catalyst turned out to be a research trip my wife, Connie, and I took to London and Canterbury early January of 2001. It was our first trip to England.

The book deadline upon me, I still had no twelfth story. Having come to the end of my rope, I turned the story over to God. This time, however, I requested an additional favor from Him: that He would not only provide me with a Christmas story plot, but that He would make it an extra special one, given that this was the twelfth story, the capstone of the collection.

Late in February, God answered my supplications. "Take your trip to England and construct a plot upon places where you stayed, places you visited, things you did, and people you met there. The characters should be limited to three: a man, a woman, and a little girl."

The dilemma I faced in the story was this: How was I to construct a believable romance out of a plot-line where the three protagonists never actually see each other until the final scene? In all my years of writing, I'd never before faced a challenge quite like this one.

I finally concluded that it could be done through the vehicle of a journal (a time-honored literary device). But it would not work were the journal the typical sequence of private thoughts and observations, for readers of such entries would generally consider them self-serving, for all of us look at ourselves through rose-tinted glasses. Perhaps a travel-related journal would work, for it could be read on many levels, and through its pages the personal revelations could be Trojan-horsed.

My primary objective was to get the woman to become so fascinated by the man who wrote the journal entries that she'd be open to love. What I hadn't counted on was Beth (who I initially considered to be a minor—almost a cameo—character), but who ended up running away with the story. She falls in love with William far earlier than her mother does; her father-hunger turns out to be more intense even than her mother's yearning for a soul mate. In fact, were it not for Beth, it's extremely doubtful whether a romance between the adult protagonists would ever have developed!

In truth, the story ended up being more about father-hunger than anything else. Since I prayed so continuously for divine guidance as I wrote, I cannot escape the conviction that God willed this unexpected shift of emphasis. Today, we are being sold a bill of goods: that fathers are optional—that a woman can do very well without a husband in raising a child. Well, we are belatedly discovering that while this may be true for the woman, it most definitely is not true for the child. When we realize that in marriage, 99 percent of the way we act as a spouse or as a parent is determined by the example-prototypes we observed in our parents, then it should come as no surprise that girls who grow up without a father-figure have no idealized prototype on which to base either a choice of a future husband or knowledge of how to jointly raise a child. Boys, if anything, are even worse off, for they face huge difficulties in learning what it means to be a man, a husband, or a father.

My heart goes out to all those children today who are so starved for a, not just father, but daddy in their lives. These children instinctively know that *they are being short-changed who daily experience the void that only a daddy can fill.*

With all these variables in mind, let us now return to little Beth. In the pages of this journal, she gradually discovers that a potential father could be a pied piper who leads her into magical worlds she has never known much about before—the worlds of the mind, the humanities: history, geography, literature, architecture, art, music, religion. Instinctively, she senses that it is this man's relationship to God that sets him apart from other men she has closely observed. In these pages she learns to trust him—the ultimate tribute a child can give an adult. Knowing her mother so well (typical of mother/daughter households), without realizing she's reversing roles, she precipitates the action that forces her mother to seriously consider marriage with this man they know only through journal pages. If this man could be brought to the point where he falls in love with her adorable mother and would promise before God to marry her and stay with her "until death do us part," and be to her daughter a really-truly daddy, who loves her as much as her mother does, then the three of them would indeed become a divinely ordained circle of three—a family.

❧   ❧   ❧

This story will be included in the trade paper Christmas in My Heart II *(published by Renew and Herald Publishing Association) and in the hardback edition (published by Tyndale House/Focus on the Family) in the fall of 2002.*

ABOUT THE AUTHOR

Joe Wheeler has been called everything from "Keeper of the Story" to "Father Christmas." He has spent a lifetime immersed in books and searching for extra special stories. In the fall of 1992 Wheeler's first book, a collection of stories titled *Christmas in My Heart* came off the presses of Maryland's largest publisher, Review and Herald Publishing Association. Since that time, he has written and compiled thirty-seven additional books, including his most recent  publications, *Easter in My Heart*, *The Wings of God*, and *What's So Good about Tough Times?*

A frequent talk show guest, Wheeler is often asked about how it all started. He tells interviewers that it all dates back to being home-schooled by his remarkable mother, Barbara Leininger Wheeler, both a teacher and a missionary in Latin America. An elocutionist of the old school, his mother memorized thousands of pages of stories, readings, and poetry, and frequently recited in public. But her specialty was the old-timey, sentimental, Judeo-Christian short story. And she poured herself—and her stories—into her son, inoculating him with a terminal case of the storyitis virus.

At Pacific Union College in the Napa Valley, Wheeler majored in history and English, then went on to secure his masters in history from that college, prior to completing a masters in english from California State University in Sacramento, and the Ph.D. in English (with a history of ideas emphasis) from Vanderbilt University. For most of his career, Wheeler has chaired departments of English and communications at colleges in Alabama, Texas, and Maryland. Today, Wheeler is senior fellow for cultural studies, Center for the New West, in Denver, Colorado, founder and executive director of the Zane Grey's West Society, and professor emeritus of Columbia Union College in Takoma Park, Maryland.

Dr. Wheeler and his wife, Connie, now live in Conifer, Colorado. Their chalet, at 9,700 feet elevation, provides a spectacular view and 200 inches of snow a year. Here they have dedicated the rest of their lives to bringing back the best of the old-timey stories and books, and helping to give them a new lease on life. Thus, though Wheeler no longer teaches full time in a traditional academic setting, his new classroom now includes the entire world.